Whisperings of Betrayal

An 18th Century tale
of
Romance and Adventure

by

Roy J. Andersen

The Moving Quill Publishing House
MQ

Copyright © Roy Andersen. 2013

The right of Roy Andersen to be identified as the author of this work has been asserted by him in accordance with the Copyright Designs and Patents Act 1988. All rights reserved. No part of this publication may be reproduced, stored in a retrieval system, or transmitted, in any form or by any means, electronic, mechanical, photocopying, recording, or otherwise, without the prior written permission of the copyright owner.

Disclaimer:

The author and the publisher will assume no liability nor responsibility to any person or entity with respect to any loss or damage related directly or indirectly to the information in this book. Neither the author nor the publisher will provide any remedy for indirect, consequential, punitive, or incidental damages arising from this book, including such from negligence, strict liability, or breach of warranty or contract, even after notice of the possibility of such damages. Neither the publisher nor the author accept any responsibility for the actions of another based on the information in this book.

\Whisperings of Betrayal
was previously published under the title *The Woman*

ISBN: 978-1-0685296-5-8

I would like to dedicate this book

to

All those who live their dream.

About the Author

Roy Andersen is a distinguished scientist, educationalist and author of 18 books detailing how society and the school work together to produce the citizen worker. As a child in school, Roy never understood what he was doing wrong to always gain low marks. He failed all of his final school examinations. Roy went back into education when he was 20 and was then an outstanding academic success. He continually gained distinctions in every examination he entered. After college, he went to sea and, through a host of adventures, before defining the purpose of his life's mission.

For more than 30 years, Roy has dedicated his life to first improving and then redesigning education. Firstly, to change education globally so that no child would fail in school as they once did. Secondly, to alter the structure of education to enable the child of today to survive in the AI-dominated world that will await them. He has written many books and lectured profoundly on the need to redesign education to prepare the 21st-century child for a world dominated by artificial intelligence. As he explains, the purpose of education is to provide a variety of capabilities for the job market.

However, AI must change the whole purpose of education, because it will take over 90% of jobs by the end of this century. This will create untold social problems. AI, itself, regards Roy Andersen as the first scientist to openly discuss the serious social problems that AI must create. Without work and a purpose to their lives, people become depressed, leading to alcohol and substance abuse. In turn, this will affect relationships, marriages and the raising of children, just as crime and rejection to the system that created these conditions will fester. Governments will seek to control public behavior through the many tools of AI, and so the whole character of the citizen must change.

Roy Andersen explains how education must urgently begin to transform from a system grading competence to one that develops greater intellectual and behavioural self-responsibility in the future citizen, so they may maintain an acceptable level of harmony in their society. It is only by this that people may be able to hold on to a level of personal freedom under AI, which is already beginning to diminish.

To give the machinery for this transformation in education, Roy has dedicated many years of research into genetics and neurology. He has proposed a new and very different version to what we think intelligence is and how it develops in the human being. This view, which he terms The Brain Environment Complex, explains how and why we have misunderstood the role of the gene in intelligence and how the intelligence capability of any individual, and so their ability to learn, is far more a consequence of the environment that is normally understood.

His book Intelligence: The Great Lie is hailed by the dean of an American university as one of the most important books published this century. All this has great meaning to the design of school, how children should be taught, and the meaning of the ability they display in their lessons and examinations. Roy has now dedicated 40 years of his life to helping children learn better in school. You can find out more about Roy Andersen, his life, and his books at

www.andersenroy.com

Whisperings of Betrayal, as not to be confused with different books by different authors using the same title, is Roy Andersen's first fictional book. Set during the time of the American Revolution, it is said by reviewers. such as Mr.Tom Wong of the book club Riverbend Readers, who wrote:

Thanks to Maria Pauling for bringing Whisperings of Betrayal to our book club. We were completely swept away by Jane's journey. The blend of romance, suspense, and historical richness sparked one of the most engaging discussions we've had in months. Several of us even reread it before the meeting. It is that good. As Emily Johnson wrote: From the windswept cliffs of Cornwall to the fiery heart of the American Revolution, Whisperings of Betrayal swept me into a world of danger, love, and destiny. Jane is the kind of heroine I've longed to see, brave, intelligent, and constantly evolving. Her journey from a frightened young woman to someone who shapes her own future was nothing short of inspirational. The historical details are immersive without ever slowing down the pace., I felt like I was there, tasting salt in the air and hearing the gunshots of revolution. A masterfully written tale, I will be recommending to every historical fiction lover I know.

As Doctor Gwen Lavert wrote:

"This novel conjures up all the love, passion, and adventure of 'Gone with the Wind'. Roy Andersen's romantic novel takes the reader from Cornish smuggling and high seas adventures into the turbulent time of the American Revolution. This book is a riveting page turner."

I hope you may find it so, and enjoy the characters as much as I did in inventing them and living through the lives each leads.

Roy Andersen

Table of Contents

Chapter One 'Them that Ask no Questions, Them that Told no Lies' - Smugglers' Proverb	3
Chapter Two Who is This Man?	22
Chapter Three Betrayal	54
Chapter Four Deadly Waters	66
Chapter Five A New Life	92
Chapter Six Tis a Question of Tax	108
Chapter Seven The Beginning of it All	121
Chapter Eight Sisterhood	144
Chapter Nine Lost	188
Chapter Ten Mathew Returns	210
Chapter Eleven The Captain	231

Chapter Twelve Leave no Stone Unturned	240
Chapter Thirteen Something Sinister	248
Chapter Fourteen A Common Bond	261
Chapter Fifteen A Dark Ritual	270
Chapter Sixteen Homeward Bound	278
Chapter Seventeen A Shadow Lurks	288
Chapter Eighteen "Vengeance Shall Be Mine!" Said the Lord	300
Chapter Nineteen A Little White Lie!	329
Chapter Twenty The Message	342
Further Books by Roy J. Andersen	350
Invitation from Roy Andersen.	369

Whisperings of Betrayal

Chapter One

'Them that Ask no Questions, Them that Told no Lies'

Smugglers' Proverb

His shadow was always in her mind. Often, she would hate him, but then, when she felt the desire most to cause him pain, a sense of desperate need to feel his loving touch would torment her. Her body ached to be with him. How she longed to hear him call her name. Just once.

The wind picked up in the valley and the crashing of the waves on the rocks below brought her to her senses. She had been out too long and the day was turning to night. It was lonely where she was, and the thought that she might be watched caused her to search the trees for a figure. None were there, but how easily a tree could pass for a man when the mind played tricks. Still, it was late in the day and poachers would soon be about. It was not safe to come across a man who was stealing rabbits and could be hanged for it.

Jane shuddered with the thought and started to run. The path was a trail worn in the ground and in parts she felt she could slip, but she kept herself upright until she reached a low stone wall that barred her way. The wall was old and in parts broken. She tried to remember where the gap was by which she had come through earlier, but the darkness was beginning to fall fast now.

This stressed her and she felt a sense of worry. Not sure if she should go right or left, she chose the latter. Jane followed the wall for what seemed like hours, although in truth it was only minutes. She did not remember the stones she had to clamber over, nor the shallow ditch she had to take a long stride to cross. She cleared the ditch but did slip on the mud and felt her ankle twist as she fell down. She was angry with herself for staying out so late. It had only meant to be a short walk, but she had remembered the man she loved and how he had left her for another woman.

It was in the pain of her mind that time passed. Her mind and her heart fought each other and with all this pained confusion, she had wandered too far. Still, the pain of her ankle made her realize her situation now, and she realized she had taken the wrong direction at the wall. Leaning upon it, she pulled herself up until she was able to stand. It hurt, but not too much. She could limp and did so back along the way she had come. Now it was dark, but not too dark not to see her way. Time was slow now and it seemed to take a very long time to reach the path she had left.

Although reach it she did, and with a sigh of relief moved along the wall towards the gap she now knew she would find. She lifted her skirt and felt a tear. The material was heavy, for now it had mud and the hem was wet. Still, all this could be mended.

Jane reached the gap in the wall and was about to step over a large stone when something caught her eye.

It was a light down on the beach. Curious, she stopped to watch it. The curiosity pulled her away from the wall and careful not to stumble, she limped a few steps towards the edge of the cliff.

Yes. She was right. There were lights. She counted one, two, three, four. Strangely, they were all swinging in unison. She watched, puzzled as to why people should be behaving as such. Then, she noticed the lighthouse on Barney's Rock was not working. She peered into the darkness, making sure her bearings were correct. Yes. There was the silhouette of Peter's Peak to the right. The highest outcrop in the area. She looked again. Still, there was no light coming from Barney's Rock, but the lights down by the beach were still swinging in unison.

"Oh Mother of God! Wreckers!"

She had heard of such men. Cruel as pirates. They would lure a ship on to rocks with their false light and slaughter all on board, as they stole its cargo.

It was as this thought went through her mind that she saw a fleeting glimpse of something white out into the darkness of the sea. Jane peered to see if she could see something, anything out over the water. Nothing. She wondered if her eyes had deceived her. There it was again. Clearer now. A sail. It was a white sail.

Not one, but a mast. Two masts of sails. All coming towards the lights on the beach.

She felt her heart pound. She gripped the knot of the shawl she wore and held it tight to her chest. She thought to cry out a warning to the ship, but held her breath. The crew would never hear her, but the wreckers would. She had heard of what they do to innocent people, and she had remembered hearing of some who were hanged after the last assizes in Tregony. Jane watched the lights swing so slowly and so enticingly pull the ship and her crew closer and closer.

The wind seemed to rise up again from the valley, but the sound, a horrible sound of breaking wood far below, kept that of the wind from her ears. She saw the lights moving now. There were more of them, as they seemed to move into the water. There was a terrible tearing of wood as the ship bore itself upon the cruel rocks. She could see the masts clearer now and saw how they lay tilted to one side. Small images of people were moving about on the beach. She was terrified. Terrified for the sailors on board and terrified if the wreckers should ever know she saw what was happening.

There was a shuffle behind her, somewhere in the dark. Jane's heart stopped. Her eyes opened wide. She turned but could see nothing.

"Hurry up!" the voice came in a hard whisper.

"Sorry, M'Lord."

A tall figure moved out of the darkness. Jane stooped as low as she could manage without falling onto the ground. Her breathing was now silent, though the sound of her heart beating felt like a church bell.

The figures moved along the side of the wall and did not look at her, only along the path they followed.

"Did Jimmy put the wagons where I told him?" The voice now lower, as the tall figure moved further into the darkness. Further, Jane knew, down towards the beach.

She did not hear the reply, but M'Lord, who was M'Lord? The thought that it might be Squire Morgan was too much and she dismissed it immediately. Squire Morgan was the local magistrate. A magistrate could not be a wrecker.

There was some shouting from the beach now and with this noise, Jane felt a little safer to move back towards the wall and through the gap she had long sought.

It was the cock crowing that woke her the next morning. She had left the scene last night as quickly as she could. There was nothing she could have done to save that poor crew, and there was no one she could have told that night. The way back to her home had gone so quickly with her mind on what she had seen. It was only the sound of her dog barking that made her give a sigh of relief as she approached the small cottage where she lived. But now, as she lay there in bed, her mind began to question if anyone else had been out there in the shadows last night. Suppose there had been. Suppose she had dropped something. Her mind raced to think if she had had everything with her that she had left home with. Surely, she tried to comfort herself, if someone had seen her, they would have caught her, wouldn't they? The thoughts were uncomfortable, and she moved to get away from them by getting out of bed. Better to do something than just to lie here with imagination, she thought.

Jane poured water into the bowl on the table and gently washed her face. She dressed, went down to the kitchen and felt a relief that Bobby was there. The dog rose from his basket and came to greet her. She bent down and felt the love of her dog lick her face. She stroked his head, stood up and went outside. It was chilly out here and she pulled her shawl more about her shoulders.

"Morning, Ma'am." It was a loud and rough voice that startled her.

Jane turned quickly to see a soldier standing at the gate. There were three of them. The one who had greeted her was a sergeant.

"Good morning, sergeant," she replied, knowing full well why the soldiers were here.

"Did you see or hear anything last night Ma'am?" asked the sergeant, once she had turned to face him.

The thought to tell him what she saw moved to her mouth. The lips moved, but she bit them closed.

Wreckers were normal people in the day. They could be anyone. You would never know. They might even be one of the soldiers, although Jane knew this was unlikely. Still, they would have families, brothers, fathers, and cousins. It was a small world in the little villages of Cornwall and no secret lasted longer than the time it took a man to drink a glass of grog.

The soldier was waiting. She could see he was in a hurry. Her mind lingered with the truth, but there was something about one of the other soldiers that disturbed her. It was this man she did not like. There was no reason for it, save a feeling. Just something inside that told her not to trust these men.

"No!" she replied. "Why should I have done?"

The sergeant touched his hat in respect.

"Sorry to be disturbing you, Ma'am." He turned and ordered the other two to move off.

She watched them grow smaller in the distance. It was good she did not say anything, she told herself, but what was it about that soldier? A shudder moved through her. Jane turned and moved quickly back into the house, but inside, she suddenly felt vulnerable. She felt unsafe alone and needed the feel of other people about her. Other people, she thought, would distract her mind and make her feel safe. She just needed to get the feeling of that soldier out of her mind. Anyway, she had used up all the salted fish in her larder, so there was a good excuse to go down to the harbor in Port Warren and buy some fresh fish.

Jane brushed her hair, placed a new shawl about her shoulders, pinned a broad-rimmed but flat hat upon her head and, carrying a shallow basket under her left arm, stepped out into the fresh air.

There was a gentle breeze about and with the warmth of the sun, Jane felt a sense of freedom after all the events of the previous night. As she closed the gate to her land, she stepped onto a common path and followed this downhill until it blended in with another, and another, until she found herself on the main road that led down to the village.

There were many red-coated soldiers about and as she walked past a group of them, she searched their faces looking for the three that had visited her this morning. She felt a sense of relief that they were not there. The sound of hooves and a heavy wheel moving over uneven ground made her turn to see a coach approaching. She stepped back and lifted her skirt to avoid the dirt the wheels were spraying out. Once the coach had passed, she stepped back onto the road and soon found herself amid many shops and people moving about. She could see clusters of women, joined by a few men, and knew well how they would be talking about the wreck but she kept clear of them, not wishing to be drawn into any kind of conversation that might cause a word to slip.

She turned into a narrow alley and saw how the sunlight twinkled on the water down at the harbor. She followed the alley until it opened out into a large square, with a line of long rowing boats beached on pebbles. The boats had not long been in, for the air was full of seagulls squawking and circling overhead.

Jane went to the first boat, looked at the fish, some of which were still jumping on top of others as they gasped for life, and asked the price. The sailor had a kind face and was polite to her, but she knew his price was too high. She smiled, refused and thanking him, turned towards the next boat, each of which were offering their harvest.

"OK! Tell you what, Ma'am," It was the voice of the sailor whose price she had rejected. "I'll let you have three of these big ones here for six pence." Jane turned to look. The fish were indeed fully grown and probably two pounds each in weight. She shook her head; four pence she offered. The man pulled a face, then laughed. "OK Miss, and you won't get a better price down the line this day."

With a warm smile for her, he took out a knife, held it by the blade and hit each fish hard on its head with the handle before laying them down on a board to gut.

"No, thank you," she interrupted the man's actions. "I'll do that myself when I get home."

The sailor wrapped the fish in old paper and handed them to Jane, who placed them in her shallow basket before opening her purse and handing the man the agreed price. In turn, he touched the hair hanging over his forehead in respect, to which Jane curtsied a little in hers to him.

What is next? she wondered. Ah! She needed salt and flour and so walked towards the merchant's shop on the other side of the square. But it was just as she was about to go in that she heard a voice that caused her to freeze. The voice sounded unmistakably like that of the man who had said "Yes, M'Lord" the night before.

Jane felt the color drain from her face; desperate not to show any sign of nervousness, she turned away from the entrance to the shop, but in her panic did so too quickly.

"Hello there, Ma'am!" It was the same voice.

Jane turned to look back and knew she could not stop herself shaking. A large man, dressed in rough clothes, bent down and picked up a fish from the street.

"You dropped 'im!" he said.

Jane glanced down into her basket and realized how the fish must have slipped out when she turned. "Thank you," she said. Her voice felt meek and her throat a little choked as she did so.

"Not a problem, Ma'am." But the man's look seemed to tarry too long into her eyes before he smiled. It was almost as if he was searching for something and the way he rose seemed to be in a purposeful sort of way, a way that made Jane feel threatened, but once upright, he turned and walked away.

Thoughts flashed through Jane's mind. What had he seen? How could he know? He didn't know, she convinced herself, but then why did he look so hard into her eyes before turning to walk away? What was he thinking?

Jane felt herself shake. She no longer wanted to be out with other people. She wished she was back home. She watched the man walk towards the end of the square. A shout from the tavern caused him to turn his head and change direction. As he entered the tavern, Jane wondered if he was new here, for she had never seen him before. A chill moved through her body. She should get home. Bobby would protect her and she remembered that she had her father's old gun. As Jane hurried home, she could not wipe the question from her mind as to why the man had looked so hard and for so long into her eyes.

Her thoughts were so preoccupied that she hardly noticed the steep climb back to her cottage. The sun was out now and the ground was dry and hot. It was just as she turned a corner and came to see around the thick hedge that she saw a rider slowly coming down towards her. He was some distance, but the light was good and Jane could see that he was a young man, not in uniform. Thank God! she thought, but there was a nervous movement from the horse and Jane could just make out a raised adder. It must have been basking on the warm rock and disturbed by the horse. The horse reared itself up. The rider tried to pull its head down, but a sudden movement from the snake, fearing it was being attacked, caused the horse to suddenly rear up again, kicking at the ground. So sudden was the movement of the horse that the rider was thrown from the saddle and fell down upon the small stone wall surrounding Jane's cottage.

She pulled up her skirts and ran as fast as she could to his aid. By the time she got there, the snake had withdrawn into the thick of the hedge and the horse had cantered off a little, but the young man lay still. When she reached him, she could see that he was about her age, had dark black hair and a fresh complexion. His eyes were closed and she was fearful at first that he was dead. But as she gently laid her hand upon his forehead, his eyes flickered open. He moaned slightly.

"My leg… My leg…it hurts. I think it may be broken," he murmured.

Jane looked down and saw that the right leg lay awkwardly under his left.

"It may be so," she replied gently. "Please lie still. I'll get some wood to lean on."

Jane raced to her home and, ignoring Bobby barking with excitement from inside, found a stout pole. With this in hand, she ran back to the young man and asked him if he could take his weight on the pole and make it to her home. As he moved his leg, Jane thought not that it was broken, but injured in some lesser way, for he was able to hobble on it using the pole she had given him. Placing his arm across her shoulder, she helped him up the path to the front door and, opening it, now told an excited Bobby to calm down and not to jump upon the man.

The man stumbled to a wooden-backed chair by the empty fireplace, while Jane took Bobby outside and closed the door lest he distress the man more. With the door locked, she took a bottle from a cupboard and passed the man a small tot of rum. "Better to ease the shock," she said.

He nodded in gratitude, but said nothing. Obviously, the pain was too much for him.

As she watched him put the mug to his mouth and slip slowly, she realized for the first time how handsome he was. His eyes were closed and so she felt it safe to study his face. He had a strong nose, high cheekbones, but his face looked kind. A lock of hair fell over his forehead and she felt tempted to brush it back, but stopped herself because a strange sensation moved throughout her body, causing her to feel a greater desire to touch him. His eyes flickered open and she pulled herself back.

"That's enough for now," she told him. "Rest and I'll find your horse."

As Jane opened the door, she saw the horse standing by the gate.

That's a relief, she thought and brought the horse into her garden and tied him to a post as a temporary measure until she could work out what to do with the animal later. Yet, she found that as she was tying the horse's rein to the post, her thoughts flashed back to the feelings that had arisen within her when she was close to the man. She felt troubled by this and wondered what it could mean. But then, something uneasy came about her. She felt a cold shiver run down her back and turned to the main path. Jane thought she saw the outline of a man disappear within the hedge, but was not sure. She felt scared and wondered if it was her imagination.

Better to be inside, she thought and hastily left the horse and only then noticed that Bobby was growling towards the main path. Jane turned again to study the scene, but nothing moved and no one was there. She did not feel safe and remembered the man in the square. Why had he looked so intently at her? She wanted protection, and in seeking it from the young man, took Bobby inside.

The man was sleeping when she entered and so as not to disturb him, she told Bobby to go and lie in his basket. Jane pulled a stool up beside the man and wondered who he was. His clothes were very fine and his boots were of very soft leather. Certainly, he was a man of means, but who was he?

It seemed a long time before he raised his eyebrows and struggled to focus on his surroundings. At first, Jane seemed a blur, but as she came into focus, he felt a smile rise upon his face.

"Thank you, Ma'am." His words were soft and gentle. Jane smiled in return.

"Are you a local here?" she asked.

He shook his head slowly. "I've come up from London to visit my uncle here. He's the local squire."

This made sense to her, for she had not noticed this man before and she knew everyone around.

"How is your leg?" she enquired, looking down for the first time at the leg that was thought to be broken.

"I don't think it is," he said, as if he could read her mind. "Just got twisted when I fell. It feels a bit better already... Must be your rum." He smiled in jest.

She felt a smile rise upon her face too. She liked this man. He was kind and good-natured.

Bobby whined from his basket and Jane called him over so he would not be left out. The dog moved slowly and sat leaning his head against her leg. How safe she felt with Bobby and this man.

"My name is Jane," she said, suddenly realizing they had not been introduced.

"And mine is Mathew Appleton." He smiled. "Please forgive me for not introducing myself earlier."

Jane felt a flush of embarrassment rise within her and turned towards the table lest he saw signs of this.

"Would you like something to eat? I bought fish," she said, and only then remembered how she had left her basket where he had fallen.

"Oh, excuse me, please. I have just remembered I left my basket outside." She rose with a sense of urgency, which prompted Bobby to stir up with his tail wagging.

Jane moved towards the door and took a shawl, which she placed about her shoulders. The day had grown since she had first met the man and now evening was beginning to settle in.

She found the basket where she had left it, but the fish had gone. Prize to some animal, she thought, perhaps a fox or even a badger, early about. It was just as she picked up her basket that she remembered the feeling of being watched earlier when she had tied the horse up, and spun around to see if anyone was watching her now. There was no one she could see, but the hedges were dense and she felt the same cold draught run down her spine again. She moved quickly now, back into her garden, closed the gate and hurried back inside, sorry she had not taken Bobby with her.

Mathew was sitting up and smiled when she came inside. She felt happy to see him. She felt safe with him and she knew Bobby liked the man too.

It was too late to go for help now and she still felt a little uneasy to go out now it was dark, but she moved the horse to a better place where there was shelter and took off the saddle, which was heavier than she had thought. Back inside, she lit the fire, made Mathew as comfortable as she could and cooked a meal. They ate in front of the glow of the fire and she found she laughed easily with the small things he said. She liked this man.

The morning came earlier than she had expected, for they had talked a long time in the night. She had been captivated by his thoughts, the places he had been to and the things he had seen. Paris, Rome, were for her somewhere on a map until he had given them vivid life with his descriptions of buildings, museums and people. She had been so enthralled with him that she had quite forgotten all the incidents of the preceding 24 hours, until in making a bed for him by the fire, a sudden wave of tiredness overwhelmed her.

She had no recollection of going to bed, only that in waking, she could feel the warmth of Bobby's body as he had come to lie on her bed. As she lay there, not quite fully awake, her thoughts wondered what it would be like to have Mathew lying by her side. She smiled inwardly and felt peace until a sudden and hard knock at the front door opened her eyes fully. Disturbed by the violence of the knock, Jane moved quickly out of bed and to the window overlooking her garden. Below, she could see two men, dressed in servants' clothes, one of whom held Mathew's horse by its rein.

She dressed quickly and with Bobby following behind, she went down below. Mathew had dressed, but it was plain to see that he was still in discomfort with his leg. She opened the door wide enough for the men to see Mathew and for him to explain simply what had happened. He bade them return to their master and thank him for his concern. Mathew, he explained by himself, would rest a few days within the house if he may, turning to Jane for her approval.

A rush of excitement rose within her, for at the sight of the servants, her heart had fallen, expecting them to take him away and forever out of her life. Now he was here. She had time with him. Hours to take care of him and hours to hold memories. She was in love with this man. How? She had no idea. It had happened so fast. All the events since leaving her home two nights ago had merged from fear to safety. She would be safe with this man. She knew it as she looked down at him sitting by the now dead fire. The fire had died in the night, but there was a fire burning within her now, and this, she would not let go out.

Chapter Two

Who is This Man?

The days passed happily between Jane and Mathew. With each day, his leg healed more and more, and as she saw him move more swiftly about, it saddened her to think he would the more quickly move out of her life.

As this thought grew in her mind, so it tormented her. At night, she would lie in bed thinking of him and in the day would watch the things he did with loving pleasure. She had memorized how his hands looked, for they were strong yet gentle. She knew most about his body, for at night, she would reconstruct him bit by bit in her mind. There was a deep need developing within her to have this man in her life but she did not know how, lest some clumsy movement brought rejection and termination to her desire. The moment came when she was not expecting it, or for that matter, much thinking about it.

He was sitting at the table, at the place she now kept for him. She had cooked food and was coming into the room. As she entered carrying two plates, she saw how he was looking at her. It was a deep penetrating look that seemed to invade not just her thoughts but who she knew herself to be. Jane saw her hand tremble as she failed in her attempt to calmly lay one plate before him. Mathew saw it too and moved his hand upon hers to steady her. How she wished he would say something. She ached inside to hear the words 'I love you'.

She felt the tensions rise within her; a flush of cold and then hot moved over her face. She breathed out to clear her mind, but she did so too fast and too hard to hide the feeling that had built up within her. Mathew rose from the table, took the remaining plate from her other hand, placed it on the table and took her in his hands.

"Ma…thew…" The words stumbled in hesitation from her lips. He gave no sound but looked into her eyes. She felt a tear move down her cheek and closed her eyes, not expecting the kiss that came upon her.

Thank you, she heard her thoughts whisper, as if to no one and yet to everything in existence, all at the same time.

Suddenly, there was a knock at the door. It was a loud knock that disturbingly woke her from the peace she held in her mind. Her eyes opened and she saw the love that she had yearned to see for so long in Mathew's eyes.

"The servants?" he wondered aloud.

"Tell them to go away," she whispered.

He nodded and rose. Both arranged their clothing and Jane opened the door.

There in front of her stood Squire Morgan himself.

"Is my nephew in here, madam?" enquired the squire in a loud and stern tone.

"Uncle!" Mathew came forward and stood beside Jane.

Squire Morgan ignored the obvious stance.

"Come lad! I can see you are better by yourself now. There are matters to attend to. You have been absent too long."

It was not a request. Squire Morgan was a man who demanded and he carried great authority in his manner.

Jane felt a twinge in her heart. Will he come back? Her thoughts danced with this worry. She wanted to reach out and hold Mathew's hand, but this would be too obvious. If the squire suspected his nephew was in love with her, it would be the end of everything. The end of her life, she feared.

It all happened so fast. One moment, she had him as close as she had been dreaming about. He was with her totally. He was hers. Then, with a cruelty, her love had been severed from her.

She leaned against the open doorway and watched as Mathew and his uncle walked to the main path, where two horses were tethered, waiting to take him away from her.

Would he turn to say goodbye? Would he care enough to look back?

The gate was closed. The two men mounted the horses. Her heart dropped. Then, the younger one said something to the older and dismounted again. He opened the gate and moved as quickly as he could—Mathew still could not run—back to her.

"Excuse me, Ma'am," he said aloud, "I forgot my riding crop." Mathew moved into the house and, when out of sight of his uncle, threw his arms about her in a tight embrace.

"God! I love you, Jane Witlaw. I will be back."

Her heart lit up.

"I love you too, Mathew Appleton. I love you so much."

She folded herself inside his arms, sensing all about him till he let go and went once more out of the house and away from her. This time, she did not watch him go. She did not need to, for she knew he would be back.

But when? she wondered.

Her thoughts were distracted by a scraping sound and she realized that Bobby had been shut out of the main room when the door had closed. She smiled to herself, grateful for the intimate time she had been allowed with Mathew, and opened the door to her four-legged friend who stood with his head to one side and his tail wagging. She looked beyond him and saw that too little was left of the meat she had left on the table.

"You rascal." She smiled, lifting the dog into her arms and giving him a warm and loving cuddle.

The following days passed uneventfully. The more time passed, the more Jane wondered if Mathew remembered her and if his love was real. She cleaned her home and was moving things about when she came to the skirt she had worn on the night she saw the ship crash upon the rocks.

It was an old skirt, but she loved the color, a faded sea green. Appropriate, she thought, for all that had happened. As she held it up and remembered she needed to wash the mud off the hem, she noticed again the tear. But it was not simply a tear. A part of the material was missing. It had been ripped off.

Suddenly, a fear ran through her mind.

What if the material had come off at the wall? What if a wrecker had found it? Then she remembered the strange way that man had looked at her at the harbor. What was she wearing that day? God! She had worn the same skirt as the night before. The skirt that had been ripped and was missing some cloth that she had not noticed till now.

Thoughts to go back to the wall and look for the fabric came and went as she tried to dismiss the fear from her mind, but the thought would not go. She had to go and look for that missing cloth.

It was windy when she opened the door and she wondered if it was too late in the day to go out, but she had to settle her mind. It wouldn't take too long, she thought. She would take Bobby for protection. The dog was little, but he was a terrier and had the courage of a lion to defend her.

Bobby was excited when Jane mentioned the word 'walk'. He was at the door with his tail wagging before the sound of the word had finished.

She opened the door, hesitated and said to herself, I have to settle this.

Bobby was already in the yard waiting for her, and before she had moved outside and closed the door, he was up at the gate waiting to go and explore.

Actually, it seemed a bit warmer than she had thought it would be and there was still enough light, so she felt happier she had made the decision and quite proud of herself for being so brave.

Jane and Bobby followed the way until they came to the old stone wall and the gap she had last moved through. Bobby was happily sniffing about, while Jane looked about the ground for the missing fabric. It could have been blown away, she thought, but if it was wet, it would more likely have gone to the ground and perhaps become wedged under a stone. She looked carefully about. The cloth was not to be seen. Slowly and gradually, Jane began to extend her search area. She was about 20 minutes in time from the gap in the wall and near the beach, when Bobby started to growl.

Jane froze. Thoughts flooded into her mind for all the reasons Bobby might growl, but the most obvious one took all the bravery out of her. Who or what was in the thicket that Bobby was staring at? Suddenly, and without any warning, a rabbit shot out of the undergrowth. Jane almost collapsed with relief, but Bobby was soon after the rabbit and fast disappearing down the path of broken stones.

Jane followed as quickly as she could, angry with herself now for bringing the dog. She could not see him anywhere. She stopped to catch her breath, walked up the path further and retraced her steps, peering into the scrub for any sign of her dog. After some ten minutes, she heard a faint howling sound coming from deep within the thicket. Cursing Bobby for running after the rabbit, she pushed herself between the bushes and overgrown scrub, hearing tears in the different skirt she had put on. Her hands were soon cut by thorns and rough wood and a few vines had scratched her face. One scratch felt deep and she found blood on the back of her hand after she had wiped her face with it.

After some time, for it was hard going, she came to a rocky outcrop so overgrown that it could not be seen from the path. A crack seemed to split a huge rock, and from the bottom of the crack, where it widened, was a space just large enough for a body to move through. It was from within here that she could hear Bobby. Cursing him more, she bent down, pulled her skirts tight to her and forced her slender body through the gap. It was dark at first when she came out into a sort of cavern, but gradually, her eyes adjusted to the light.

"Oh! Mother of God." There, in front of her, was much of the goods taken from the ship that had been wrecked. Quite by accident, Jane had discovered the secret hiding place of the wreckers. Now, she was in much more mortal danger than she ever had been.

Where was Bobby? Why had he not come to her? Why had he howled?

Jane was too frightened that there could be men about, so she could not call out his name. She was shaking with fear, but she would not desert her little dog. The cave she was in was dark, but a little shaft of light came from the gap in the rocks she had entered through. With a shaking hand, Jane slid off her right shoe and then her left so that no sound would be made as she walked upon the floor. As Jane moved past some wooden crates piled on top of each other, she felt the rock give way to sand. Still there was no sound of Bobby. As she moved deeper and deeper into the cave, it seemed to become strangely lighter. She could not hear anyone, but where was Bobby?

Slowly, ever so carefully, she moved closer and closer towards the light. Desperate not to make a noise, she held her breath for as long as she could, but then when she released it and inhaled, she thought she made more noise than if she had just breathed as quietly as she could. The light ahead flickered and she knew now that it was a fire. God, where was Bobby? She dared not go on, but she would not leave her dog. Step by slow step, each taken with a shaking leg, she moved closer to the light. Suddenly, there was a sound from behind. Her heart stopped and she turned wide-eyed in terror. She could not see anyone, but then below and by her feet, she could hear the panting of Bobby.

The dog must have entered the cave looking for the rabbit, somehow gone right through it to the outside, circled around and come to look for her and traced her back into the cave.

Too nervous to be relieved, she picked up the little dog and held her hand over his snout so he could not make a noise. As quickly as she could, Jane made her way back to where she had left her shoes, picked them up with her free hand and moved out of the cave, back into the dense but now happy, happy freedom of nature. She was free.

Quickly, but still carrying Bobby, she pushed her way back to the path that she had left not so long ago, not caring now for the rough thicket that caught her clothes and cut her arm. It was almost dark, but she hurried as fast as she could back to the gap in the wall and back home. All thoughts of the torn fabric she had come to look for were gone from her mind. All she wanted to do was be safely in her home, with the door locked and Bobby by her side.

Once inside her home, Jane went over to the fire and in lighting it, placed a large log by the side to warm up. Wood always burnt better when it was drier. As the flames began to splutter from the bracken she had laid and soon warmed into a fire, she wondered where Mathew was. Why had he not passed by? It was only a few days, but to her it seemed an eternity. Had he forgotten about her?

Suddenly, she felt very lonely and even Bobby coming to sit by her side and in front of the fire did not lessen the isolation she felt. She needed a man. A man to love, a man to care for and a man who would protect her when she was frightened.

Why the hell had Mathew not come? She stoked the fire in anger. She felt angry. She felt frightened. She felt lonely. She needed him. She felt jealous that there might be another woman with him now. She tried to dismiss the thought, but the more she looked into the fire, the more she felt that she only had Bobby in the whole world.

When she awoke the following morning, the air was cold and damp. A mist had come in from the sea and covered the landscape. When she looked out of her bedroom window, she could see little beyond the wall of her garden. Seagulls were crying overhead, but apart from their noise, she could have been living on the Moon. She felt so isolated, so deserted. She had not known it, but Mathew had come to see her while she was out with Bobby; in the long time she was trapped in the cave, he had assumed she had gone to visit a friend. Jane, however, knew none of this, and the cold, damp morning made her feel unhappier than when she had gone to bed.

Still, she thought to herself, no use feeling sorry for myself, and opened the window to feel the cold even more. Pain, although she knew this really wasn't, grounded her feelings. She pulled a blanket over her shoulders and went out from her bedroom down the cold stone steps of the staircase and into the living room. Standing in front of her was Mathew, and behind him, the fire was blazing.

"How…how did you get in?" she stumbled to say, while she flew into his arms.

God, he felt good. He was strong.

He held her tight and kissed her frantically.

"I am so sorry. I could not get away from my uncle and I could not risk a message. There was no one I could trust. I managed to come briefly yesterday, but—"

She held him tight to her bosom, not caring for his words now. His body was warm and hard. Her's soft and cold. She shivered and he led her to the fire by her hand.

"I missed you so much. I thought you would never come back."

"I came yesterday but you were out," he tried to explain again, holding her head to his chest as they stood by the fire.

Jane felt the heat of the fire warm first her legs and then her body, but Mathew's presence warmed her soul.

"How long do we have?" she enquired, a little frightened it was only minutes.

"Don't worry, my darling. We have all day…a very long day. My uncle had to travel to meet people, and I told him I had some business to attend to in Tregony. He won't be expecting me back until very…" He smiled… "…very late."

Jane felt a great happiness rise up from within her. He was hers all day.

Suddenly, the cold misty morning seemed to know of her happiness and rapidly disappeared to allow a warm sunshine to fall down upon the land. Jane thought of all the things they could do together.

"Sit yourself down, Mathew Appleton. I shall make a fine breakfast for you and then, we can take Bobby for a long walk and make a picnic."

At the sound of the word 'walk', Bobby stood upright, ears up and tail wagging. Both Jane and Mathew smiled at each other.

"How about I take Bobby for a short stroll while you ready our breakfast?" he suggested.

They both looked at Bobby, who was now standing by the front door, whining.

"Do we have a choice?" She laughed as she kissed him full force on his warm lips and felt the rough skin of an unshaven face. It made her feel excited. She turned with a girlish giggle and went into the kitchen, while Mathew donned his heavy coat and took Bobby outside.

It was nice and fresh in the early morning now that the mist had lifted. Bobby was happily sniffing about and making adventures for himself. Both were unaware of two men, rough cads, who walked up the lane and passed by.

"Mor'n, Squire!" said one, as both touched their hats in respect.

Mathew acknowledged them with a short wave of his hand and watched them pass Jane's gate. One of the men whispered something to the other, as both looked past Mathew to Jane's cottage.

Mathew felt uneasy with these two, as did Bobby, who was now barking at them. Mathew gave them a steady stare, and it was this, with Bobby's increasing barking, that drove the pair on their way.

"A shifty pair if ever I saw two," muttered Mathew to himself as he pulled back on Bobby's lead and led him back into the cottage.

"What was Bobby barking at?" called Jane, leaning half out of the kitchen doorway. Her face was radiant. She was happy. He would say nothing to dampen this day.

"Oh, I think he saw a rabbit," lied Mathew, holding his crossed fingers behind his back to lessen the fib.

"Rabbits again!" teasingly scolded Jane to the dog, as she gave him a loving gesture. Bobby dropped his head to one side and still wagged his tail.

"Now! Sit ye down there." Jane pointed to a chair at the table. "Warm bread and mutton are on its way."

She found it a great pleasure to make breakfast for Mathew. She simply wanted to make him happy, and in his happiness, feel a sense of purpose for herself. The mutton, however, had not been salted properly and as she took it out of the barrel, she questioned whether it was wise to eat.

Better not, she thought and took two eggs from the shelf. The dough was easily cooked on the fire. It was a simple meal, but the herbs she collected from her small garden dressed the plate well, and she smiled at Bobby, who was making short work of the mutton.

Mathew was sitting at the table when she entered the room. It felt so good to see him there. She felt a smile broaden across her face and saw the same upon his. She felt Bobby behind her. He did not want to be left out. Mathew held his hand downwards and the dog moved to it. My family, thought Jane. She could not remember feeling so happy before.

The breakfast passed quickly and with the sun now shining and the day beckoning, all three left the house and walked up the main path towards the old mine. Hammerhouse Mine had once been a good producer of tin, but the seam had run dry and the owners did not have the money to invest in new equipment to search for other seams, and as one accident had followed another, it was decided to finally close it down. It made Jane feel a little sad to pass the abandoned houses where once children had played outside, wives had cooked food and waited for their men to return after a long, hard day. Now the buildings were empty, ghost-like. No sounds, no cries and no laughter. She wondered where the people were now and what they were doing. Probably America, she thought, and if unlucky enough, Australia—the land where criminals went and those unfortunate enough to pay the debts that life heaved upon them.

As she looked at the now empty houses, her gaze took her thoughts beyond and to the blue sea. What land lay beyond, she wondered. As she saw how calm the sea was and how pastel the clouds seemed, her mind was suddenly brought back to that dreadful night when the wreckers had lured the hapless ship upon the rocks. A cold shiver ran through her and she grabbed Mathew's hand. His hand was strong. She felt safe. She moved towards him, but there was a cold feeling from him. He seemed strange and not like she had known him. She looked into his eyes and saw that he was hiding something.

For the first time, Jane felt strange with this man. A thought flashed through her mind, which caused her to wonder if she could be safe with him. It was as if he sensed it, because he suddenly held her hand reassuringly, but it was not the same feeling. This feeling was a pretense, and she knew it.

"Come!" he said. "I don't like it here."

"Why?" she asked.

"Nothing…I just want to go."

Jane knew this was not the truth. Mathew was not telling her something, but now was not the time to enquire more. She moved as he did and they passed by the empty houses and were soon over a hill and away from a place that had opened up a deep question in her mind. Who really was Mathew Appleton?

She tried to think nothing more about it, and when Bobby began barking at some seagulls that were flying too close to him, her mind seemed pleasantly to relax again. It was warm now and after some thirty minutes, they found a nice spot to lay the blanket he carried and begin to enjoy the picnic they had planned.

Jane thought how beautiful the sea was. It was so calm now. Only occasionally, whiffs of white broke the calm deep blue far below and beyond from where she sat. Mathew sat close to her and unwittingly, she touched his hand. It was an innocent touch, but the warmth she felt made her feel good. They fell back upon the grass and looked up at the rich blue sky to watch a white, puffy cloud slowly drift into view.

Somehow, she felt protected by his presence now. All thoughts of his strange behaviour so recently were soon forgotten. She loved him. She knew it and she wanted him forever. His head moved until his lips touched hers and a feeling of inner intensity filled her body. She could feel her heart move as he touched her tenderly. The sun was warm. The air fresh. The waves, far below from the cliff where she lay, could be heard lapping onto rocks. Their sound was gentle and as he breathed and she listened to their lapping against the shore, a feeling of completeness overtook her. She knew at that moment, in a strange kind of way, that he would always be a part of her life.

The rest of the day seemed to roll into one of happiness, laughter and fascination, as he told her of the lands he had been to and the things he had seen. Her world seemed so small and so insignificant to that which he knew. How she had long dreamed to travel beyond Cornwall. London had always been her dream. Streets filled with great wonders. Shops she could endlessly explore. Great buildings higher than the church steeple in Truro, it was said, but she had never thought of Italy until now. As Mathew laughed at her thoughts of London, she felt her eyes widen with a world unfolding before her when he told of Constantinople, of the great buildings there and of its people and the great markets he had walked through where everything was sold—even girls, he slyly winked. She laughed at the thought, but then felt a nervous twitch inside. There was something about this man that compelled and confused her at the same time.

The sun stayed for a long time in the sky, but soon its warmth began to fade and a wind picked up from the southwest. Perhaps, it was a sign the day was over, for they hurried to collect the things they had brought and return to her home. There was another path there and Jane chose it to avoid the old houses where Mathew had seemed troubled. It was late in the afternoon when they arrived at her home. She had hoped he would stay the night, but it was not possible, he explained, for he had business with his uncle to attend to. She did not like that old man, not for the way he treated others but because he seemed to be behind Mathew, always leaving her, and so she watched, lonely, as he lifted himself into the saddle, touched his hat with respect and with a wave was taken by his horse up the common path and beyond her sight.

Bobby jumped on the bed first and took his position at the bottom. It had been a long day and Jane fell within the sheets easily with her mind wondering once again why Mathew had pulled away from her at the old mine.

What thoughts did he have? What disturbed his mind? she wondered.

Once again, the thought seeped into her mind, Who is Mathew Appleton? But just as these did, so then did thoughts of another man come. She had not thought about Joshua since that dreadful night of the wreckers, when she had hated him so much for leaving her. So much had happened, so many things had disturbed and frightened her, until she had met Mathew. Now, as she lay there in bed and sleep overtook her, she wondered how the two men compared.

She was woken early the following morning by a sharp knock on the front door. Bobby barked and ran down the stairs while Jane wrapped a shawl about her shoulders and opened the window. Down below, she could see two soldiers. One of them looked up as she opened the window.

"Morning, Ma'am. Sorry to be disturbing you, but we have orders to search all the houses hereabouts."

"Search! What for?" she asked.

"Ship things. Open up, please."

Jane felt frightened, but had no reason to avoid the order. She quickly pulled her dress on, ran a brush through her hair and went downstairs. Bobby was growling at the door and she hesitated, wishing she was not alone. She picked Bobby up and opened the door.

The soldier she had spoken to touched his hat in respect.

"Sorry Ma'am. We have to look for belongings."

"What do you mean?" Jane enquired.

"Belongings from the wreck."

Her mind woke up now. They were looking for things that belonged to the ship that had been wrecked recently. The one she had witnessed. In other words, they were looking for people involved with the wreck. They were searching for wreckers. Wreckers were hanged.

Jane had nothing to hide, but she felt guilty that her home was about to be searched. She remembered her father's old gun and wished she had brought it down with her, but all this was so sudden and she felt dazed until she had stood in front of the soldier.

"It's OK." Jane stood back to allow the soldier to enter. It was only as this soldier entered that she could see the face of the second soldier. It was the one who had carried the horrible expression she had seen on the day after the wreck, when the three soldiers had come. It was the same man.

He looked at her with a snide kind of smile as he followed the other into her home.

Jane felt an instant dislike to him. He was not honest and she knew it. Worst was that he knew that she knew. Bobby growled at this man and showed his teeth. Jane held him tight.

"Please hurry up. I have a visitor coming soon." It was a lie, but she wanted to feel safe and she did not.

The second soldier paused as he entered the threshold. He looked deep into her eyes. This was a bad man. Jane hated him and did not want him in her home. He looked at the dog and growled back in jest.

Bobby lunged forwards at the man, but Jane held him tight and pulled his snout close to her chest in case the soldier hit him.

"Please hurry," she begged.

The first soldier had already moved from the living room and had disappeared into the kitchen, while this soldier she disliked went up the stairs. The thought of him searching her bedroom gave Jane a feeling of distaste. She wanted to go up there to see what he would do, but she knew it would be too dangerous. She waited by the door, thinking she could run out and escape if they tried to hurt her.

"Nothing!" shouted the first soldier. "Come on," he shouted to the one who had gone upstairs. "Found anything?"

The soldier upstairs did not reply. Jane felt unease at what he might be doing. Why had she let this man into her home?

It seemed a long time before she heard his boots coming down the stairs. She held her breath. Bobby snarled again as he reappeared in the living room.

"No!" he stated, looking at Jane again. He stopped at the foot of the stairs and leered at her. Jane felt very frightened, but tried not to show it.

The man lingered with indecision and Jane knew what was on his mind. Suddenly, Bobby flew from her arms and pounced at the man's leg.

"Get off!" he snarled as he tried to kick the dog.

"Fool!" the other soldier said and pushed him out of the door with Bobby's teeth fastened to his trouser leg. The soldier raised the butt of his gun as if to hit the dog, and Jane shouted, "No!"

Just at that moment, the neigh of a horse broke the scene. It was Mathew. He had come to save her.

"Oh. Thank God," Jane muttered as she felt safe enough now to go near the man and pull Bobby back. The dog barked, but the soldier laughed.

"What's going on here?" demanded Mathew as he jumped down from his horse.

"Nothing, Squire! Honest to God," said the first soldier. The second said nothing, but turned his face.

"Get ye gone," commanded Mathew. "Your officer shall hear about this."

"But we ain't done nothing," protested the first soldier.

"Go!" Mathew pointed to the gate with his riding crop. "Before I lay this about your backs."

Both soldiers moved off and Jane flung herself at Mathew, but as she did so, Bobby jumped out of her arms and ran at the soldiers.

"Oh! Thank God, you came. I was so frightened."

She held him tight as he put both arms about her.

"Get this dog off me." It was the soldier Jane most hated. "Get it off before I kill it."

Mathew strode to the soldier and picked up Bobby. "If I ever see you a mile from here, I will whip the hide off you. Do you understand?"

He stood tall and strong. The soldier backed away, and the other grabbed his shoulder and pulled him off Jane's property.

Mathew turned to Jane and, with Bobby under one arm, held her tight with the other.

"It's OK now," he said. "I am here."

"Oh, I was so frightened, Mathew. I hate that soldier."

"Why? Have you ever seen him before?"

"Once! Just after the wreck. Three soldiers came here. He was one of them."

Mathew said nothing, but guided her into the house and put Bobby down once the door was closed. "You are shaking, Jane. Here, sit down. I'll make a warm drink for you."

"No. Please. You sit down, Mathew. Let me look after you. It will please me."

She held his hand and, in letting it go, gently begged him to sit at the table while she went into the kitchen.

She felt dirty. The soldier had made her feel this way and she wanted to wash herself, but she was embarrassed to so clean herself with Mathew so close. In the kitchen, she ran water and washed her face and tried to tidy her hair. She wished she had made the time to look better before he had come, but he had come when she had most needed him. Perhaps he hadn't noticed the way she looked. She pinched her cheeks to make each a little rosy and herself look more cheerful. She had lit the fire and by now, the water had boiled. She took herbs from a jar and sprinkled some into two mugs, then added water.

It was as she brought the mugs into the living room and sitting next to Mathew, that he looked at her with a slight frown.

"Tell me what you know about the wreck?" he asked.

Jane could not stop but look at his face. Somehow, it had changed. He seemed strange again, just as he had done the day before.

For the second time since she had met Mathew, Jane felt a sense of wariness. Suddenly, she felt unsure of what was wise to say and what should not be said. She hated this feeling. It bred mistrust, yet there was something in his manner that warned her to be careful. Jane looked directly into his eyes, trying to convey honesty when she said, "Oh, not much. It was just what I heard in the village."

"What did you hear?" There was a look in his face, as a cat may have when it plays with a mouse. He was playing with her and it made her feel uncomfortable. Where is this coming from? her mind asked. What is Mathew doing? But Mathew gave no hint as to where he was going with his questions. The air between them had become cold and still; even Bobby noticed it for he whined at Jane's feet and gave her excuse to be distracted.

"Off you go," she said, brushing him away from her skirt and looking down at the dog, breaking the stare that Mathew had caught her in. Free of the stare, she attempted to stand up but his hand moved upon hers and held her firmly to the table.

She looked at him, now more wary than ever of what might come next, but he spoke in a calm and reassuring voice, "Jane, these are dangerous times. Wrecking is a serious business, but what happened recently is more so. More soldiers will be brought in to find those involved, and those who are, will slit a throat as easily as breathe through their own."

"Why?" She sat down from her half-raised stand and looked curiously into his face.

"The daughter of the Duke of Northumberland was on that ship. She was slaughtered with the rest of the crew. The Duke has promised to have every tree along the coast decorated with every man and woman involved. This is why those two were here this morning. Any artifact found in a home that can be connected with the vessel is enough to lead the entire household to the scaffold."

He waited a moment and watched her face.

"If you know more than you have told me, Jane, please tell me now. These villains will hunt anyone down and rid them, before the soldiers and the coastguard find them."

Indecision filled her mind. Could she trust this man? Why was he so strange yesterday and just now? But had he not saved her from those soldiers and did she not love him? How much did he love her? What did she really know about him, and who was M'Lord? Could it be Mathew? If it was he, she may be dead before the tea went cold.

Jane stared down at the cup in Mathew's hand, as if it could tell her what she should say.

She trembled inside. Looked into his eyes.

"I saw it all, Mathew." She had given him all her trust. She had placed her throat against his knife. God would guide his hand.

"I love you so much, darling." The game she had imagined no longer played in his eyes. Mathew was full of sincerity. He was strong and powerful. She would be safe with him. She knew it.

"Tell me all."

Jane recounted how she was out late and how she had hurt her ankle and become lost in the dark along the wall. She gave all in detail to Mathew, who listened very carefully. It was when she explained how she had heard the name M'Lord that the change came upon him again.

"Do you know who M'Lord is, Mathew?"

He nodded in silence. "But it is not something I can tell you or even dare to tell you. Does anyone know you were there?"

Jane shook her head, but thought then about the man in the square who had picked up the fish she had dropped. He knew something, she had seen it in his eyes. Jane described the incident to Mathew.

Mathew let go of her hand and pulled himself upright. "It cannot be safe for you here, Jane. Least, not for a long time."

A cold fear ran through her body. She had always felt nervous since that night, but the thought that her life could really be in danger had not so occurred to her.

"What should I do?" It was a plea. A fear that sought release. A summon for safety.

Mathew leaned forwards and once again took her hand within his own.

"We must go away from here. We must travel a long way and we must not dally, my darling."

Mathew looked out of the window. It was still before noon and she could feel the thoughts as one worked to another in the construction of a plan. A plan for her safety. A plan for a new life. A life with Mathew.

"We should go tonight!" he said suddenly. "There is a frigate we could take to France in the morning from Mevagissey."

"France! Why France?" The thought of leaving England was first a shock, and then an adventure. "I thought London."

"No! My sweetheart. We have to leave this merry land, at least for the time being. There is going to be a lot of trouble here, at least until the Duke feels righted." He paused in thought for a moment.

"It's better we leave tonight. I'll go now. I have things that need to be done. I'll be back just after dark with my uncle's coach. I'll tell him I have to do some business in Truro."

"We'll be ready," she said with a smile, stroking Bobby who had stayed by her side.

"Hmm. It's better not to take the dog."

"I can't go without Bobby."

"We'll have to. Is there anyone you can leave him with?"

"Leave him? How long will we be away?"

"I don't think forever… Maybe just a few months."

"But why can't we take him with us?" The dog looked up at Jane as if he sensed what was happening.

"It's better to leave him here. We'll travel a lot and it won't be easy to lodge with a dog in different places at night."

Jane looked down at Bobby and felt a sadness come upon her.

"Well, my sister could look after him. She would love him. But do we really have to go?"

"There's no doubt. If they suspect you know about M'Lord," his tone dropped when he spoke the word, "your throat will be cut readily."

Jane swallowed. "Alright," she said solemnly. "I'll take him once you leave."

"Good! Then, this is our plan."

He stood up, kissed her forehead and moved towards the door.

"Are you sure we need to do this?" she asked once again.

It was his look more than the words he spoke that confirmed what must be done.

"I'll do it. Will you come back soon?"

"After it is dark," he said, moving out of the door.

Jane remained sitting and looked down at Bobby. She felt a tear come to her eye.

"At least you will be safe, my darling," she said, stroking his head. Mathew's horse could be heard and suddenly, she realized he was gone.

It took Jane only a short time to dress properly, and with Bobby by her side, she walked the two hours to her sister's home.

Alice was outside hanging up washing when she came into view. The sisters waved to each other and Bobby ran on ahead to greet her sister.

"You look as happy as a bee, Jane. What's ahead?" Alice greeted her.

The sisters hugged and Jane entered Alice's home to explain all that had happened.

"Then you must let me read your tea leaves before you go," said her sister with a little look of intrigue.

Jane responded with a girlish giggle. She was so happy for the new life she was about to embark upon, and it would be interesting and exciting to have a happy time confirmed. But after Jane had drunk the tea Alice made for her, the serious look on her sister's face as she stared down into the tea leaves caused her to doubt that this had been a wise decision.

"What is it, Alice?" Jane could not contain herself.

"Well, this man of yours loves you for sure," began Alice, "and you will go on a long journey, but it will not be the journey you have in your mind." Alice put the cup down and looked directly into her sister's eyes.

"Take care, Jane. There be many dangers ahead. Be very careful whom you trust."

Jane's happy inquisitiveness turned to concern and she felt worried about what this could mean, but Alice could not or would not say more. The sisters talked for a while, but time was pressing and Jane knew she had to leave, but it made her feel happy that Bobby had a safe home while she would be away. Maybe everything is turning out as it should, she thought, thinking of Mathew, their new life and not too much about Alice's tea leaves. Besides, Alice was very happy to take the dog; her own had recently died and she had much lost love to give. So it was that later in the day, Jane parted from her sister, waved a final goodbye and left with the sound of Bobby barking from inside the house. Still, he will be safe, she thought to herself.

The wind had picked up now and Jane fought it most of the way home, adding another hour to her journey. It was getting dark already and she had little time to think about leaving her home. A new life was beginning and Mathew would be here soon. Jane went straight to her room and suddenly wondered what clothes she should take. She had no case, for she never left her home for more than a few hours. She took three dresses and some toiletries and carefully laid them within a shawl, knotted it and wondered if she should take more, when the sound of heavy wheels on the path outside made her hasten to the window. It was too dark to see if it was Mathew, but it must be—no coach ever came this way. She grabbed the shawl, it was heavy but Mathew would carry it for her. Quickly, Jane went down the stairs and to the living room. She took one last look about her home, opened the door and was out in the darkness.

She looked at the path and could just make out the outline of a carriage. It was dark and there was no sound, save for the slight neigh of a horse. Suddenly, there was a sound behind her. A foot heavy upon the ground. Jane turned quickly but not quick enough to avoid the cloth placed forcibly over her mouth. She struggled against the hand that held the cloth but it was too strong, then a great pain came upon her head and a darkness greater than the night came upon her mind.

Chapter Three

Betrayal

Confusion and pain greeted her from within the dark room she found herself in. Jane tried to sit up but the room was rolling from left to right and she realized she was in some kind of a ship.

"Help!" she called, but her voice was weak and frail. Her head hurt too much to think clearly and the movement of the boat made her feel sick. Her head hurt, but her heart hurt more than she could imagine. Did Mathew do this to her? Why? What harm had she ever done to him? She cried. Her heart cried for injustice. How she missed her home and Bobby. Why was this done to her?

There was little light in the room and the foul stench within it was overpowering. She heard a noise outside the room and suddenly, the door to it opened. It was darkish outside and Jane could just make out stars in the faint distance. The open door brought a rush of fresh air and Jane felt a sense of freedom with it. But within moments of it opening, a small man with one tooth in his mouth appeared and passed in two buckets. One slopped with water.

"Here," he said abruptly. "One for pissing in and one for drinking out of. Don't mix them up." His laughter was cruel and it left a chill within her as he slammed the door shut and sealed off the fresh air. Jane felt frightened of what hell she had been thrown into.

With the door closed again, the room seemed to smell even more of foul air than before, and the buckets she had been given soon became demons that played on her mind. One gave her life and the other allowed the equally foul man to know her privacy. He came the next day, brought bread and cheese and changed the buckets. He did not speak to her. His eyes gave no compassion. They were as empty as his heart.

On the second day, when he brought new buckets, she asked: "When will we arrive in France?"

The cold and only reply he gave was, "We ain't going to France."

Where then was she being taken? Mathew had told her he would take her to France; maybe that also was a lie. She cried long and deep at the deception he had done to her. In the darkness of the room, she remembered how he had changed when she had said the word, M'Lord. Was Mathew M'Lord? Could it have been he who had walked past her on that dreaded night? The dark plays evil games on the mind, and all Jane had was darkness now.

She curled herself up and cried. There was no one to hear her and no one to care. All had been taken away from her. She had nothing. Nothing, except the question, why?

The sea was rough and the ship she was in rolled mercilessly from side to side. It was, she was sure, the third day and she tried to think of how to escape. The man who came was strong and, she knew, would have no qualms about hurting her. Yet the thought of escape did not go from her thoughts and so, Jane began to wonder how she could trick him into the room, just long enough for her to slip through the doorway, but what then could she do? She could not swim.

Suddenly, a sharp cry came from outside the door. Voices were shouting and all went quiet with a sudden pistol shot. Jane stirred in terror towards the doorway, dreading what may befall her now. There was a heavy sliding sound, as if a large sack was being moved from somewhere outside. Suddenly, the door burst open.

Jane could not see clearly. Her eyes were blurry with so much darkness. All she could see was the outline of a man at the doorway.

"My God. What have they done to you?"

It was Mathew. Mathew had come. He had saved her. But fear lingered inside of Jane. How could Mathew save her? It was he who had put her here in the first place. It was Mathew who had betrayed their love. She had left her home, believing he would rescue her and instead, he had had her brutally kidnapped.

Jane cowered in a corner as Mathew took a step into the room. She could not look at him.

"Jane. It's me, Mathew. I am so sorry, darling. I knew none of this."

Confusion twisted her thoughts. Would he hurt her? Did he still love her? Why was all this happening? Suddenly and uncontrollably, she burst into tears. She cried and cried and felt Mathew lift her up and carry her out of this damp room that had been her prison.

The light was bright and as she closed her eyes because of this, she felt closer to the man who carried her.

"Oh, Mathew. Why did you do this to me? I trusted you so much."

"It was not me, my darling."

Jane opened her eyes to look at him but as she did so, she could see bodies lying about the deck of the ship. Red blood ran from the body of a man, and the man who had brought her the buckets and made fun of her lay by the side of the door.

"Oh Mathew, I was so frightened."

"I know, darling. I will explain all to you, but first, we have to get off this boat."

A marine came forward and tried to put Jane in a sling so that she could be transferred to another ship lying close by, but she would not let go of Mathew. It was only after he promised to come with her immediately that she released her grip of him. The marine tied the sling, gave a loud whistle and Jane saw herself move up and away from Mathew. He looked intently at her, but as she moved further from the ship, she could see more bodies lying about. There were shouts coming from the ship she was being transferred to and as she looked down, she could see some sailors waiting for her. Many men were moving about quickly, some in white and some with red coats. An officer was pointing to something she could not see and as she came to land on the deck, he moved forwards and took off his hat.

"Welcome, Ma'am, to His Majesty's ship, Valiant. I am Lieutenant Hathaway. Would you please come with me, Ma'am? Mr Appleton will join you shortly."

Jane turned and could see Mathew waving to her. She felt safe now. She felt too tired to dwell on all that had so recently happened. She was just so grateful her hell was over. She took one last look at the cruel ship full of cruel people and turned to follow the officer off the deck and into a room brightly lit by lanterns.

It seemed a long time, too long, before she heard sounds outside the door of the cabin she had been placed in. Her mind had gone over everything that had happened since she had met Mathew and she could find no explanation for the recent events of her kidnapping. Jane knew Mathew was good. She knew it in her heart, but why was he not here with her now, comforting her and telling her the truth?

It was as the word truth moved through her thoughts that the handle of the door suddenly turned and the door was opened wide. Mathew moved quickly into the room and embraced her strongly as she stood up to meet him.

"Oh my darling, darling Jane. I am so terribly sorry for all that has happened to you. It's all my fault. I should have told you about my uncle when I first met you."

His words moved past her mind as if they were not meant for her. All she could think of was of Mathew holding her. He felt so solid, so strong. She inhaled deeply the smell of his body. She knew this man. She knew his scent, she knew his soul, how could she ever have doubted him? He would never hurt her. Jane knew it now. All thoughts of why or if had gone. He was with her, and that was all that mattered.

Mathew made way for her to return to where she had been sitting.

"I have so much to explain to you, my darling."

"It's OK, Mathew, I don't—" but she could not find the words to finish her sentence as she saw a tear leave his right eye.

"I am so, so sorry, my darling."

The fear of her danger and of the pain of thinking that she had been betrayed welled up inside her. She felt tears coming from her own eyes. They flooded down her face as Mathew moved to place his arms about her once again.

"Oh Mathew! Please don't ever leave me again."

"I won't, Jane. I never will leave you again, my darling."

She missed him. She needed to feel him, to know he was hers again. He felt the need too and held her tight.

A dry cough came from beyond the door and Jane felt her cheeks burn in embarrassment.

"Oh, Mathew!" She held a hand to her face, dreading that someone was outside.

"It's OK, my darling. I had a guard posted in the gangway so we would not be disturbed."

She looked at him, a little confused at first, then smiled. He would always think of her. He would always look after her.

"One moment!" he commanded to the man waiting outside the door.

Hastily, they straightened their clothing and after Jane had brought order to her hair, Mathew invited the intruder in.

"Begging your pardon, Master Appleton, but the captain requires you on the bridge if you please."

"Thank you. I shall come in a moment. Please wait outside."
The marine bowed to Jane and closed the door behind him.

"Oh, Mathew, I need you with me. Please don't leave me again."

Mathew looked into her eyes, "I never will again, Jane. Never." No tear came, but his eyes held so much water he had to wipe them with the back of a hand. "Rest, please," he asked. "I must see the captain, but only for a short time."

Jane watched him move across the small room and remembered only the door closing after he had left. She felt unsure of herself now in an empty room. Thoughts of the dark one she had been held in came flooding back and Jane turned the wick up in the lanterns to bring more light into the room.

The door opened and she woke with the sound. Jane had not realized how she had fallen asleep, but the tension of all the past few days and the sudden release of it all safe in Mathew's arms had brought a peace upon her that took her into a deep sleep.

"I am sorry, my dear. I was too long and now I have disturbed you."

"No! No, please stay, Mathew," she pleaded as he moved to leave the room. "Come and sit by me. Tell me what I need to know."

He took off the hat he was wearing, one that he must have put on to meet the captain, and placing it upon the table, sat down opposite to her.

"What happened, Mathew?" Her eyes held a tiredness and sadness that caused Mathew to drop his head in shame.

"I am so, so sorry, Jane. I thought it would be best if you never knew and in your ignorance be safe."

He lifted his gaze to meet hers and she could see the pain he could not conceal.

"My uncle was behind the wreckers. He was, to my knowledge, the organizer and the profiteer." He hung his head in shame now. "I did not know what kind of man he was until it was too late."

"What do you mean too late, Mathew?"

Once again, he lifted his eyes to look directly into hers.

"They knew about you, Jane."

"Knew about me, why? How?" She was startled by what she heard.

"Do you remember the night of the wreck, when you saw them on the beach and heard men pass you by as you hid?"

She nodded her head slowly, remembering clearly that night.

"Well, as you moved from your spot to the wall, one of them glimpsed you. Well! They did not know it was you at first, for they only saw the outline of a woman move and then they were distracted by the ship crashing onto the rocks. Anyway, M'Lord was informed…" Mathew paused for a moment when he said this name and bit his lip before continuing, "…and the next day, they began to think who you may have been. Perhaps, it was my accident that saved you, because they were intent on doing away with you, reasoning it was you who lived so close to the spot and lived alone."

A look of horror passed over Jane's face. The thought she would have been murdered had not entered into her head.

He looked sheepish and explained how he had stumbled across a tunnel in his uncle's house and how he had found many valuables taken from the ship. His uncle had caught him and sworn him to secrecy, to which he had agreed, providing he looked at her directly now, "—that you would not be harmed."

"Oh, Mathew!" Jane moved closer to him and held his hand. "I would have gone anywhere with you."

"It was my thought, Jane, to take you to a safe place, but events went faster than my plan. In all my naivety…" Again, he dropped his head but in clear regret now. "…I went to my uncle and asked for a loan so that you and I may begin a new life in France, where we would never trouble him.

"My uncle agreed and promised a good sum so that we could be safe and away, but in the drink he gave me was a draught. When I later woke from it, I found myself locked in my room. This was why," a look of such deep pain came upon his face that he raised to hers, "I was not in the carriage that night we had agreed."

"But where were they taking me?" she enquired.

Mathew let out a long sigh. "After two days, my door was unlocked and two of my uncle's men took me to him. He was so evil that time. I had never seen a man so possessed with evilness.

I felt deep inside that they had indeed killed you, but then, with a cruel laugh, my uncle explained how you were to be taken to the colonies to be sold there as an indentured slave. The ship we rescued you from was only a coastal ship that was to rendezvous with a larger ship that would have taken you…" he paused momentarily before solemnly saying, "…across the Atlantic…"

"Slavery!" A feeling of horror passed over Jane. Then suddenly, she remembered Bobby. "Oh, Bobby! I must get back to my sister, Mathew. She is holding Bobby for me there."

This time, a warm smile came upon Mathew's face. He said nothing, but stood up.

"We can never go back to England, Jane. Never, do you understand?"

She felt confused and worried now about little Bobby. He was always her best friend. Her companion when all had left her. Why had she not thought to keep him with her that night?

"Wait, my dear."

Mathew turned and left the room again. It was some time before he returned, but when he came once more into the room, he held in his arms a small scruffy-looking terrier.

"Bobby!" she cried. "Oh, Bobby!" Jane moved up and towards Mathew and took hold of the little dog, who, in making such a great fuss, nearly fell from Mathew's arm.

"Oh, now we can go, Mathew. Thank you so, so much for this." But then, she looked up at Mathew in puzzlement. "Where can we go, Mathew?"

"Well, darling, I managed to escape from my uncle and, in knowing a colonel of militia, went straight to him. It seemed this man and my uncle had long been foes and so it was only a short time before soldiers went to arrest him. But…" he held his breath for a moment, "…the bird had flown! No sign of my uncle could be found and while many of his gang were caught and confessed, nothing more of my uncle was heard of again. So, you see, my dear Jane, we can never be safe in merry England again. It is a new country for you and for me now, and a new life."

"And one for Bobby too." She smiled, looking down at the little dog who, with tongue out, sat panting on her lap.

They both looked at Bobby as he in turn looked at each of them. Jane looked back to Mathew.

"Where will we go, Mathew?"

Chapter Four

Deadly Waters

"Our ship is headed for Virginia, Jane. A new land with new hope, but this time you will arrive as my wife and not a slave."

"Your wife?" A smile lit up her face and a gleam shone from her eyes.

"Providing that is, that you will accept me?"

"Oh yes, Mathew."

He nodded. "It was for this very reason that the captain called me before. He will make the necessary ceremony as soon as we are ready."

"I am now." She stood up and held her hands out to him.

Mathew stood up and took her hands in his. "I will ask the captain for his instructions in this. But first, you need to rest. You have been through more than I would ever have dreamt in my worst nightmare. Come, there is a cabin and clean clothes for you."

"Clothes!" Jane looked down at her dress. It was filthy and the material ripped in parts. She had not thought how she looked until this moment. All had happened so fast and she had been so confused by all the events that had passed with so much turmoil.

"Oh, Mathew, I look awful."

"It is all over now, Jane. Come with me and I will show you to your cabin. I had the mind to bring clean clothes for you."

She looked into his eyes. Mathew really cared about her. How could she ever have doubted him?

Jane awoke to the gentle roll of the ship. It was, she learnt, a merchantman of war. A large ship that carried both sailors and marines, many of whom always seemed to be moving about doing things. The constant movement of men made Jane feel idle and with Mathew's permission and in ignorance of his warning, she made her way to the galley to see if she could help the cook with the many meals he must make.

The sight of the huge negro made Jane feel a little frightened at first, for he did not look the happiest of men in the happiest of times and to see a woman on a ship—"The worst luck in the world," he muttered when he first caught sight of her; it did not cool his temper when she asked to be of assistance. But despite all his sullen ways, he was a kind man at heart and saw how lonely the woman was without a purpose. He suggested she would be better sewing sails, but he found a use for her in preparing meals for the officers. A task that most pleased the captain, and as days went by, her singing in the galley area had a calming effect upon all present.

Gradually, a happy companionship blossomed between the cook and "the lady", as he called her, as with her feminine charm, she found a way to make him smile, although he was quick to hide it if a crew member appeared.

The first leg of their journey was uneventful. The Atlantic could be as calm as a millpond, the cook explained to her, but with little warning could be a nightmare of monstrous waves that would engulf the biggest of ships and so, warned her how to be about in the galley if the seas should rise and how hot pots could roll about if not set properly where they should be. Jane's duties, as she liked to call them, did not take much of the day and she and Mathew began to talk more and more about the world that lay somewhere over the horizon as yet unseen.

The day of the wedding came and all aboard the ship made it special. Sailors had prepared knots of white sail to decorate the bridge. Jane, with only the simple dress she had and no other woman to help her, made the best preparation she could. The captain was a kind old man, nothing like the rough sea dog she expected a captain to be, as she told Mathew. The first officer had volunteered to be her stand-in father and give her away, but Jane thought he was too keen for others to see how important he was; besides, he was more her own age. No! Jane asked the cook, who seldom smiled and often cursed.

"But why him?" Mathew had asked.

"I like him," said Jane. "He is honest, and I know he is kind at heart, even if he doesn't show it."

"Well, he doesn't have many teeth to show," remarked Mathew as he ducked the towel Jane threw at him in jest and, moving out of the cabin, turned back and blew her a kiss.

She felt so happy. She had Mathew and now Bobby. She had her family; everything else would be in God's hands. She twirled around in happiness and felt her skirt rise with the motion. What a wonderful day it is going to be, she said to herself. Mrs Mathew Appleton!

The ceremony was a simple but very joyous one, for the main deck and much of the riggings were filled with sailors and marines cheering as the captain pronounced them man and wife. Everyone was happy, even the cook was smiling and felt bold enough to ask to kiss the bride. One of the officers tried to take the chance, but Jane flung her arms around the cook and gave him such a huge hug that many sailors shouted greetings that the cook's face reddened with embarrassment. Then, two sailors cleared a space on the deck and began to play penny whistles, while two more moved into the clearing and began to dance the hornpipe.

"Come on." Jane took Mathew's hand as she pulled him towards the dancing sailors. More space was cleared for the couple as Jane and a too stiff Mathew danced the hornpipe with the sailors.

"Oh, this is so much fun," she laughed as she lifted her skirt and danced outwards with her toe. The dancing continued as more sailors and even a junior officer joined in. Suddenly, the swirling of the dance went to Jane's head and she grabbed Mathew's arm.

"I have to sit for a moment, darling," she said, full of fun.

A rough-looking man in his 50s, with few teeth in his mouth and a nose that had been broken on more than one occasion, offered Jane a grog of rum. "Excuse me, Ma'am, but would you drink with a poor sailor?"

"To be sure I will," she replied in his Irish brogue and with such a smile that the man leaned backwards in play, but then lost his balance and, falling upon another sailor, slid to the floor, too drunk to get up. A roar of laughter came from the surrounding sailors, causing Jane to laugh again.

Mathew looked at his new wife. She was so beautiful and so full of life. Here was a woman who could and would talk with the king and with a common sailor and treat each as equal. He had a fine investment for any political work ahead, he thought. With a woman like this behind him, he might even be a governor of the colonies one day.

The thought of the new land they were sailing for sobered his thoughts, and he moved slightly from Jane so he could turn to face the sea and lean on a railing.

"What is it, Mathew?" she asked, as she placed her arm within his and followed his gaze out towards the endless sea.

"Oh, I was just wondering what lies ahead, darling."

"A new beginning," she said happily.

Mathew's face was stern, though, for he was in deep thought.

"What is it?" Jane asked, trying to encourage a smile upon his face.

He turned and, looking into her eyes, smiled. Their eyes held each other and each felt the happiest they could ever be.

"Nothing at all." He shook his head. "Just wondering how we will make out."

Jane looked with a joking sternness into his eyes. "Mathew Appleton, we will make out, and we will make out wonderfully, do you understand me?"

He looked deeply into her eyes. This was the woman he needed.

A polite tap on his shoulder caused Mathew to turn. It was the first officer.

"Beginning your pardon, Master Appleton, but may I be so bold as to ask your wife for a dance?"

Jane felt sorry for the man. He did not know how to be happy. She thought that his whole mind was set that he would one day be a captain, and as such, he should be distant from all on board. The master of the ship.

"Of course you may, Mr Felling," said Jane as she curtsied and took his hand. She turned back to smile at Mathew and gave a huge wink to the cook who had caught her eye from beyond a group of sailors.

But Mr Felling was even a worse dancer than Mathew and it was a relief to Jane that he soon excused himself, having played an honorable part.

"Ship Ahoy!" came a shout from the top of the main mast. All heads turned up towards the lookout and then east in the direction of his outstretched arm. There, on the horizon, the outline of a ship could be seen.

"What is it?" asked Jane, who became concerned by the gravity on Mathew's face.

"I don't know, my darling."

But as these words left his mouth, they were drowned by the words of the coxswain.

"Battle stations! Battle stations!" Marines started to beat their drums, which until now had been silent.

The gaiety and happiness of her wedding would have to be postponed.

The captain moved to Mathew. "Better take the lady below, and good to stay with her, Mr Appleton, if you please."

"But why, Sir?" asked Jane.

"Pirates probably, Ma'am!" The captain touched his hat in respect and shouted orders to those about. Sailors were moving quickly now, huge guns that had not been noticed before were now rolled to openings in the side of the hull.

What had moments before been a happy carefree assembly was now one of the finest organized body of men, all held in unison by the terrible discipline they had been taught to fear.

"Quickly, if you please, Mr Appleton, follow me," came the voice of the first officer who may have been awkward on the dance floor but was now showing himself to be the man of action that he truly was.

With cutlass in hand, he pushed through the throng of moving men, watching that Mathew and a now much frightened Jane were close behind.

"If you please, Sir, take the lady below deck and to the captain's cabin. It may be the safest place to be, and hurry past the centre of the ship."

"Why?" asked Mathew, baffled with all this new confusion.

"It's where the gunpowder is stored."

Jane felt her hand press hard against that of Mathew's. "Will we be alright, Mathew?"

"Of course, my dear. This is His Majesty's warship." But his words did not carry the conviction he had hoped to give.

Just then, there was a loud explosion in the water close to the ship and a huge spray came down upon them.

"Oh, Mathew. I am frightened."

"Haste, Sir. Haste!" shouted the first officer, as he turned away from them and shouted orders to sailors standing by guns.

Jane pushed her hands to her ears as a deafening roar blew from the guns on the side of the ship.

"Quick, my dear, follow me." Mathew took her hand and, pushing a door open, led the way to a wide staircase.

"No! We must get Bobby."

"But Jane—" Mathew's face held a pain of worry. He had to get her to a safe place.

Her face was not to be moved. "Bobby" was the single word she said.

Avoiding the stairs, Mathew and Jane moved further into the ship until they came to a row of small rooms. Barking from one told them where Bobby was.

"Oh, Bobby, you must come quickly," said Jane, but as she bent down to pick him up, Mathew had already grabbed the little dog and, holding him strongly under his left arm, pulled Jane with his right hand back the way they had come.

Suddenly, there was a deafening explosion and a shower of splintered wood blew into the air. Men screamed as limbs were broken or smashed. Blood was running freely over the deck and the air was so heavy with smoke that Jane could only cough and squint her eyes to wonder which way she should run. Mathew was straight by her side. He said nothing, but grabbed her arm and forced her forward. She lifted her skirt to avoid stepping upon a man who did not move on the deck and wanted to help another who begged for help, but Mathew did not stop his pace. She turned to look at him and winced to see blood on his face.

"Oh, Mathew." She reached up to his face to find where the blood was coming from, but he held her arm steady.

"It's nothing," he said, as he fought a path through the mayhem. Suddenly, they were at the top of the stairs again but just as they began to move down, their ship fired a whole broadside towards the enemy ship and rolled fully to the left. Jane lost her balance and began to fall, but Mathew grabbed her shoulder. "Steady," he said. "Quick! That way." He pointed to a door at the end of the lower deck, but reaching the door was no easy thing, for sailors were moving about quickly and had no time for manners. This was life or death, and the latter if you dawdled.

Just as they reached the door and Mathew opened it, a sailor came up to him and, touching the lock of hair on his forehead, asked, "With the compliments of the surgeon, Sir. Would you care to assist him?"

Mathew's mind swayed with indecision. He did not want to leave Jane, but he knew the surgeon would need all the help he could get. He knew many would die, if there was not enough help for them.

He forced open the door to a cabin to find piles of canvas. "Darling, please lie on the floor and hold Bobby tight. Protect your bodies with the sails." But he did not wait for her to do it. It was then that Mathew realized how the little dog was limp. Bobby was not moving. A splinter from the explosion had killed him.

"Oh my God, Jane, I am so sorry."

The agony that rapidly spread over Jane's face told its own story. "Oh, Bobby," she cried.

She took the little body from Mathew and held it tight to her. Tears flowed from her face, but then there was a sudden tilt of the ship and Mathew grabbed her to hold her upright.

"Please lie down, darling. It is not safe for you."

Jane had lost all reason. She could not make sense of the words that were coming from Mathew, but she made no resistance as he laid her down on the deck and began to cover her with heavy canvas. She kept the lifeless body of her little dog close to her, unable to think about anything clearly. All she was aware of was Mathew placing more canvas upon her and how the weight became heavier and the light beneath it darker.

She heard his voice saying, "Please do not leave this place. I will be back as soon as I can."

Weakly, she called his name, but he was already moving down the deck with the sailor.

Another explosion somewhere above made Jane cry in fear. "Oh God, please help us! Please God, please protect Mathew."

An explosion so loud that Jane felt her ears would burst, suddenly shattered all thoughts. She clung tightly to the little dog's cold body in her darkness. Jane had never imagined to be so frightened in her life in the silence that followed the explosion. There was no sound. It was as if the world had completely ended. All was silent. For a long time, there was no sound of any description. Then, and suddenly eerily, the sound of a shoe slowly walking upon the wooden floor brought her fear to a new height.

Pirates! Jane shut her eyes tightly and dared not to breathe.

The footsteps moved slowly and uncertainly about the room. They sounded fainter and Jane prayed they were moving away from her. But then, they stopped momentarily and turned about. One…two… Jane counted the steps coming slowly towards where she lay hidden. Her heart was beating beyond her body, and in her terror, she tried not to breathe, praying she would go unnoticed, but slowly, very slowly, the canvas was lifted slightly off the ground until Jane looked straight into the face of the cook.

Jane was so relieved and so happy to see her friend.

"Oh thank you, Tom. I was so frightened you were a pirate!"

He smiled from his toothless mouth. "Some say I am, missus. Come on! Let us get you out of here. Master Appleton asked me to fetch you. He cannot leave the surgeon yet, too much to do."

The thought of Mathew helping the doctor, and then of so many injured men, brought Jane back to reality.

"Bobby," she said and held the little body for the cook to see.

"I am sorry, Mistress Jane. I am sorry, but there are men badly wounded. Bobby has moved to Heaven. There are men living in Hell. We must think of these poor souls now."

Jane understood what he was saying. Bobby was in Heaven. He was not here now. Now he was safe, she told herself, then asked, "What was that awful explosion, Tom? It felt like the end of the world."

"It was for them pirates, Miss." His face went hard at the thought of those evil men and what they could have done had they boarded the ship. "We blew them to kingdom come. Hit their magazine and the entire black ship blew up. Not a worthless soul left." He crossed his forehead.

Jane did not really understand what the cook had meant, but she knew the pirates were no more and now she and Mathew were safe again.

"Can you take Bobby and me to Mathew, please?"

"I can't do that, Ma'am. It's not a sight for a woman with all those damaged men about. Many lost a limb today."

"A limb!" The horror of amputation brought a gasp from Jane.

The cook cast his eyes down. "The good captain an arm."

"Oh my God!" Jane covered her mouth to disguise the horror she felt. "Please take me to these men, Tom. I can help. They need their mother now."

The cook looked into her eyes momentarily, unsure of what to do.

"Please," she pleaded.

"It's best I take you to your cabin first. Master Appleton will have to decide this, but let me take the little dog. I will see he is buried rightly."

"No, Tom, I want him with me."

The cook nodded. "I understand. It's OK, Ma'am, please follow me."

As Jane and the cook moved through the ship, she was horrified to see how much damage had been done in such a short time. Splinters of wood, large and small, lay over parts of the deck, which was spoiled with red stains of too recent blood.

Sailors were moving about, bringing things into order. Eventually, they approached a doorway, which Tom opened for her, and asked her to wait in the room beyond.

It seemed only moments before she had seen Mathew handsome, clean and sweet. Now, in a time too short, he looked tired and covered in blood. Not his, thank God, but that of sailors he had labored to save with the surgeon.

"It's not the place for you down there, Jane. You must listen to me." He paused and looked at the little body she held.

"Let me take Bobby. I will make sure he is buried like the sailors today he died with."

She looked into his eyes and felt the suffering he had just lived through. She knew Bobby was not now with her, but to let go of his body felt wrong.

"The men need their mother now," he said. "Would you be their mother?" He was thinking to distract the pain in her mind. "Some are very young and this is not the world they belong in." He added, "Some will soon be in another."

She nodded and did not resist as Mathew took the little body from her and gently placed it on a bunk.

"It won't be pretty, my darling… But I know you can handle it."

He turned, opened the door as if in haste and closed it after she had walked out. Outside the room, the atmosphere was much noisier than Jane had noticed before. Perhaps it was the quietness of the cabin that had made her more aware of what was really happening in the ship, or perhaps her mind had been distracted by the relief she had felt in being met by the cook and not a pirate, but now she could smell the smoke in the air and hear more the sounds of men groaning in pain as she followed Mathew further into the depths of the ship.

Men were lying in rows, either side of the deck. Many were bandaged, with red stains on the white cotton. Some seemed unconscious, others awake but silent as they watched her pass. Jane felt their pain and bent down to reassure a young boy, too young to be here, that he would be alright and his father would be so proud of him. Mathew had moved into another room, but as she turned to seek him, she saw the captain propped up against the wall.

"My place is here with my boys," he managed a smile as he understood she expected to see him placed in better surroundings.

"Oh, Captain. I am so sorry." She looked at his eyes, deliberately avoiding the empty sleeve to his left.

"Still a good arm left, my dear."

"Jane! In here, if you please." It was Mathew's voice and as a stern instruction that she had never heard before.

Jane excused herself from the captain and moved into the place Mathew had called her.

"Hold his hand," Mathew said, as she saw a young sailor upon a table.

The surgeon looked up at her momentarily. "Thank you, Ma'am. Show your love."

Jane looked into the eyes of the man and tried with all her might to ease the terror from his eyes as the surgeon's saw cut into his flesh. Strong men were holding him fast, locking him to the table, but his body struggled for freedom from the pain. It was over in half a moment and the useless foot was placed into a bucket. The stump of his leg was sealed with tar, and Jane bit her lips to hold back the tears as the eyes of the man closed.

"He'll be alright in a while," the surgeon tried to comfort her.

"Thank you, Jane. He needed his mother then." Mathew looked into her eyes. "Well done, darling. He was the last."

She felt angry with herself for hiding under the canvas when she should have been here, where she was needed, but she knew that she had not known of this place or what was going on here. It was a new world to her and one she hoped never to visit again.

The unconscious man was lifted gently off the table and placed among others on the deck. Jane moved to be with him, but others called to her for attention. All each wanted now was love. They had moved with strength to fight, but while in their pain, all they wished for was love. Men, old and young, would not admit it, but while in pain, they wished for a mother. Jane had found a place where she could be that to each and every one of them. Taking time to smile at each and share her love, she moved from one to another, until a sailor next to the man she was moving to said, "Sam won't be needing you now, Ma'am. He's gone to a greater place than this."

She looked down at the still body and knew others were watching her. Jane would not cry in front of these brave men. She struggled to keep her composure, nodded reverently and moved to the next man.

"Here, Ma'am, take a swig. It will help." A sailor passed her a mug containing rum. Jane looked down into the drink. There were so many here who needed this far more than her, but she smiled a thank you at the man and pretended to take a drink before passing the mug back to him. They needed to feel she was one of them. She needed this too, right now.

"Come, my dear." Jane turned around and was relieved to see Mathew standing above her. "You need to rest."

"No. I'm alright, Mathew." Though she knew she was not and Mathew knew it too. He held his hand out to her until she gave in and gratefully was pulled to her feet.

Jane looked about her and felt sad to see so many young men now disabled for life. She wondered why this had happened. What had all this really been for? She saw bodies being stitched up in canvas, being made ready for sea burial and thought of the mothers, wives and lovers in England who did not yet know what they had lost and must live with this loss all their lives. A man moaned near her and she was brought back to thinking of those who survived, and wondering what sort of life they would lead with only one arm or one leg. Mathew put his coat over her shoulders and led her to her cabin.

She could not sleep much that night, and after dressing, made her way to where the wounded sailors and marines lay. There was a horrible smell when she entered the part of the deck reserved for the wounded, and Jane felt the death of those dying and sadness for those in pain all about her.

The surgeon was still there. She did not think he had rested since the pirates had attacked. He was only in his thirties, but he looked so old and so worn in the dim light of the lanterns. He smiled to see her and nodded his head towards a pile of clean bandages.

Jane was tired too, but smiled back at him, moved over to the bandages and, lifting a new set, went to assist the surgeon. Every man she tended moaned. The pain must be awful, she thought. Jane had no idea that war was like this. She had only ever seen soldiers about her local district and down at the harbor back home. Many of them seemed bored when not being shouted at, and Jane thought how the life of a soldier must be one of complete boredom interspaced with a few moments of complete terror.

She wondered why men were so willing to join the army. She knew that sailors were pressed into service. Her cousin had been. He had a wife, Betty, and went down to collect tackle for his boat in Plymouth, but never came back. Betty had told how he had been press-ganged by sailors when he came out of a tavern near the dockside. She remembered his fair hair and strong blue eyes. She wondered what became of him and, in seeing so many wounded on the deck, prayed to God that he was still alive and well. The groan from a man to her left distracted her thoughts and she moved to comfort him.

There seemed so many who needed her attention and Jane helped the surgeon the best she could. Suddenly, she remembered the captain but could not see him. At first, she thought he had been moved to better quarters; asking the surgeon, she was saddened to learn he had not survived the night.

"I could not stop the gangrene," the surgeon solemnly informed her, as if he had lost a member of his own family. The death of the captain seemed to hit Jane more than seeing the bodies about her. He had been such a nice and jovial man, who had always been kind to her. Now he was gone. Jane thought of the first officer and how he must now be in charge, but she did not like him and hoped not to meet him too often. A wave of tiredness came over her and she knew she must return to her bed. Mathew would need her in the morning.

The ship seemed to be rolling more than before as she made her way back to her cabin. Once, it lurched hard to the left and Jane had to grab hold of some frame of the ship to steady herself. As she stood upright and was able to let go of the wood she had held to, to steady herself, her thoughts went to the wounded sailors and how they must have been affected by the roll. Their pain must be awful by the movement of the ship. Jane turned around and returned to the wounded area. The cries were indeed loud now and entering the area, Jane saw how men had been rolled on top of each other and how this had worsened their pain.

"We need to lash them down," the surgeon shouted to her, as he asked Jane to help him with ropes he held in his hand. Jane knew nothing about ropes or knots and felt angry with herself for not learning just simple tasks, but she did the best she could as she watched how the surgeon and his assistants worked. She was not able to move the men herself, for they were too heavy, but she held their hand and forehead as abler men lifted those that had rolled on top of others.

The ship rolled again and Jane was thrown off balance and fell upon a sailor. The man cried with her weight and she felt herself cry for the harm she had done to him.

"Move lightly, girl," shouted one of the surgeon's assistants angrily at her. This was the first time she had been treated as a nuisance and not as a gentle lady since she had been on the ship. Jane bit her lip, angry with herself.

Pull yourself together, Jane, she said in her mind, but the rolling of the ship seemed to increase and she struggled more to keep balance.

"We're in for a storm!" the surgeon shouted to Jane. "Do your best, please, Ma'am. These brave boys will need all the mothering you can give them."

Jane felt a sense of purpose when she heard the word 'mothering'. She had forgotten how tired she was and even how she may look. She wiped a tear from her eye with the back of her hand. A hand that, she now realized, had blood on it.

Suddenly, a sailor who was lying behind her vomited and others moaned in their pain as the ship rolled again.

"What are you doing here, Jane?" Mathew was standing at the end of the room.

She looked up at him. "Please help me, Mathew," but he was already moving towards her.

Mathew reached her as the ship rolled more violently and managed to hold her and himself firm. Wounded were not so fortunate and once again, those not yet lashed down were thrown agonizingly upon comrades. The screams and moans of agony were the worst hell Jane could imagine. For three hours, the torment did not stop. When finally it did, too many wounded had died of their pain or the opening to their wounds, which the violent tossing of the ship had brought upon them. To see so many dead was too much for Jane, and Mathew quickly took her away from the scene lest it demoralize the living wounded. Once away from the area, Mathew lifted her up and carried her to their cabin. She was too exhausted to walk unaided and as he lifted her up to her bunk, he saw that she was already asleep.

Jane was hazy when she woke some hours later and quietly asked Mathew to hold her hand. The storm had passed, but in its constant rolling of the ship, she had been drained by the energy needed to counter each roll.

"Oh, Mathew, what of those poor souls?"

"It's alright, my dear Jane." Mathew held her hand and stroked her forehead with the hand that was free. "The surgeon and his men have all in order. They could not have done so well without you."

He smiled at her with deep pride.

Jane tried to smile back, but felt too weak and, closing her eyes, drifted back to sleep.

It was two days before she finally woke, and when she did, Mathew was sitting by the side of her bunk.

"Finally," he smiled.

"Thank you," she quietly muttered. Her smile was slow, but the gaze she placed into Mathew's eyes was long and peaceful.

"Your friend, the cook, has been missing you," he jested.

"Oh, I am so sorry." Jane tried to rise but Mathew held her back.

"Just jesting, my darling. He is burning the food as normal."

She gave a little laugh.

"How are the wounded?"

Mathew nodded. "As well as can be. Things are more ship-shape now the storm has gone."

"That was a terrible storm."

"Indeed, but it's passed now! All is well, and we have full sails for the colonies again."

"There were times when I thought we would never get there."

"I know. Me too; but with God's hand we are well on our way now."

A great calm came upon the sea after this and Jane could not believe the ocean could be so calm. On many days, there were almost no ripples on the surface. The water seemed so calm she almost felt she could walk upon it. The new captain was doing well. The high airs of the first officer seemed to have disappeared with the real responsibility he now had, and Jane began to like him more. They even laughed a little during mealtimes, for now the cook had finally banned her from his galley, insisting that she had done too much work and now really needed to rest. Her work with the wounded had gained her a special recognition with the men and, with respect to Mathew, she began to receive gifts of carved items from one or two of the sailors.

It was later in the month when she awoke from a deep sleep during the night. It may have been the creaking of the lantern that woke her. She looked over to Mathew's bunk but could not see his outline in the dark. Gently, she raised herself and moved to touch him, but he was not there. She missed him and reasoned that he had gone up onto the deck. Jane pulled on her dress, brushed her hair, yawned a little, and, with a shawl about her shoulders, moved out of their cabin and up onto the main deck. The night sky was clear, and she was surprised by how many stars lit up the sky. It was very beautiful. She could see a few outlines of men on the high bridge and, looking for Mathew, found him leaning against the side of the ship, staring out into the distant sea.

Jane moved over to where he stood, gently placed her arm about his waist and lay her head upon his arm. He lifted it up and placed it about her shoulders.

"Missed you."

"Me too," she said quietly.

He leaned down towards her and gently kissed her on her lips, then looked out to sea again.

"What are you doing?" she asked.

He did not speak immediately, but when he did, it was in a quiet and peaceful mood.

"Just wondering what awaits us beyond the horizon. I am told we shall sight land soon. It has been a long time since we left England. I kind of miss her."

"Me too, but we can't go back, Mathew, can we?" It was not really a question, for Jane knew the answer and wondered why fate had placed them on this journey. A journey to a new land, with new people and new ways. Suddenly, she missed her home —remembered the table she used to sit at, the fireplace she would clean at five in the mornings. She thought about her dresses and wished she had some with her now. Jane leaned more into Mathew, for he did not reply to her question. "We will be all right. I know we will," she added.

"I know, darling." His words were quiet and strong.

They stayed watching the starlit heaven for a long time, The ship gently bobbed upon the sea and a great peace came over both of them. He tightened his grip upon her shoulder.

"We'll be alright."

They turned and walked quietly back to their cabin.

Chapter Five

A New Life

It was the sound of barefooted men running about that awoke them early in the morning.

"There's land," was a shout that made them both sit up quickly from where they lay. Quickly, they dressed; Mathew opened the door for her and holding hands, they both ran up to the deck. The morning sky was bright and clear of clouds. The sun shone warmly down upon them, and there, out into the far, far distant, could be seen a faint grey mass on the horizon.

"Is that the Americas?" she asked.

"I think it is," he said. "We've made it, Jane. New land. Our land."

A sailor ran past and touched his forehead.

"Morning, Ma'am." There was an infectious happiness with all on board. They had made it. No more pirates and no more storms to wreck their lives. The sails high above them were full of wind and the small ship bore straight and sure to the new land.

Mathew turned to look into Jane's eyes. They were as excited as his own; with his mind on their new life, he asked, "Are you ready, Mrs Appleton?"

"Yes." Jane looked steadily into his eyes. "I am, Mr Appleton."

Both turned to look out to the horizon and to the faint grey mass that slowly, but only slowly, became larger and seemingly more real. After seeing only an endless and empty horizon for so long, all were joyful the next day at breakfast to be told by their captain that they would dock just before noon this day. All at the table congratulated this new captain on bringing them to safety. It brought a happy smile to Jane's face to see how this once superior-minded first officer now seemed humble with such recognition.

The captain held his hand up to silence the excited assembly.

"Please, gentlemen," and then, looking at Jane with a kind smile, added, "most revered lady, please let us hold silence for a moment for those who cannot be with us now."

All held their heads in silence, until the captain held up a glass of wine.

"And here's to our late Captain Jarvis. May God bless his soul. A wonderful captain, a most admirable gentleman and the bravest man I have ever known."

All raised their glasses and drank the toast to their dear departed captain, who had most recently died following the pirate attack.

When the glasses were placed on the table, the captain begged to be excused for he now had much to do. It was the signal for all to rise and to be about the tasks that awaited them. For Mathew and Jane, there was nothing to do, and so as all began to move about in haste, they alone quietly walked up to the main deck and leaning against the side of the ship waited and watched as the wooden houses and waterfront buildings came ever closer, and with these the new life that awaited them. Winter was just beginning here and Jane felt a cold wind in the air. She cuddled into Mathew as he wrapped his coat about her.

"Jane…" His voice seemed awkward and not as she had known him to sound.

"What is it, darling?"

"There is something…I have to explain to you."

Jane looked up sharply and into his eyes. She saw only concern and honesty there. "Tell me."

Mathew was silent for a time. He heaved out a heavy breath.

"Jane…the idea to have you sent to the colonies was not that of my uncle's."

"What do you mean, Mathew?" She looked confusingly at him.

"He wanted you murdered, darling. There was a plan to have you removed from being any future witness."

She looked deeply into his eyes, waiting.

"It was my idea to have you sent to the colonies," he spoke sadly and with regret, "…as a slave." Then, more rapidly, he added, "It was all I could think of at the moment. It was just a means to keep you alive until I could find a way of getting you out of danger." His voice took on a desperate tone. "He meant to have you killed, darling." He looked deep into her eyes. "They would have you dead, Jane…I am so, so sorry."

Jane placed her finger upon his lips to seal all sound. She smiled. She understood. He had saved her life and now she was alive.

She looked out to the distant harbor. "Let's put it all behind us, Mathew. He was a bad man. We are free of him and now… We have a new life in a new country."

He said no more, placed his arm about her and held her tight. Gradually, the ship approached the harbor, but it moved slowly and seemed to take an eternity to dock.

Jane turned to her husband with an air of positive energy.

"Let us go and thank all who have helped us and saved us on this long journey, Mathew."

He smiled. She was right. Together, they moved first to the captain, then to the other officers and finally, to a young midshipman barely old enough to hold a uniform. While Mathew was encouraging this boy on his career and talking of the adventures he may have, Jane excused herself and went to the galley. Tom was there as always. The cook looked at her when she entered and knew she had come to say goodbye. True to his nature, he never showed a weakness.

"Thank goodness we are losing the lady!" he said, as if talking to everyone and no one in particular, but Jane knew his heart and, moving closer, kissed his cheek and thanked him for making her travel a happy one.

The huge man looked out of the corner of his eye and, seeing a galley assistant smile at the kiss, barked an order to have pans cleaner than they were. The assistant took the smile from his face and picked up a pan as instructed.

"Thank you too." Jane turned to the assistant in her usual happy nature, said goodbye once again and now finally to Tom, then left the galley. She found Mathew on the bridge.

"Are you ready, Mrs Appleton?"

Jane curtsied before taking Mathew's hand and moving down the gangway.

It was strange to walk on land again and she felt herself sway as she had done naturally on the ship, but the land did not move and Jane felt awkward in walking as she followed Mathew.

"Where are we going?" she asked, turning left and right, amazed at all the many different people about her. She had grown used to the small company of the ship and suddenly, she felt as if she were now in the centre of London.

"First to a dressmaker's and then to register with a bank."

"Why not the bank first?" she enquired.

Mathew smiled and looked down at her dress. He raised his eyebrows as if in a knowing manner and smiled again.

"Wouldn't you like new dresses and a pretty hat, my darling? Besides, it is December now and you will have need of a heavy cloak."

Jane loved this man. He was so considerate. "Where do you come from, Mathew?" she enquired. "I have never known a man so kind and considerate."

Mathew did not reply and instead turned to ask a passing lady if she may know of a dressmaker.

The lady looked at Mathew and then at Jane, smiled at her and directed the couple towards a narrow street and gave directions beyond it. As they began to move in the direction of the street, Jane suddenly grasped Mathew's arm.

"Let us go to the bank first, Mathew. I have a bad feeling about this street; besides, it would be best for us to have your letter of credit approved so we can look for a new home."

Mathew smiled at her and then at her dress.

"But tell me, how can I present my wife with this dress, my dear? People will think me a poor man."

"I'll take a seat over there and wait for you, Mathew." Jane pointed to an area where people were sitting.

"Oh no. I will not risk you being kidnapped again. The dock is not a safe place for a lady like you. We are going to a dress shop." Mathew continued in the direction and Jane hugged his arm. She loved this man and she knew he loved her.

As the street gradually began to widen, Jane felt excited by so many shops. In her village in Cornwall, there had been shops, but not as many as she could now see, and not with so many fine things on display. She passed a shop selling fine china plates directly imported from England, a shop selling an amazing number of cheeses, one selling fine leather boots and then more dressmaking shops than she had thought possible in a town.

"This is Boston, not Cornwall, my dear," remarked Mathew as he saw Jane's eyes open with excitement.

The first shop they entered was small and tightly packed with layers of rolled material on shelves, but the glare of the elderly looking woman behind the counter at Jane's appearance disturbed her feelings and she whispered to Mathew to seek another shop. The third shop they came to was larger than the preceding two and a girl, the same age as Jane, greeted them in a most pleasant and unassuming way when they first entered. A man, the girl's father with small round glasses near the tip of his nose, introduced himself, his daughter and their shop and welcomed Jane to examine his store. The material was very light and held a beautiful texture. It took her only minutes, with a delight that much pleased Mathew, to select clothes for three dresses. Upon being told they would be ready in two days, Mathew took Jane to find lodgings for the night. The bank can wait, he told her, as she was eager to walk the cobbled streets and hear the strange and new tongue of how people spoke English here.

The room they found was simple but clean. Jane felt wonderful to lie in a real bath again and then to climb into a bed of fresh white linen. She felt herself relax in a way she had not done in a very long time. "Pure heaven," was all she could say, but Mathew was not listening. He was fast asleep. Jane looked at his face. She loved this man. Who he was and where he came from, she was never really sure, but he was with her now, and that was all that mattered. The wick of the candle in the room had burnt itself out and as the light finally flickered, she closed her eyes too.

They were woken in the early morning by the strange noise of wagons and carts and shouts in the street below, as people were getting ready for another day of business. He leaned over onto his side to face her and asked, "So, my dear, are you ready for another day ashore?"

Her face lit up as she suddenly remembered her dresses would be ready soon. At last, she could discard those she had worn too much and bore so much sadness since she had first thought to leave her home and go down to meet Mathew in the carriage on that dark night. It was in remembering the carriage and the way she was brutally abducted that brought thoughts that saddened her face. It seemed that Mathew understood what she was thinking, for he took her hands in his own.

"It's the past, Jane. We have a new future now."

She smiled at him and looked into his eyes, as he did into hers.

"Come! Mrs Appleton, let us get on with our new life."

Their affairs with the bank were soon resolved for, unknown to Jane, Mathew's family were of good security. Indeed, it was a surprise for her to see the manner in which they were welcomed in the bank. After a pleasant morning, which included more shopping for Jane, they entered a coffeehouse to take refreshment. It was in here that Mathew took a chance reading of a newspaper.

"What is it, darling?" Jane could see that Mathew was reading something intently.

"It seems we've landed in a hornet's nest." He looked up at Jane seriously.

"What is it?" She felt pensive.

He put the paper down, leaned back in his chair, looked up at the ceiling for a moment, as if clearing his thoughts, and then looked once again at Jane.

"This distant part of England—the colonies," he corrected himself, "is comprised of 13 actual colonies. Each of these has a representative for the British parliament. It seems that the British parliament has just passed a law whereby tea can be imported here with a tax levied by the government and without the opinion of the colony's representatives."

"Is this a problem, Mathew?" She looked slightly mystified.

"It could be." He chewed the top of his lip. "It could be a very big problem, Jane. It means that the people here have no say in their own livelihood."

Jane searched his face for an understanding.

"It means," he helped her, "that legislation is being imposed upon the people here. Essentially, it means no right to vote, or at least not being able to have a vote that matters."

"Why?" She stumbled with her thoughts. "What's this law called?"

"Apparently, it's called the Tea Act!"

At that precise moment, a voice boomed from the far side of the room. "By Gad, Sir. We'll make the Wigs sit up with this one."

Both Jane and Mathew turned to the direction from which it came, to see a large man in his fifties suddenly stand up, and with a paper in his hand, and march briskly out of the shop.

"I thought so," nodded Mathew. "There will be trouble with this."

A voice from another part of the room could be heard to murmur,

"Townshend's ghost is behind this, I'll wager." Followed by the voice of another:

"Aye, Peter, and I won't be taking the wager."

Jane leaned over the table. "Who is Townshend?" she asked in a low tone.

"He was the Chancellor of the Exchequer. Not a name welcomed in these parts, I understand."

"Why?" asked Jane, becoming increasingly more intrigued to all that was happening and thought how this place was such a far cry from her Cornish village where nothing happened…except for wrecked ships, she added as an afterthought.

"Townshend fell in favor with the king because he found ways to fill the royal purse by a number of acts designed to tax the colonies."

"Was he behind this tea thing?" She was beginning to think a plot could be uncovered.

"Well! The Tea Act has its roots in Townshend's plans; this is for sure."

Another voice rose above the increasingly angry chatter as more people were reading the newspapers.

"Dam them! It's the British East India Company behind this. They can't get rid of the huge amount of tea stored in London warehouses and are going bust. Not at our expense, they aren't."

At that moment, the sound of boots marching in step could be heard outside, followed shortly by the sight of red coated soldiers marching past the window of the coffee shop.

"There'll be another massacre," said a young woman, watching the soldiers pass as she carried cups to a nearby table.

Jane could not resist herself and leaned towards the woman.

"Excuse me, Miss. Did you say massacre?"

"Ah! You're not from these parts then, are you, Ma'am?"

Jane shook her head, feeling slightly embarrassed that her Cornish accent made her out to be a stranger.

"Three years ago, soldiers murdered innocent people here."

"That's not the way of it, girl," said a man at the table she was heading for. "The mob got out of hand. They were defending themselves."

"Not so, William," challenged a red-haired man on his table. "They were tried and convicted for the incident on King Street."

"You're as patriotic as your head," remarked his friend with a laugh that dispelled the tension building around the room as others joined in the laughter.

Jane turned back to Mathew. "What happened? Please do tell me?"

"Well! As I had read in the papers back in England, it seems that this good City of Boston has taken the brunt of heavy taxes for quite a while. Some three years ago, tensions over

Townshend's tax acts blew up and a mob assembled around a sentry. The crowd became increasingly angry and stones were thrown at the sentry; other soldiers moved to protect him and the situation became so desperate that the soldiers felt it necessary to fire into the crowd."

"English soldiers firing at English people," gasped Jane.

"Well, it's not the way of it here. They were British soldiers who fired upon British subjects living in the colonies. There is a distinction."

"It's a small one," she countered, but began to realize herself that she was no longer in England and wondered if they may take more refreshment.

"Indeed it is, my darling. Indeed it is," replied Mathew as he called the girl over. Suddenly, Mathew slapped his forehead.

"Oh my God! I forgot to tell you."

"Tell me what?" Jane looked disturbingly at Mathew.

"We are invited to Lord and Lady Rathbone's for dinner tomorrow night."

"Tomorrow! What am I going to wear? Oh, why didn't you tell me, Mathew?"

"I'm so sorry, my darling. It was while I was with the bank manager, a man came into our meeting and introduced himself. He explained he has some land in Cornwall and upon hearing you were from there, asked…well, he rather demanded that you and I attend a small dinner party…tomorrow night," he said a little meekly, then added, "I shall ask if we can borrow a dress for you."

"Mathew Appleton, do you make your wife a pauper? I will have my own dress."

Mathew felt the temper of his wife and smiled.

"I was not so serious. Come, let us go immediately back to the dressmakers and have a fine dress made for you for tomorrow night."

Jane could not change the indignation on her face as quickly as her heart, but slowly, a look of endearment came upon it, which gradually changed to one of love. With this, and now in the need to hurry, Mathew pulled coins out of his pocket to pay the shop assistant and wondered as he put the change back how much this new dress would cost.

The shop owner had a little worried look when the little bell rang over the door, as Jane, followed by Mathew, entered his shop.

"Is there something wrong with a dress, Madam?" he enquired, moving over to greet the couple.

"No! No Sir. I love all you have done for me."

The relief on the man's face was evident and worry quickly changed to a smile with a hint of pride.

"But may we please ask for your immediate assistance?"

"Of course, Madam. What may I do?"

Mathew interrupted the dialogue, seeing it was not going anywhere very fast.

"The problem is that we have been called early to an evening dinner and my wife has nothing to wear."

The sharp look that Jane shot at Mathew warned him not to say more.

"As my husband explains, Sir, I am in need of your most urgent service."

"The matter is already underway, Madam. Please let me show you some suitable material." The man turned and stood back slightly to allow Jane to move further into the shop. Mathew stood by the door and smiled the same at each material that Jane showed him, until one came that lit his eyes.

"That would look beautiful, Jane."

She held the cloth up to the light and thought deeply about it, then suddenly turned to the owner.

"May we take this please for wearing tomorrow?"

The owner struggled with his thoughts for a moment, then quickly promised all would be ready by three tomorrow. Details were discussed and the couple left the shop.

"Now, Mathew, I shall need shoes."

The happy look upon his face fell slightly as he wondered how long this dressing adventure would last, but being kind and loving by nature, he gestured along the row of shops that lined the street and took his wife's hand as Jane went off to explore.

It was late in the afternoon by the time they returned to their lodgings; they were both tired but Jane was happy with her many small purchases.

"I can't wait to see what my new dress looks like," she said happily as he sat upon the bed.

"I like the one you're wearing, darling. The blue flowers lift your presence in any room."

"Do you think so?" Jane turned to admire herself in the full-length mirror, but as she did so, she saw Mathew in the reflection. She smiled inwardly and moved over to where he was.

Chapter Six

'Tis a Question of Tax

The next day was one in which Jane had much preparation to do; having been to the dressmakers with the dress all ready and fitting, the couple prepared for the coach that would take them to Lord and Lady Rathbone's home.

The coach came at the expected time and took the couple down towards the harbor. Jane felt excited and enchanted by the sight of so many masts along the skyline. The driver followed cobbled streets past a large warehouse and then into a row of fashionable houses. Eventually, he stopped outside a well-lit terraced house and waited till a servant came from the house to open the coach door and assist Jane out.

She felt happy to hear so many voices coming from inside the house and excited for an evening so far removed from one she would have had in her small cottage in Cornwall. The dress was light and the cloth moved freely. The dressmaker had done a wonderful job, and Jane felt confident and ready for the other ladies, whom she well knew would cast their eyes and minds upon her.

Yet, it was not quite as she had expected. Lady Rathbone moved with ease to greet her warmly as she entered the house and was introduced by Mathew.

"We are not so stuffy in the Americas, my dear," she greeted Jane. "Come! I want you to meet Phyllis Colbere."

Jane was ushered off to meet a group of ladies, while Mathew was engaged by an officer dressed in a red tunic. Eventually, all were called to dinner and entered the dining room, whereupon Jane walked towards a place next to where Mathew would be seated.

"Please sit here, my dear," called Lord Rathbone, gesturing to a chair next to himself and beckoning Jane over with an insistent wave of his hand. "I would like very much to hear about Cornwall and all that is happening there."

"Martha," he called to his wife, "can you put Clara Mackenzie next to Mathew? I want to talk to Jane here."

His wife gave her husband a rather stern look, indicating she had spent much time wondering where to place each guest so that all could be best entertained.

"Do you mind, Sir?" he called to Mathew.

"No, Sir, it is my pleasure," returned Mathew, giving Jane a small and quick wink with a smile.

Jane moved next to Lord Rathbone, raised her dress and sat neatly upon the cushioned chair as it was gently pushed towards the table by Lord Rathbone himself.

"Now then, tell me about the tin business. How is it doing?"

Jane knew little about this, but steered the conversation towards her new country. She was intrigued and a little disturbed to learn there was much unrest and many soldiers about.

"What is happening, Sir?" she asked as the first course of dinner moved to the second.

His lordship leaned over towards Jane, a little awkwardly, being a stout man and not young in years. "Well, on the other side of the water, it's all about money, my dear."

"Is it not so here also, Sir?"

Lord Rathbone rolled his bottom lip inwards, "Indeed so, my dear. Mind you," he paused, "there are some who have higher ideas than coinage."

"What would those be?" Jane knew well enough, but she was charming the old gentleman on.

Why not? she thought. What would the harm be in bringing life into the old man? Mathew was sitting near and no harm was being done.

"Honor. What else! The very right to govern oneself. Independence."

"Would that not be treason, Sir?"

"Indeed, Ma'am. Indeed, it would."

"Then, must we not talk of it?"

"We are all free Englishmen now and loyal to His Majesty here."

"Then why such need for independence?"

"I talk of freedom of choice, my dear, to defend our interests here. The right to have our hearts heard in the matters of His Majesty's government, and not to have all dictated by those politicians in London."

"But pray tell me, Sir Rathbone, what is the root of all this?"

"Ah! May you well ask, my dear." Rathbone took a sip of wine that gave him a moment to present the situation.

"Well, it is very costly for the crown to pay for the military here, you know. The land here belongs to His Majesty and he will raise taxes for its upkeep, but if the taxes are not fair to the good people of this land, what is there to do?"

"It should be fair, Sir."

"Indeed, so should life, but you know the way of men."

"Pray tell me the root, Lord Rathbone."

"Well! It lies in the Seven Years' War back in '63, when we beat the Frenchies. The British won, thank God, or we'd all be…" he cut into the chicken on his plate and, pausing with a piece on his fork, continued, "…eating frog legs now." He paused to talk while he chewed the chicken.

"Perfectly cooked! We have a very good cook in the kitchen. A lass from the Caribbean. Used to work on a sugar plantation. Mind you! She knows how to cook." He gave a knowing wink.

Jane wondered what life the woman must have had. She had heard how negroes were treated, whipped and abused on those sugar plantations, and remembered the destiny Mathew's uncle had planned for her.

"Anyway," resumed Lord Rathbone, "the war had cost the king a great deal of money. They are not free, you know. Things have to be paid for and the last thing the king wanted was another war."

"But the French lost."

"Yes. Yes, but the problem then and still now is not with them."

"With whom, Sir?"

"Indians."

Jane had heard of Indians. She had heard stories on the ship from the sailors of how they attacked and killed settlers, cutting off their scalps as trophies. The stories lay in the back of her mind as the ship had come closer and closer to land, but she had kept them out of her conversations with Mathew.

"You see, we have many more people coming here from Europe, too many of them now, and they want new land to make a new life. Fair enough I say, but they need to be protected and that means soldiers and this means forts, equipment, payment…in short—money. Well! The people here don't want to pay for these soldiers and neither does the British government, so the king, God bless him, issued a proclamation that people were not to travel west of the Appalachian mountains into Indian territory without permission from the Indians. Otherwise, another Indian war would start, more forts needed and more solders, horses, guns and the upkeep of it all. Do you have the gist of it, my dear?"

"Where are these mountains, Sir?"

"Oh, there's a long line of them running down the country. Beautiful land, but full of copperheads and Indians. Not the place for the likes of you and me." He gave Jane a look of acceptance to her companionship, as he sliced more chicken off the breast on his plate.

"Copperheads, Sir?"

"Snakes, my dear. Very dangerous, you know. But there are plants just as poisonous out there, and disease and… Oh, quite horrible, you know."

The thought of Cornwall's pleasant green and rolling hills, cliffs, coves, small fishing villages, seagulls and rolling sea seemed another world now. Jane looked over at Mathew and he smiled at her. Rathbone looked over at his wife and realized he was leaning too close to Jane and sat more upright, for Jane was well-breasted. A fact that Rathbone had well noted, and his wife of him.

"Anyway..." he continued with a side glance at his wife, "...the idea that the king should say who can go where, and where they may not, got the back up of many fellows here. We have a pioneering spirit, do you know." It was a statement, not a question, for Rathbone gave no pause. "Well, in short, people here began to develop ideas that they should decide their own lives. This is the root of it." Rathbone looked forward to eating his food, which he feared was going cold, but Jane's mind held too many questions.

"Was this all, Sir?"

"Where there is a purse to be filled, it never can be," he remarked with his own mouth fairly filled. "It was the Sugar Act that really stirred things up."

"Do you grow sugar here?" Jane knew nothing of how sugar was grown or the climate needed for it, but it was a woman's innocence that encouraged the older man.

"Not hot enough, my dear. It comes from the Caribbean, same as the cook..." Then paused to wonder if his cook used sugar to aid the flavoring. "Could be!" he thought aloud and to no one in particular.

"No, my dear, you see the merchants in London want their investments in the Caribbean to do well. So, they pushed the

British government to make this Sugar Act, which put a very low tax on their rum and other such stuff." He leaned over again to emphasize the point—"Too cheap to resist!"

"But why should anyone object to this?'

"Ah! That is not the game, do you see? To deter smugglers, the government set up a court in Halifax where all smuggling cases would be heard with the presumption of guilt."

Jane looked slightly confused as to what this meant.

"Hang 'em! My dear. Anyone suspected of smuggling…and if a fellow has an enemy…well, that's it! No justice there. Do you see what I mean? Anyway," he continued, "this court stirred up a hornet's nest. There was widespread protest across all the colonies."

"Because smugglers were hanged?"

"No! Damn it, Madam. Because the right…the right, do you understand?" Rathbone lost his mood for a moment and Jane felt a little frightened. "The right to control our affairs and not have these dictated from across the water. This! Is what it is all about, Madam."

"Did the government stop then, Sir?" Jane knew a little of this and was feeding him to keep the conversation going.

"Not then, by Jove. Not enough complaint here yet. Too many, too loyal to His Majesty. Well then," he gave a laugh to himself, "the next thing those rouges over there did was to create a tax on paper. Paper! Do you understand? Any paper used by any civilized person had to have a watermark and this tax. It meant that we were taxed to understand what we could read. Phew…" He blew out loudly. "Well…it was this Townshend fellow that really upset the applecart."

Jane remembered hearing the name before and at first could not place it, then recalled Mathew explaining how Townshend had been the Chancellor of the Exchequer.

"I know he used to be the Chancellor of the Exchequer."

"Yes, 'used to be' is very apt, my dear. It was Townshend, ever after a knighthood from His Majesty, who thought up lots of Acts that would tax the colonies out of every penny they earned. Do you see," he looked Jane directly into her eyes with the most urgency, "all this is a natural violation of the natural charter and constitutional right of us people over here. Anyway, Townshend is out of it now, the fellow died a couple of years ago, and now we have this Lord North fellow and his Tea Act. The East India Company have 17 million pounds of tea stuck in warehouses that they can't sell, about to go bust, and North and his government see to save it. I'll wager he has his finger in the pie."

"What will they do with so much tea, Sir?"

Rathbone gave a small laugh to himself. "Dump it over here, my dear; at least, they'll try!"

"But how?"

He trust his fork into a potato roasted in honey. "She's a marvel, this girl," he said, referring to his cook. "Well, they'll put such a low tax on their tea so as to close the competition," Rathbone said, returning to the point at hand. "People must have tea, you know! But the real point here is not really about tea, you know."

Jane felt confused to what all this meant.

"It's the principle of it. North is just putting more wood on the fire. This tea is a taxation tyranny! What will be next, and what after that? There is no stopping the fellow if we let this one go. It's all too much, my dear. Too much." Placing the potato into his mouth, he added, "There will be blood over this one, mark my words."

In the coincidences of the moment, the attention of every single person in the room was captured by the sound of a distant musket fire outside. Then, one more, and then a volley. Mathew and two other men quickly moved to the windows.

"It's coming from out in the harbor," said a man standing next to Mathew.

Jane stood up to join Mathew and as she did so, all the other men and ladies left the table.

Two men had rushed outside and were looking out over the water.

"It's coming from those ships," he shouted as he pointed.

"Oh, I do hope it's not another massacre," said a rather fashionable lady standing behind Jane.

Mathew pushed his way through the assembly at the windows and ran out of the house to join the two outside.

"Look! There is a ship on fire," shouted his companion. By now, all the guests were outside and watching the distant scene as flames lit up the night sky, illuminating the harbor.

Shouting and more firing could be heard out in the distant waters.

A soldier ran past.

"What is it, man?" shouted Lord Rathbone.

"Indians, Sir." The soldier stopped and took breath, as he spoke, "They've thrown much tea into the harbor."

"From the ships?"

"Yes, Sir." Gaining his breath, he touched his hat in respect and started to run again in the direction he was going.

"Indians be damned," laughed his lordship. "Indians don't throw tea into water. They take scalps."

A lady standing next to Jane put her hand to her mouth in horror, before closing her eyes and moving unsteadily on her feet. Jane moved to catch her, but a man standing next to the woman already had her.

"She'll be alright in a moment, Madam," he said, thanking her.

"Oh, John! Do you think they are Indians?" asked a lady standing next to his lordship.

"Not a single one of them, my dear. They'll be local lads dressed up."

"But why?" asked Jane, interrupting their thoughts.

"Because, Madam," said a singularly tall man standing next to her, who seemed to carry a very agreeable if not happy face, "we're not paying the tax for those fat rascals in London."

The intensity of the firing began to dwindle and a quietness came from the distant waters.

"Well! Whatever it was, it seems to be over. Come, gentlemen, we must get the ladies inside. There is a nip in the air."

Jane had not felt cold until she heard this and realized that she did indeed feel cold now. Mathew placed his coat about his shoulders when he saw her shiver.

"Let's get inside, Jane."

They both paused together and turned to look back over the dark waters, as the rest of the guests moved steadily into the house.

A small white spot suddenly appeared on Mathew's shoulder and Jane looked up into the night sky.

"It's snowing, Mathew. Oh, it's snowing. It's so romantically beautiful."

They stood there in the dark, overlooking the waters of the harbor as gentle snow began to fall upon the scene.

"You know, Jane," said Mathew, a little grim and his mind on other things, "I think this is far from over yet."

Chapter Seven

The Beginning of it All

There were many soldiers about the harbor and the old town in the following days, once it had been discovered that it was not actual Indians who had destroyed the tea, and a great deal of it, but Bostonians so dressed up. These Sons of Liberty, as they called themselves, were being hunted earnestly by the authorities.

"Do you think they were right, Mathew?' asked Jane when they sat in a discreet corner of a tavern one evening.

Mathew looked at her, slightly taken aback. "How can it be right to destroy the property of another? Do you know there was nearly ten thousand pounds lost? It is a capital offense."

"But look at the wider issue, Mathew."

"What do you mean?"

"I see the people here increasingly losing control over their rights. As I can understand it, they are being taxed heavily to keep an army here they don't need or want, merely because it keeps the land under control of England."

"Shush, Jane. This is sedition. We must be careful in these times what we say. Indeed, what we think." He looked over his shoulder. "You never know who is listening or what they may do with what they hear."

At that moment, a very large man came over to their table and placed a mug of ale on their table.

"If you don't object, I would be grateful to join you," he said.

"And who may you be, Sir?" enquired Mathew, alarmed and ready to fight if need be.

"Relax, good Sir. My mind is in sympathy with what the good lady has said. Our rights are being eroded by a king who does not care for us, and a government too intent on lining its own pocket at our expense."

"Have a care, Sir. These are dangerous words you use."

"Not in here, my friend," replied the stranger. "This is an alehouse where no government spy would risk to be, or live beyond the door if he were discovered."

Jane shot a look of alarm towards Mathew, and he one of concern to her. It seemed that innocently, they had taken refuge for refreshment in a tavern frequented, if not owned, by revolutionaries.

"And why do you think we are not spies?" Mathew looked directly into the eyes of the man, but as he did so, he saw honesty and courage staring back at him.

"This is a port, Sir. We have many people new to our land. They carry themselves in ways we know to be new. I would guess you came recently." He paused for a moment. "I would also guess you were a guest of Lord Rathbone three nights ago."

A look of alarm spread over Mathew's face.

"How do you know this, Sir, and what business is it of yours?"

The stranger took the mug from the table and leaned back in his chair. His head tilted slightly to the left as if he were weighing Mathew up. He slowly took a drink and placed the mug back upon the table, leaning towards Mathew as he did so.

"Let's say there were people there…friends there…who noticed you."

"Is Lord Rathbone a revolutionary?" asked Jane, quicker than her mind wished she had not.

The stranger held his head towards Mathew, but rolled his eyes towards Jane.

"Would you have a man so easily hanged, Madam?"

"Oh! I am so sorry, Sir. I did not mean—"

"We did not mean any harm by all we have said, Sir. If you will excuse us, we will be on our way." At that point, Mathew began to rise to his feet, but the stranger gently placed his hand upon his arm.

"Please stay a moment, Sir. No one here wishes you harm. Enjoy your drink. The fire is warm," he nodded to a large burning fireplace on the other side of the room, "and forgive me for the intrusion." The stranger stood up. He was taller than Mathew had first thought, broad and strong.

"May we be introduced?" asked Mathew.

"No names, Sir. Just good friends. Free men sharing free thoughts." With this, the stranger touched his head in respect to Jane, turned and walked calmly out of the tavern.

"What do you make of him, Mathew?" Jane did not take her eyes off the door, thinking the stranger might return.

"I don't know, my darling," he replied, and then more slowly repeated himself with a quiet deliberation, "I don't know."

Mathew turned to look at the doorway too. "We need to find a purpose for ourselves in this new land. I have an idea to buy into a wine import company. I will talk with some people I know tomorrow."

In the morning, Jane was awoken by seagulls crying overhead. It was a common enough sound in any harbor, but it reminded her of home. She remembered how she would lie in bed in the mornings in her home in Cornwall, always happy when the sunlight burst into her room, and ever ready for the first seagull to cry out, but this morning, Mathew needed to be up early and had already left before the sun had come up. It was agreed that while Mathew met people he knew and discussed all with the bank, Jane would spend the day shopping. So, she arose alone and, having dressed and eaten, left their loggings soon after ten.

The streets were already bustling with people, merchandise being delivered to shops and potential customers examining the shop windows. It was while Jane was looking at a window dressing that she happened to turn to her left and for a moment just glimpsed sight of the man who had talked with them in the tavern. He was, as she had remembered, a tall and well-built man, but in a strange way he did not stand out, for as he moved, he seemed to blend into everywhere he went.

A sudden impulse took hold of Jane and she could not resist the urge to follow this man. At the moment, it did not occur to her that this may be a dangerous thing to do. Her mind was so much caught up in the mystery of who he could be that she was already following him before she realized it. After following him down two main streets, he suddenly turned into a very narrow road that had many taverns along its sides. Jane should have stopped but she was curious about this man and wondered where he would go. She stepped into the narrow street and ignored the inner feeling that she should not have done so. Mathew would be furious with her, but she had come this far.

The taverns were noisy and Jane felt more afraid as she walked further into the street. A beggar with one leg sat on the street floor, and three prostitutes standing in a group turned to eye her finer clothes as she walked past. A rough-looking man, half drunk and leaning against an open doorway, lustfully examined her as she approached. Jane felt very unsafe but tried not to show it as she quickened her pace to get past him as quickly as she could. The street ahead looked no safer than that she had already walked through, and a feeling of indecision took over. She dared not go back past that man and yet felt the street ahead was no safer.

"You shouldn't be here!" It was a hard voice that spoke from behind. At first, Jane froze. Then she knew it to be the man she had followed. Slowly, Jane turned around.

"Oh, Sir, I was…I was lost…" she stumbled over her words, trying to find a way to explain why she was here and why she had followed him.

"My name is Jane Appleton," she said firmly, as she tried to take control of the situation.

"I know," replied the man.

"And you are…Sir?"

"I am who I am." He looked grimly at her.

Jane felt the power in his body. He was as strong with his mind as he was with his body.

"But your name, if you please?"

The man looked down at her as if he was tired of such games.

"These are dangerous times, Miss. My name's for those I chose to know." Suddenly, his manner changed. "Come now. Let me get you back into a safer street and back to the protection of your good husband." With this said, he placed an arm about Jane's shoulders and turned her fully about in the direction she had come.

The drunk at the doorway, seeing Jane escorted by this strong man, melted into the rooms behind him. Thank you, God, for this man, thought Jane as she saw the drunk disappear and felt safe enough to pass by where he had stood.

Out of the narrow street, the sun shone and a warm, bright, and cheerful air, so very different from that of the narrow street, greeted her. At first, the light was so bright she felt the need to shade her eyes with a hand. Shameful of her rudeness, she thought to apologize to the man who had just saved her, but as she turned to talk to him, another man accidentally bumped into her and by the time she had composed herself, the stranger had disappeared. Jane looked about, and although there were people in the street and she was sure she could mark the presence of her tall savior, nowhere could he be seen. Jane looked at the street from which they had just emerged, but he was not to be seen there. She turned her head, searching the people moving in the street, but nowhere was this man.

Just like a phantom, she said under her breath, but then felt a sense of protection. He had not harmed her. In fact, it was this man who had saved her and sought no return for doing so.

He is my friend. Our friend, she thought, as she began to make her way back to the logging house where they were staying.

When Mathew returned later in the day with news of his business venture, Jane told him all that had happened.

Mathew looked at her very carefully. "My darling, this is not Cornwall. I beg you to promise me you will never again go into such a street alone and without protection. Far worse could have happened to you there than you have the imagination for."

Then he saw that he had frightened her and was sorry for what he had said, but he felt the need to be a stern father to protect her in such a circumstance. Once Jane related again how this man had behaved, Mathew held her close.

"I do not know who this man is, Jane. I feel I should not pry into his identity. If we are to know, then the truth will come upon us when it is ready. Let us be thankful that he seems a good man with good intent."

"Yes," said Jane. "A good revolutionary." At that, they both looked at each other in silence, but Jane felt that a bond had been made with this stranger. A bond that would only be strengthened in the days to come.

The following day, Jane received an invitation to take tea with Lady Rathbone at 4 o'clock in two days hence. Mathew was now fully engaged in setting up his new business and promised her that they would soon look for a home of their own. It was the happiest words she had heard since leaving her own small cottage, and Jane had begun to think of where their new home could be. This thought much occupied her mind over the days that went by, and it was a happy Jane who arrived at the home of Lord and Lady Rathbone on the appointed day and time.

"Come, my dear," were the words used to greet her by Lady Rathbone, "we shall have tea and chat about the old country. Oh! And you may please call me Martha."

Jane was ushered into a room where she found two other ladies.

"Pray, let me introduce you all," said Martha Rathbone. "Here, ladies, a newcomer to our land, directly from England, is Jane Appleton, and this, dear Jane, is Abigail Adams," Jane curtsied, and the lady replied in fashion, "And this is Sarah Bradlee Fulton," continued Martha.

Jane and Sarah greeted each other similarly, and Jane found herself seated next to Abigail. There was something in this lady that Jane took an instant liking to. She had an amazingly strong character and was clearly of wise mind. A mind that Jane found great comfort with, and while Martha and Sarah sat talking together, Jane found herself in great company with Abigail.

Abigail wanted to know all about England and in particular, the part of Cornwall where Jane had lived. Jane found it wise not to reveal too much about how she came to come to the Americas and mentioned nothing of Mathew's uncle or the wreckers, although she did mention the pirate boat. An incident that caused the other two ladies to look up in shock, while Abigail held a sense of compassion and respect for all Jane had been through.

The time seemed to go all too quickly and Jane felt very happy for her new companions. At the time they were to depart, Abigail invited Jane and Mathew to spend Christmas Eve with her and her husband, John Adams.

Mathew had heard of Mr Adams' reputation as a lawyer and, it was whispered, a patriot, so he was both intrigued and a little excited to meet the acquaintances that Jane had made. It was snowing heavily when they arrived at the Adams' home, and Jane was greeted lovingly by Abigail, while John Adams introduced himself to Mathew more formally. The evening was a great success and a good friendship was established between all. John was a sharp-witted lawyer that Mathew enjoyed sharing thoughts with, and Abigail a woman with no lesser a mind. She had a great ease to see what was the crux of any issue and to present thoughts by which it could be overcome. Her knowledge of history and people amazed Jane, for she had never met this intelligence in a woman before.

What John found in Mathew and Abigail in Jane, they did not dwell upon. They were accepted into the home of another, found the people to be kind, generous and sensitive to all issues. John had not spoken too heavily about the trouble of the colonies. It was early times and new ground for this couple straight from England, but Abigail had been more outright. She applauded the act of destroying the tea in the harbor a few nights earlier, explaining how a stand had to be made lest this disease of taxation move beyond all sense and sensibility to the people living here. Nor were her words simply those of emotion, for she understood perfectly well the politics of the British government and the economy it moved through.

"Politics is not war," she told Jane, "as some say of it. Politics is about money, pure and simple. Who may have what and who may be deprived of it."

Jane had witnessed hunger in Cornwall and seen people desperate for food and hanged for it when they took it unlawfully from those who had too much. She had grown up to see justice to lie in the heart and not in a book of rules. She was never sure where this heart and mind of hers had come from, but in her discussions with Abigail, she began to find a home for them. So it was that just two days later, the day after Christmas, Jane had just popped out to buy some fresh bread when she came across Abigail in the main street.

"How nice to meet you again," she greeted Jane.

Jane curtsied in mock fashion and gave her new friend a gentle kiss on her cheek.

"Shall we take tea together?" she asked Jane.

"But I'd heard it said that we," Jane dropped her tone with the word we, "refuse to drink tea, lest it is British tea."

"So true, dear Jane. So true, but we have beaten them at the game, for we make our own tea here from boiled basil leaves and," she gave an encouraging smile, "…it is tax-free."

The bread had not yet been bought and as she wanted to take it back to Mathew warm, Jane thought it would be fun to talk with her new friend. The ladies arrived shortly later at a tearoom on the corner of Queen Anne Street.

"So, my friend, pray tell me what was Christmas like?"

Jane told of the presents she had bought for Mathew and the beautiful brooch he had bought for her, which she displayed it for Abigail to see a little proudly.

"Yes, it is indeed beautiful, Jane, and how wonderful it is to meet again.

"Indeed so, Abigail. We were so happy to meet you and John."

"Isn't it strange," remarked her friend, "how this day is called Boxing Day. I imagine it has something to do with the sport of men."

"Oh no, my dear. I know the root of this."

"Then pray tell me, for I have long wondered on this."

"I had once pondered upon this myself and was told by Mr Green, my local pastor, that in medieval days, noble people would take small boxes down to the church containing food for poor people on the day after Christmas."

"Ingenious!" remarked Abigail. "Why did I never think of that…the Day of the Boxes becoming Boxing Day. Oh! It is so simple. Goodness me. Well, Jane, you have enlightened me on a mystery I have long had. But tell me, is Mathew's business sound?"

The ladies talked for the good part of a half hour more, but in realizing Mathew would be waiting, Jane begged permission to go about her shopping.

"Then let's meet again soon," prompted Abigail.

"That would be so delightful," replied Jane with a smile towards this lady whom she liked increasingly the more time she spent in her company.

"Good! Then we shall invite you both to join us for a very small get-together on New Year's Eve."

"But I will have to ask Mathew first," said Jane a little thoughtfully.

"Nonsense. We women decide all things like this. Anyway, if you tell him I have arranged it, he can hardly refuse, can he?" She gave a purposeful wink to Jane and added, "And tell him there will be good contacts for his new business. That will seal the issue!"

"It is to be a party affair," Jane explained to Mathew when she returned, apologizing that it would demand a new dress. So, it was decided and with Mathew eager to build up more contacts, they left immediately to the dressmaker's shop.

By now, the dressmaker had become accustomed to Jane's urgent need and always held a kind smile behind the wire-framed glasses held down on his nose. Jane had an air of innocence and excitement for life that attracted older men, she had long discovered, and she found how she could feed this with her charm and manner to gain the help when she needed it.

The party they had been invited to turned out to be a lavish affair, for John and his wife were very popular in the city. Jane was not the best-dressed lady, not that it interested her. She would just not be seen to be below others in circles where such things mattered. She had learnt many things regarding Boston society and how to handle its society ladies from Abigail in the few short days they had known each other.

It was mid-way through the evening, when Jane and Mathew found themselves sitting in a dining room with a few other guests to hear the exploits of William Fraser. William was a survivor of the '45 rising, some thirty years earlier, and a man who had narrowly escaped the slaughter that had befallen his comrades after that fateful Battle of Culloden.

"Tell us," asked Abigail, "what was this prince of yours really like?"

"He was a fine man, Mistress Adams...a true prince." William's mind seemed to drift back to another time and place as he spoke. "He was the most chivalrous of men. He had great courage and was always most gallant to the ladies." He cast an eye around the table and saw how the ladies there could dream to meet his prince.

"But his heart was taken," he added with a bitter smile to dispel what dreams they may have."

"Pray tell us who she was," pleaded a lady from the far end of the table.

"Her name was Lady Anne Mackintosh. Aye," he added, "she was a rare lady if ever there was one."

"Why so?" asked another lady, deeply intrigued.

"Well," said William, "her husband was a soldier in the Black Watch regiment on the side of the English, but Anne's heart was with the Scottish and the prince."

"Oh!" gasped the same lady as she leaned forwards, eager to hear more.

"When the prince arrived in Scotland, he had too little money and men; the French who had promised him both were distracted by attacks in Canada and left him too little for the enterprise he was embarked upon. It was this lady who, with a pistol in one hand and money in the other," he smiled in admiration, "travelled Scotland and, it is said, 'menaced, gave and promised' to pull together 600 fighting men within 15 days to fight for her prince."

"Oh, what a lady! Why have we not heard of her before?"

William cast a look at the lady. "And who, Madam, controls the news?" said he, meaning only the victors.

"Well, you do now, Sir," responded Abigail with a smile of determination, "but tell us, was the Battle of Culloden a near loss?"

William dropped his head for a moment and lifted it to show a different face. Now was the face of a tired and weary man. A man who had seen tragedy. "No, my lady, it was far from this."

No one spoke; all were listening and waiting for William to speak again. It was a long minute before he did so, with a long sigh.

"We were all lined up, ready to charge. A whole highland army. Men dressed in their finest tartan, swords at the ready. All waiting to scream and charge upon the silly little soldiers dressed in their pretty uniforms."

One of the younger ladies gave a short giggle, but was quickly ushered into silence by others around the table, intent to hear what had happened.

"But our order did not come. We were told to wait and wait we did, while the English fired cannon after cannon into our ranks. It was a terrible sight. Brave men standing tall one moment, the next, a gap in the lines where they stood. Only mangled bodies and blood upon the moor."

"Was it not dry land?" asked John Adams.

"If it were, Sir, it would be a different story I would be telling you today."

"Pray proceed, Sir," remarked John.

"Well, then, the order came and we charged. Our blood was up. It was a fine sight. It must have sent a shiver through the spines of all our enemies."

It was at that moment that Jane realized that she had not seen the red coat of a British officer at the party. This was most unusual, for red-coated soldiers were a very familiar sight in Boston, and officers were normally present at every social occasion. But not here. Not this night, she remarked to herself.

"Bang!" William slammed his fist upon the table, taking all the ladies by fright and pulling Jane's attention back to the battle.

"All we could hear were the thunder of cannons about us. We ran fast over the moor, but then…" he changed the mood of his speech. "Then we fell into the waterlogged moor. It was hardest for those on the left flank, the men of the Glen Garry, for they could hardly move through the bog. And therein lies the tragedy. As men on the left flank edged to their right, and those in the centre, similarly being slowed down in the wet ground, all moved to the right flank. It was a mass of brave men screaming death to the English." William fell silent for a moment. "But it was not the English who would die that day. We were barely into their ranks, slashing with broadsword, when the whole air we breathed was a mass of lead balls. The English had well inspected the land and were prepared for the way things would go. We were mown down within minutes. Before ten were over, 600 men lay dead or dying."

"Oh!" One of the ladies shot her hand to her mouth at the thought.

"Well, then, it was lost," remarked William grimly. "No quarter was given. The butcher, as we call him, that bastard Cumberland," he gave no excuse for so swearing, "ordered every soldier and Scottish civilian in the area to be slaughtered."

"How, then, did you survive, Sir?" asked a young man who was clearly in esteem of William.

"They were bayoneting the dying and the dead. A bayonet came through my left thigh. I pretended to be dead and bit my tongue to sound so. When the night fell, I crawled off the moor and was found three days later by an old man who risked his life to save mine."

"Incredible story, Sir. Thank you for sharing it with us," said John Adams, "and a toast to you."

He held up a glass of wine he was holding in his hand.

"And a better toast to your prince," interrupted Abigail.

"Indeed! Indeed," raised a chorus of voices.

"To the Prince!"

It was as the glasses were emptied that a servant came into the room to whisper something into the ear of John Adams. Adams nodded to himself as if in thought and asked to be excused from his guests for a moment. Jane's eyes watched as their host rose and moved through the doorway held open by his servant. She was not sure, for it was only a fleeting glimpse, but she saw a man walk past the open door to greet John Adams after he had entered the adjoining room and thought she knew who he was. She had the distinct feeling it was the big man who had come to their table in the tavern soon after their arrival, and so also the man she had followed into that dreadful street and been saved from its horrors by him. She strained her ears, desperate to hear a voice to so recognise if it was indeed this man, but all she could hear were very faint whispers. Then, with steps of clear decisiveness, Adams suddenly returned to the room, his face now more serious than when he had left. Jane, who was sitting opposite Abigail, pretended innocence as she caught her eye, but Abigail had seen into her mind and she knew it.

Throughout the remainder of the winter and the following spring, the friendship between Jane and Abigail blossomed, as Jane felt much sympathy with Abigail's thoughts upon the struggles of those in the colonies and the increasing military presence, which was taken more as a threat than a measure of their safety for the people of Boston. Indeed, every ship entering the harbor soon had a number of armed soldiers to guard her cargo while she was tied up, and more and more red-coated soldiers seemed to be present in the streets and alehouses. Attacks upon them by rough locals were becoming more common to be heard of, just as the hangings that followed.

It was on a warm summer's day that the Appletons called upon the Adams, as they had been invited.

"Have you heard the news, Mathew?" asked John Adams as Mathew and Jane entered his home.

"No, John… What of it?"

"Take a look at this…" He angrily thrust a newspaper into Mathew's hand. "It's fresh news, but I'll wager it won't be for long."

"What is it?" Jane leaned over to look at the paper that Mathew was reading.

"My God! They've passed another act."

"An act of war!" replied John, his face stern and angriest Jane had ever seen in him.

"What is it?" persisted Jane.

"One moment, please, my darling. I need to digest the facts fully."

"Jane! Welcome to our home. John, don't keep our friends at the door." Abigail moved out of a room off the hall and gestured to a servant to take Mathew's hat.

"Come, my dears," as she led them into the parlor.

"Well! What do you think, Mathew?" inquired John, once all were sitting.

"I'm not sure I fully understand what it is all about."

"It's simple, man." John was in a state of anger and not easy to reason with.

"But dear," interrupted his wife, "they have only just arrived. "Abigail looked at Jane's state of confusion, for no one had yet told her what all this was about.

"I don't understand," pleaded Jane, asking for clarification for the state of John's alarm.

"Well, it's to be expected, because nobody," Abigail cast a momentary glare at her husband to reprimand his rudeness, "has had the calm decency to explain to you what is causing such commotion…at least in this household."

In response to Jane's plea and to help Mathew gain a full understanding to the headlines, for he had not yet had the chance to read much of the article, Abigail, able to be calmer than her husband, explained the situation.

"As you know, the British government increasingly embark upon a strategy of taxes, until…well, finally, we had to demonstrate that their action is not acceptable to us."

"The throwing of nine thousand pounds worth of tea into the harbor," nodded Mathew.

"Precisely! What has now become the 'Boston Tea Party'," added Abigail with a smile. "Well, in retaliation, His Majesty's government has now sought to make an example of the good people of Boston."

"How?" enquired Jane with a look of suspicion mixed with puzzlement.

Abigail nodded towards the paper that Mathew was still holding. "By an act of parliament that effectively cancels out the charter our forefathers were granted in 1691, enabling us free right in the government of our state."

"Can you please explain precisely the meaning, Abigail?" Jane looked at her friend.

"It is to say that we have no representation in laws that govern how we may live.

"What is the act called?" This time it was Mathew who asked.

"They call it the Coercive Act."

"More likely Intolerable Act," broke in Mr Adams. "We won't stand for it."

"What will you do?" asked Jane, looking directly at him.

At that moment, Abigail stood up and addressed Jane. "I think we should leave the men to discuss this. We have other things to share. Come, Jane, let us take tea in the other room."

Chapter Eight

Sisterhood

"Dear Jane, we have become close, very close if I may say so, over a few months."

Jane nodded pleasantly. She liked the character of this woman.

Abigail looked deeply into her eyes. "Can you keep a secret?"

"For you? Yes, I will, Abigail. Is it about John?" She looked a little worried.

Abigail shook her head. "No." She hesitated for a moment, staring deeply into Jane's eyes. "Jane, there is going to be war soon."

"War!" Jane's eyes opened wide, but in truth, she had long suspected that the troubles could not be contained.

Abigail nodded. "If it comes to this, our men will fight and many will die for their freedom."

Jane now looked directly into Abigail's eyes, wondering what she would say next.

"War is not won on the battlefield. It is won by intelligence. The gathering of information, and we women are better at this than our menfolk." Abigail watched her eyes very closely, trying to measure Jane's reactions before proceeding. The pause she gave was long. "I am part of an organisation to collect information that will save the lives of many of our men."

"You mean, spying?" whispered Jane.

Abigail ignored Jane's direct question. "Our organisation is called 'The Daughters of Liberty'."

"You mean after 'The Sons of Liberty'…who destroyed the tea?"

"There is a longer association, my dear. It goes back nearly ten years."

"I love it. May I join you, please?"

"I am delighted to hear you say this. Yes. Absolutely…yes, my dear Jane, but we must keep this a secret."

"Can I tell Mathew?"

"Well, our organisation is well known here, but not at the dangerous level you and I are going to make it. A level we could be hanged for."

"But I don't keep anything from Mathew."

"My dear, we wives must always keep a little something from our husbands. A wife who is known is boring, but a wife who has a little mystery to her…well…she will keep her man desiring her."

Both women laughed.

"In time," Abigail continued, "we shall tell Mathew, but for now let us think what we can do and how best we may do it."

"Oh, I have a thought." At that moment, Jane remembered the three prostitutes in that dreadful street.

"Pray, do tell me, Jane."

"Well," she felt her cheeks rise in embarrassment, "I just thought that if we could get very close to British officers, then we would know their plans."

"Of course, and how should we do this?"

"Well, I don't mean that we should, but we could engage some ladies to do this."

"You mean prostitutes?" Abigail laughed. "Yes, they would be the ideal spies for our cause."

Jane nodded. "All we would need to do is to find a high-class brothel that the officers frequent and engage the madam."

Abigail nodded with glee. "It is so the way of the world, dear Jane. We shall make discreet inquiries to find our madam!" Both the women laughed more, and then Abigail's eyes held a certain gleam.

"You have met Thomas, have you not?'

"The name is not familiar with me," declared Jane.

Abigail smiled to herself. "Come now, my dear, you noticed Thomas when he called upon my husband at New Year's Eve."

Jane's mind raced to recollect the events of that evening. Then her mind understood.

"You mean, the man who came to see John after meeting the Scotsman who talked about Culloden?"

Abigail smiled with a slight nod. "You thought I did not detect your interest."

"I thought I had seen him before. He ...."

"He saved you from the alley after you had followed him," interrupted Abigail, "and he was the one who met you and Mathew in the tavern."

"How...how did you know?" Jane was flabbergasted; she looked incredulously at Abigail.

Abigail smiled back. "I have long had my own network for information. We knew about you at the Rathbones."

"You mean the night of the Tea Party."

Abigail merely nodded.

"But how...but why?"

"Let me just say intuition...that you would be on our side."

"A woman's intuition," replied Jane.

Abigail looked at her friend. "I will introduce you formally to Thomas soon. He will protect you as you begin our work. He moves like a ghost, but sees and hears all. He is our best servant."

"You mean...the prostitute network?"

"Let us call them courtesans, for we will distinguish them from camp followers and use only those with access to the mind of senior officers. We are embarking upon a mission to save our men … and our country, Jane. But come! My dearest friend, we have been away from our husbands too long…and we have a very important guest arriving soon. In fact, he may be here by now."

"Who is it?" asked Jane, full of suspense.

"All in good time, my dear Jane." Abigail's voice had a tint of tease about it, suggesting she wanted to tell who it was, but wanted Jane to be the more surprised by not telling her.

As the ladies entered the parlor, there was indeed another man in the room. He was tall and elegant, but it was not this that intrigued Jane, it was his bearing. He had the presence of a nobleman, and yet his mind was very quick like that of a lawyer. He gave a broad smile as Abigail entered the room and directly addressed her.

"My dear, how are you? John has been telling me all about your new friends. Ah, this must be Mrs Mathew Appleton?" He bowed politely and Jane curtsied.

"Your servant, Sir."

"Come," remarked Abigail, "let's move on from formalities, we are all friends here." She gave Jane a look of sisterly affection she had not previously shown.

"Jane here is one of us." It was the single word 'us' that told its own story. Now, Jane had been accepted into a highly selective and secret organisation.

"Jane," continued Abigail, "I would like you to meet Mr George Washington."

She was not sure if it was the presence of the man or the reality of a personal meeting with such a famous man, but Jane suddenly felt weak in her legs. She tried to hide her excitement, but could not stop a tremble in her hand as she extended it outwards.

Washington took her hand in his own large and strong one and gently kissed the back.

"I am deeply pleased to meet you…Jane."

He called me Jane, raced her mind. She looked at Mathew, who stood beside John Adams, and saw how proud he also looked to be in such esteemed company. This will do our wine business nothing but good, she heard her own mind say to itself or was it Mathew's mind she was thinking? But Jane dismissed the whole business of profits and margins quickly as Washington encouraged her to sit down. Abigail sat next to her.

"I assume, George, that you know the news?"

"Indeed, Abigail, I was already acquainted with it before I arrived."

"You see, dear Jane," whispered Abigail, "the acquisition of information is what brings success. See how he knows it already." She quickly turned her attention back to their guest.

Washington surveyed his friends, old and new. "This..." he said with an air of disgust and pointed with a finger to the newspaper now lying upon a table, "...is an invasion of our rights and privileges. We must take action and defend the state of our free minds. I have already sent a message to George Mason back in Virginia, to whom I must urgently return. I shall call for a review of our Constitutional Rights. For what right has a man to put his hand into my pocket, if he will not let me put mine into his? We can no longer consider ourselves a part of a country that does not treat us as equal citizens."

Jane shot a look at Mathew, who had already understood the consequences of such words. War! This was not the new life he had desired to give her. But he knew enough of life to know there was a greater purpose to everything, and that he and his wife would find their purpose in all this coming tragedy.

With great energy in all he did and thought, Washington shortly excused himself with the need of a long journey. As the Adamses and Appletons waved him goodbye and bid a safe journey, Abigail turned to Jane, "Now, my comrade, we have a mission upon ourselves, do we not?"

"What is this about a mission?" asked her husband, standing too close.

"Oh nothing, my dear. It's a women thing." She gave a brief wink of an eye to Jane, and all returned inside the house.

Washington did not waste time, for news soon reached Boston that he had chaired a meeting in which the Fairfax Resolves were agreed upon and adopted.

"Read this," exclaimed Mathew to his wife. "Washington calls for a Continental Congress. Things are boiling fast in the pan."

Jane listened quietly but did not show more interest than she thought necessary to satisfy her husband's attention, for she was now engaged with Abigail in the setting up of a network to collect information from British officers. Many of whom were patrons of Mathew's wine business, for Mathew was now regularly sending crates of wine bottles to the military headquarters and was increasingly invited there.

"You know what this will mean," remarked Abigail to Jane when they met at the tea room, now to be their own headquarters with a secluded table reserved exclusively for them, "it will unite the colonies."

"How so?" asked Jane, as she sipped from her fine bone china cup.

"Once delegates in other counties recognise a shared interest, as they must do, there will be a call for unity and, in turn, the formation of a single body of thought."

"You mean a country in its own right! I also have seen this coming. It is enviable, unless the British government backs down."

"And that they won't do. There is too much money at stake and now, too much pride."

"The pride before the fall," replied Jane, but then held back an obvious thought.

"What is it?" Abigail knew too well her friend.

"I was just wondering if we take it for granted that all 13 colonies would unite."

"Oh, if only one or two colonies stand against the British, it will be a very courageous but I fear a disastrous result. We must pray that all 13 will see sense and unite immediately."

"But Abigail, the minds of men are a fickle thing. They must have a cause greater than their contentment and a leader to die for."

"That, my dearest friend, is why God has given us Washington. There is no other man who can unite the colonies and beat the British in war. We must prepare our intelligence network to assist him, for surely he will need us."

"I am so happy to have met you, Abigail." Jane reflected on how quiet but meaningless her life had been in Cornwall. She would probably have died an old maid or at least had a life just raising children. But here, now, she saw how she could take part in the raising of a nation.

"Have you heard from Mother Macquarie yet?" asked Abigail in this regard.

Jane nodded. "She has recruited the prettiest and most smart-minded girls to attend to the higher-ranking officers."

"It must be awful to sell your body to men," remarked Abigail. "I have heard it is a dangerous occupation; some can be most violent."

"And some, I understand…a little sadistic, shall we say." At least, those frequenting Mother Macquarie's officers' brothel. The stories recounted to her by Mother Macquarie, whom she found a lovable and kind woman in her early fifties, had educated her in the ways of the world. Jane was not now the naïve country girl she had once been when she first set foot on Boston's wharf.

Abigail put down the cup and saucer she was holding and opened her purse.

"I have a little present for you, my dear." Abigail, teasingly and with a smile, slowly took out a silver chain with a small locket attached to it.

"Oh, it is so beautiful." Jane examined the front and, turning it over, examined a leaf beautifully engraved on the back."

"Oh, thank you, Abigail. I shall always treasure this." She studied the engraving. "The leaf is so beautiful, does it have a meaning?"

"It's a tea leaf." Abigail teasingly smiled.

"A tea leaf! But why—"

"It's going to be our symbol. The symbol of the 'Daughters of Liberty'."

"But…but…why a tea leaf?"

"Because the British are going to lose this country over their tea!" Abigail burst into laughter.

"It's ingenious, Abigail." Jane laughed with her. "Tea, taxes… freedom. Oh, I do love you."

Abigail leaned forwards and lifted a necklace from her chest. "See, I have one too. Now we really are sisters."

Jane looked again at the leaf engraved on the back of her locket.

"It really is so beautifully crafted. Who did this?"

"A friend of mine, and I think also a friend to you. I would like you to meet him."

"Who is he?" Jane leaned across the table, expecting Abigail to mention his name quietly.

"His name is Paul Revere, and he is the most famous silversmith in these parts. But he is interested in other things too."

"Such as?" Jane's face lit up in expectation.

"Well, let's just say 'other things', for now. But he is expecting us. Come, my dear, let us go and meet him."

The ladies left their tea room and took a carriage to the North End section of Boston. It was a rough area and Jane felt unsafe as she saw too many hard-looking characters in the streets.

Eventually, however, the carriage came to a halt outside a silversmith's shop. Having alighted from the carriage, Abigail opened the shop door, causing a small bell to gently tingle above their heads. Inside the shop, there were many glass cases displaying a wide range of finely crafted silverware. A man sat behind a counter, working on a watch. He looked up and smiled as the ladies walked into his shop.

"Jane," said Abigail, "I would like you to meet one of the original founders of the Sons of Liberty. Mr Paul Revere."

Jane stared wide-eyed for a moment. "You mean, of the tea party?" Then realized she was being rude. "Oh, I am so sorry." She put her gloved hand to her mouth. "Oh, please forgive me, Mr Revere."

Abigail was laughing, and Revere smiled.

"It's alright, dear. Paul is a very close friend…and a great patriot."

Jane curtsied politely, to which Paul smilingly bowed.

"You see," Abigail tenderly held Jane's arm, "our network expands! Paul here has been informing us about the activities of the British for many years."

"Ever since they started to tax us without representation," added the kindly bespectacled gentleman with a smile behind the counter.

"Let me tell you," Abigail proudly recounted Paul's activities. "Way back in '65, Paul made the first protest against the Stamp Act."

"Well, there were nine of us actually," remarked Paul shyly.

"But it was the year you formed the 'Sons of Liberty'," remarked Abigail enthusiastically.

"Well, again, I was only one of many."

"Oh, don't take any notice of him, Jane. He is just being polite. Come now, Mr Revere, would you close your shop so we can become better acquainted? It wouldn't do for a redcoat to want to buy some silver at this moment, would it?"

At that moment, both ladies spun around as the door opened and the bell above it tingled again. A warm and welcoming smile spread over Abigail's face as a lady slightly older entered.

"My dear Sarah, I feared you would be waylaid."

"I could have been," said the lady as she quickly moved into the shop and abruptly closed the door behind her. The lady rearranged her dress and stood proudly before Jane.

"Well, well, well! So, we meet again, Jane." The lady stood with arms held out, waiting to embrace her.

Jane moved quickly into the embrace and was warmly hugged. As their bodies touched, she felt a strange sense of energy move between them. It was loving and secure, but a little disconcerting for Jane because she had never experienced this before.

Once released from the embrace, Jane pulled herself back slightly, a little confused. "Pray forgive me, I know we have met before, but at this moment, I cannot place it."

"Indeed you have, Jane," laughed Abigail. "When Martha Rathbone first introduced you to myself and Sarah here."

Jane then remembered how she was struck by the strong but different sense of strength in the two ladies on that occasion. Sarah had appeared more distant, while Abigail warmer, and how this had caused their friendship to bloom from the beginning.

"I am so delighted to finally meet you again Jane," responded Sarah in her turn. "I have heard so much of you from Abigail here. Welcome to our sisterhood."

"Are you also belonging to the 'Daughters of Liberty'?"

"Jane, my dear, Sarah is the mother of the Boston Tea Party," laughed Abigail again.

Jane was taken aback by surprise. "Really?" she exclaimed with astonishment.

"It was Sarah who helped disguise our menfolk as Mohawk Indians in her home just before the raid."

"Oh gosh! It is such a great pleasure to meet you, Sarah." Jane felt a flush of excitement.

"You should meet my brother Nathaniel," responded Sarah. "It was he who partook in the raid itself."

Jane was suddenly hit with a sense of great awe. Here she was, a simple girl from Cornwall, now bonded with such strong-minded and influential people determined to risk their lives for the pursuit of liberty. She reached up to her chest and felt the locket, then noticed with surprise that Sarah was also wearing a similar one.

"Yes," remarked Sarah, "we are here now to protect our men and the right of our colony to decide our own fate."

"Enough here, my gallant ladies, we should retire into the backroom, it will be safer to talk in there."

Paul came out from behind his counter, walked over to the door to the shop, placed a sign outside—Closed for Business—and, having locked the door, led the ladies through a doorway at the back of the shop and into a small room, darkly lit by a single candle placed upon a table in the centre of the room.

As Jane entered the room, she could see the outline of a man sitting at the table, but the light was too faint to recognise his features from where she was.

"Jane," spoke Sarah in a tone not missing proudness, "we would like to introduce you to a great founder of our cause, Mr Samuel Adams."

The man rose from his chair and moved swiftly around the table to warmly take both of her hands within his own.

"My dear Jane, I have heard so much about you. We are all happy to have you with us in our strivings to break free of King

George's shackles and those of his lackeys. Please sit down, ladies." He spread his arm out to invite them to choose a chair.

"You look very well, Sam," remarked Abigail after she had embraced him and sat next to Jane at the table. Shortly and only a little later, Sarah and Paul entered the room and all sat about the table.

"So, tell me the news," inquired Sarah.

"It's grim for today," spoke Paul. "The redcoats have put a warrant upon Sam's head here for treason and rebellion, and are searching for him."

This, thought Jane, explained why she had seen so many redcoats in the streets and forcing themselves into people's homes in a manner she had not witnessed before.

"It took them long enough," smirked Abigail. "You have been a thorn in their side for a long time, Sam."

"We are lucky enough to have got so far," he replied.

The word treason held a terrifying thought to Jane. If it should be high treason, the kind and good-natured honest man sitting opposite her could be hung, drawn and quartered. A fate that had once been explained to her, and its horrific process had given her nightmares for a week. It was only then, at that moment, that the true reality of what it must be like to walk upon the gallows and feel the rope around your neck and to know that all would cease permanently for you in the next second, struck home to Jane. No more life. No more memories; she thought then of Mathew and dreaded what she could have pulled him into.

"Come, my dears," interrupted Sarah, noticing a paleness in Jane, "we must properly introduce the father of our cause."

"I am hardly that," protested the man Jane had just met and taken an immediate liking to on account of his strong bearing. Here was a man who would bow to no man. A strong man of mind and words, she imagined him to be.

"Well, to begin," spoke Abigail, "Sam here is of our family. He is a second cousin to my dear John."

This explained the family name Adams, thought Jane who had initially been confused as to what relation he may be, if any. The thought that all about this table could be walking the steps to the gallows would not leave her mind. How brave they are, she thought. How incredibly, incredibly brave to risk your life for a cause for others, who too often would not be near you when so needed. But the word 'freedom' had such a compelling nature. It could not be ignored.

"Come," said Paul with a smile, who also had noticed a seriousness in Jane's face, "we are all family here."

"So indeed, Paul," sounded Sarah. "Well, may I continue please, dear Abigail?"

"You are better for it than me, sister," replied Abigail.

Jane turned in her chair to see better the lady as she spoke.

"Sam was one of the first men, and one of the strongest in mind, to stand up to the tyranny closing about us. I remember very clearly his wording in '64." Sarah held pause for a moment to clear her mind, then spoke with great passion:

"For if our trade may be taxed, why not our lands? Why not the produce of our lands and everything we possess or make use of? This, we apprehend, annihilates our charter right to govern and tax ourselves. It strikes at our British privileges, which, as we have never forfeited them, we hold in common with our fellow subjects who are natives of Britain. If taxes are laid upon us in any shape without our having a legal representation where they are laid, are we not reduced from the character of free subjects to the miserable state of tributary slaves?"

"Well done," cheered Abigail. "You have recalled it word for word."

"I taught my children to memorize it," replied Sarah with a proud smile.

"They are fine words, Sam," added Paul.

Jane wished she could know them too. They stirred a sense of pride deep within her and inspired a greater commitment to the cause she had only recently become a member of, and yet had been set in such noble company.

The silence of their conspiracy was suddenly disturbed by violent hammering on the door to the shop.

Jane felt her heart thump and looked at Abigail for reassurance.

"It's redcoats," Paul spoke with a tone of urgency. "We must get Sam away from here quickly."

All stood up immediately and stood back from the table as the men moved the heavy table aside. Once out of the way, Paul lifted up the rug that had lain under it, allowing Jane to see the handle of a trapdoor laid into the wood of the floor.

"We have no time, Jane, we must move quickly, Mathew will never forgive me if you are caught here. Quickly, pray, down into the cellar."

Paul and Sam had pulled up the heavy door, to which Sam moved swiftly down the steps.

"Come," he beckoned to Jane who, gathering up the hem of her dress to more clearly see the steps, took hold of Abigail's hand and descended down into the darkness below. A hand reached up to hold her steady, and soon she was standing beside Sam. The cellar smelt damp and in the darkness, she wondered how large it was.

Abigail's foot descended down onto a step and Sam moved forwards to assist her.

The voice of Sarah came down to them in a hushed whisper, "I will stay here with Paul, in case I was spotted entering the shop. They will expect me here. Go quickly to the waterfront and make your ways home. I will contact you soon."

With this said, a lit candle was passed down to Sam and the heavy door was laid flat again, entombing them in the cellar. The table could be heard being moved back into place, as the hammering on the front door seemed louder with words shouted to open the shop.

Sam moved the candle so all could see the size of the cellar. It is not large enough to hide us if they search here, thought Jane, but as this thought crossed her mind, Sam laid the candle upon a large wine barrel and began to move another. The barrel was heavy, and he struggled until a small entrance was revealed behind it.

"Take the candle, Abigail, and please you both move into the tunnel with haste."

Jane followed Abigail in bending low to enter the tunnel entrance and then stood upright waiting for Sam, who was pulling on a heavy rope and moved the barrel back into position.

"Sealed!" he exclaimed. "Now they will not find us here, but we should move to the waterfront and make good our escape."

There was a box of candles lying on a shelf just inside the tunnel. Sam lit two, put a couple in his pocket and passed a lighted candle to each of his two companions.

"Try not to slip," he called back as he began to lead the way down the tunnel, which on occasions had small pools of water.

They had been walking for about ten minutes, but it seemed more like thirty, when a rat appeared some distance ahead. Abigail went to scream, but Jane put her hand over her mouth and Sam stamped his foot on the ground. The reverberations scared the rat away, but Jane wondered if there were more ahead. Eventually, the small escape tunnel they had passed through ended and opened into a larger underground tunnel. Jane wondered what this could be for, but she saw dark and natural light ahead and this was all that concerned her.

"The end," gasped Abigail. "Thank goodness."

As they approached the end of the tunnel, the party could see that they had been brought out to the harbor above the waterline. Ships of different sizes could be seen in the near distance. Jane's thoughts were to get back to Mathew, for he would be worried and angry with her, but how could she explain why she was so late.

It was just as this thought occurred to her that a large shadow appeared in front, then one more and then another.

"Hold back," said Sam sharply.

"And where are we going to?" asked the rough voice of a man coming towards them.

Jane and Abigail moved closer to each other.

"Who are you, Sir?" demanded Sam.

The man did not reply until three others had joined him.

"Ain't no business of yours."

"Then let us pass."

"Oh, we will," smirked the stranger, "but there is a little matter of tax to be paid."

"Tax! What are you talking about, man?" replied Sam in a voice becoming increasingly angry.

"They are deserters from the army," whispered Abigail to Jane.

"Enough of this nonsense," demanded Sam. "Be good enough to clear the way."

"Like I said, this is our place and if you want to pass through it, you have to pay for it. It's just a tax," smirked the man.

"Not without representation!" snarled Sam as he lunged out at the man's head and caught him squarely on the chin, knocking him down. At that moment, two of the other men moved upon Sam and the last one came to Abigail.

"Away from me, you scum," demanded Abigail, but the man ignored her warnings and grabbed her hair, intent on kissing her. Abigail tried to push him away, but he was too strong and grabbed at her bosom. By now, the ringleader was up on his feet and, ignoring Sam, who was struggling to defend himself against his two assailants, moved towards Jane. There was a loud scream from Abigail as her assailant pulled open her dress and then suddenly a deafening bang.

The man upon Abigail turned to look towards Jane only to see his friend lying on the floor, grasping his stomach in agony. Blood was flowing freely upon the floor. Jane's right hand held a small pistol. Smoke curled from the end.

"That'll bring the Watch," shouted one of the thugs standing above Sam, who had now been knocked to the ground. For a moment, the man hesitated, unsure of whether to fight or run, but in fear of the rope that would soon be waiting for him if he were caught, he chose the latter and moved quickly out into the darkness. His companion, also unsure of his actions, lingered in his own indecision, but looking into the steely and defiant eyes of Jane, turned and ran after his companion.

The man holding Abigail reached out for Jane's pistol, but Sam reached further and, grabbing his leg, pulled the man to the floor. As he fell, the man raised a fist high and brought it down upon Sam. Abigail grabbed the man's hair, thinking to pull him away, but the man only turned his head and snarled at her. Jane moved into the entanglement and hit the man hard on the top of his head with her pistol. It was not hard enough to render him unconscious, but enough to numb his mind for a moment and enough time for Sam to push him off and rise to his feet.

"Bill," groaned the ringleader in a plea of agony, "get me out of here, mate."

"Enough," swore his companion and ran towards the exit as his friends had done.

"Thank goodness you had that pistol, Jane," remarked Sam.

Abigail looked at her. "You saved us all. Where did you get it?"

"Mathew bought it for me soon after we arrived. He taught me how to fire it, but I never had until that moment." She looked down at the ringleader. "Shall we help him?"

"We must help ourselves," warned Sam. "That shot could bring the Watch, soldiers or more of his kind. We must get you safely away."

"And you too," remarked Jane, remembering there was now a price on this good man's head.

"There is no point," said Abigail, looking down at the now still body. "He's dead."

Sounds of boots running somewhere outside ended all discussion. "We must go back and pray the British have left."

Hastily, the party retraced their steps through the tunnel. Jane, leading the way with a quickly relit candle, and Sam, the last, occasionally glancing over his shoulder to make sure they were not pursued. They seemed to cover the distance in far less time this time, and when Sam began to push the barrel to open the entrance into the cellar, he now did with caution and as much silence as he could manage. Stopping and listening every so often, until the barrel was sufficiently moved to allow each to enter the cellar again.

He did not replace the barrel immediately, in case they needed to return to the tunnel; instead, all listened keenly for voices from the room above and from sounds in the tunnel in case they had been followed. But all was quiet; neither from the tunnel nor above was there any sound to be heard. Jane began to relax and noticed how Abigail's dress had been ripped.

"It's not bad," she said, looking at her. "I can repair it easily with a needle and thread if Paul has any… That was so scary," she added.

"Thank God you had that pistol." Sam looked at her. "You really are one of us now."

A sense of deep pride came over Jane, a feeling of acceptance into a body of people she had come to respect and admire.

A noise from above caused all three to look upwards and hold their breath. The slow moving of the table, the sound of carpet being slid, caused all to wonder if they may have to flee back into the tunnel. Sam stood ready to grab the handle on the inside of the door and hold it fast, giving the ladies time to run, but a friendly voice called down, "Are you still there?"

"Yes, Paul," replied Abigail. "We are here."

Immediately, the heavy door above their heads was pulled upwards and Paul's face appeared in the light of a brightly lit room.

"They have gone… But I thought you had gone to the harbor."

"Help us up, please." Abigail moved past Sam and up into the room, followed by Jane and then Sam, after he had pushed the barrel back in place and sealed the entrance to the tunnel.

"My God," cried Paul. "What happened?" he asked, turning to Abigail and seeing the state of her hair, her torn dress and then Sam's wet and dirty coat.

"It's a horrible story, Paul," replied Abigail. "Ruffians set upon us as we came out of the tunnel."

Paul bit his lip as his face dropped in shame. "Oh, I did not expect that."

"Never mind, it was not as bad as if the redcoats had caught us," responded Abigail. "But thank God for Jane here. She saved us all."

Paul looked at the younger woman, as he eyed her up and down and with a sense of admiration.

Once all four were seated around the table and Paul had served wine and cheese, the story was fully related.

Paul shook his head slowly as he heard how the deserters had threatened and then assaulted his friends. He let out a sorrowful breath. "I will talk to others about this. We will clear the scum off the waterfront."

Paul asked his new wife, Rachel, to come down from seeing to their children, to meet Jane, and to help Abigail with her dress. With this done, and as it was now late in the evening, Jane reminded all present of how she must return to her husband without delay and of the problem she now had in explaining her absence.

"We will take a coach," suggested Abigail, "and once we can quickly repair this dress, I shall come with you and together, we will concoct an explanation that will satisfy Mathew on this occasion."

"But I do not wish nor like to deceive him," responded Jane.

"You are a very good and a very brave young woman," remarked Paul, "but in these times and especially with Mathew's business connections at the military headquarters, you would keep him safer if he did not know too much of what we are embarked upon. Especially," he added, "after the incident tonight."

Sam hung his head in shame. "It's my fault. If I had a pistol or two, as Jane did, I could have ended the trouble before it began."

"There is no responsibility for any here," interrupted Abigail. "Such incidents occur, and we should just thank the Lord for our safe return."

"Then perhaps it is really my fault for suggesting you take that old passage in the first place."

"Nonsense!" Abigail stood up. "We could not have known the redcoats would come. We did what we thought was the right thing at that time. We have survived and we have a lesson learned. Come, Paul, please lend me some thread and a needle; we must get this young warrior of ours home without further delay."

Mathew was concerned, deeply concerned, and at first angry when Jane arrived to their home, for he had been walking the streets looking for her and in desperation would have soon called upon his military friends to conduct a search for her. A thought that had not occurred to Jane. But Abigail was well prepared with an elaborate explanation that soon turned Mathew's concern into a happy relief.

"There now," Abigail remarked as all was settled and Jane was cradled in Mathew's arms. "It is time for me to be on my own way, for John will also be concerned." She did not tell Mathew, but she had already sent a message to her husband informing him of her delay with Samuel and Paul, who were a family and a close friend, but she needed to complete the setting of the account she had invented. Abigail lingered for a moment at the door. "I know! Why don't we have a ball? There is someone you really must, must meet here, and with whom you have not yet done, I think."

"Who is this?" enquired Jane.

Abigail gave no name, only a tilt to her head and a smile that told its own story. "Shall we say on the last Saturday of the month?"

"I have business in that morning, but we would be both delighted and grateful to come in the evening," explained Mathew.

"Splendid! I shall arrange it."

Jane moved to her friend as the door was closing. "Pray don't keep me in suspense. Who is it?"

Abigail played her game further. She touched the tip of her nose and giggled a little. "Wait…wait…my dear Jane." With this said, she was gone, the door closed and Jane and Mathew fell into each other's arms and then to bed.

Mathew had learned how government soldiers would be reinforced in Boston to control the increasing disturbance in the colony. This was valuable news, which Jane soon relayed to Abigail and to her inner circle of conspirators. Mathew was too kind a man to keep a dishonest face, and he was the safer for not knowing how useful his information was, although Jane never revealed anything that would have placed him in any danger. Only news that a day or so later would be common news, and yet there was always the thought that one day a most vital piece of information may come her way that could have the greatest of consequences. Indeed, time would show that this would be very much the case and how Mathew's news would save a massacre of colonist soldiers. On account, that is, of the Daughters of Liberty!

Over the following days, Jane felt an increasing irritation with all about her. She understood it had something to do with the danger she had faced in the tunnel, but she could not settle it and became increasingly irritable with Mathew. Mathew, for his part, was spending more time in the British headquarters, where meetings turned to card-playing and then drinking. It was on a Wednesday that he arrived home in the early hours to find Jane sitting up waiting for him. She had felt increasingly abandoned by his activities, and in this felt a frustration she could not explain to herself. As words passed between them, they became increasingly angry with each other, until Mathew scolded her.

"I have had enough of your girlish attitude, Jane. I work hard to keep you in fine clothes and to make a future for us."

"I never asked for any such thing, Mathew Appleton. And! You can keep what you bought."

He turned to look directly at her. His fury excited her in a way she had long forgotten. She had needed this feeling of life from him for too long and goaded him on lest for some reason it should dissipate. She turned to deliberately ignore his presence.

"Enough," he snarled angrily and spun her to face him. His grip was strong upon her arms, but she resisted any sign of weakness and reached out for a hairbrush that lay on the dressing table.

"Not for this," came his words as he pulled her hand back and forced his lips upon hers. Jane tried to pull away but he was too strong, and then without realizing it, she felt the passion inside her too strong to resist.

The two weeks passed quickly, and with clothes, outfits, and all arranged, Mathew and Jane arrived at the Adams' house at the time agreed. There were many people already there by the time their carriage pulled up outside the house door, for music could be heard from the inside of the house and people moving freely from room to room and so into the rear garden where lights had been hung and a large banquet table laid in the warm evening.

Jane loved to dance and while Mathew knew too little how to do so, he attempted to please his wife as best he could. As partners were changed from dance to dance, Jane was always keeping an eye on Mathew to see if he could handle the delicate movements of a particular dance. She smiled to see him struggle on one particular dance, but his partner was Abigail and she carried him around as if he were sliding skilfully on ice.

Jane had chosen a royal blue color for her dress, with a wide white sash tied around her waist. She had thought red would be more noticeable and pleasuring for attention, but in the present political climate, ladies tended to avoid the color of the soldiers who were increasingly making themselves more and more obvious as tensions were building up.

It was at the height of the ball, when Jane was laughing with Mathew on some humorous point, that she became aware of the rustle of a dress behind her.

"Dear Jane." It was Abigail's voice. Jane turned and was closely confronted with a tall, strangely eccentric kind of man standing beside Abigail.

"Jane, I would like to introduce you to a very dear and personal friend of mine, and a very," she leaned forwards to stress her meaning, "a very, very close comrade of ours…whom you have been in so much suspense to meet… Please allow me to introduce you to…Mr Benjamin Franklin!"

Jane curtsied as the man bowed and, without any formality, burst forward with a sharp question.

"Abigail here tells me you're from England." His eyes were intense with intelligence and Jane could feel they were searching deep within her to understand who she really was.

"Cornwall, Sir."

"Ah. A delightful part of the South. Ideal for the production of tin and, more to the point, a people earnest in evading King George's taxes."

All about laughed, as did Jane, finding herself in relation to the high smuggling activity Cornwall was well known for.

Jane found she took an instant liking to this man. "Do you not agree then with tax, Sir?"

"Not without representation, my dear," smiled the man with a play on the word representation.

"I think we all would agree with that, Sir," responded Jane.

"Indeed! Indeed, we would, Madam," interrupted a man standing close, and who, with a number of other people, had come to listen to any thought Mr Franklin may share.

"And have you been to England yourself, Sir?" Inquired Jane.

"Indeed. A pleasant land. I shared many an interesting talk with scientific friends in Birmingham once."

"Did you belong to an association?"

"Indeed. The Lunar Society!" smiled Franklin with an air of intrigue.

Jane felt puzzled. "Why such a strange name, Sir?"

"Oh! Very simple, my dear. We were all busy men and we only had occasion to meet in the evenings. With the danger of robbers and highwaymen, we were forced to meet only when the moon lit the highway and so on the occasions of a full moon."

'Ah," smiled Jane, recognizing the moon as being lunar.

Franklin saw the intelligence in Jane's eyes and smiled approvingly, but just then a man approached and asked the great man to come and meet other guests. With a courteous bow,

Franklin retired, but not before insisting that Jane call upon him the next time he should return to Boston.

"You made quite an impression on the great man, I do think, dear Jane," whispered Abigail as she took her arm and led her away from Mathew and the other men who had gathered around him.

"Come! Let us ladies discuss more important things."

There were many people in the house, and Jane was intent in telling her friend of the excitement she had felt in the presence of Mr Franklin.

"Indeed!" replied Abigail. "He is the most remarkable of men. You are not the first lady to feel herself in much need of him."

Jane turned to her friend with a look of mild shock. "Abigail! How could you talk of such things?"

But her friend only smiled to herself and, raising her eyebrows, countered, "And nor will you be the last, my dear."

Both ladies hid their faces behind the fans they carried in girlish embarrassment.

It was as they moved into a smaller room that Jane saw three ladies sitting on chairs in a semi-circle. A negro boy stood behind the eldest lady, but as Abigail entered the room, the lady turned to the boy and told him to leave and to close the door as he did so.

"My dear," spoke this lady to Abigail as they both now approached, "so finally, we are to meet our new sister. Pray be seated, child." The lady nodded to a stool by her side, which Jane sat on.

"I will introduce you to Betsy Morgan and Martha Washington." It was the second lady who caught Jane's eye the most, for she knew this must be the wife of the man she had met earlier. Martha now sat erect with a clear, distinctive presence that beamed intelligence and directness.

Not a woman to be easily crossed, thought Jane, and yet she felt a strange and immediate bond with her, for it seemed that this fine woman had also taken an immediate liking to Jane.

"Abigail has spoken exceedingly well of you, dear Jane," spoke the woman, looking so deeply into Jane's eyes that she could feel the woman knew her heart.

Jane returned the stare with full honesty, until the other woman momentarily, with an act of shyness, dropped her eyes as if to acknowledge that a bond was made.

"Should I show her?" asked the woman, a little apprehensively, sitting next to Martha.

Martha Washington did not take her now kind-looking eyes off Jane and only nodded in consent.

Slowly, the woman took a small bundle out from where she was sitting and placed it on her knee. Jane watched curiously, but tried not to show it as she wondered what would be revealed to her.

After the woman had unravelled the bundle, she held in her hands a rectangle of silk made of many stripes of red and white sown together.

"Oh, it is so pretty," exclaimed Jane. "The stitching is so neat it is almost invisible."

The woman tried to hide her pride.

"Thirteen strips for thirteen colonies," thought Jane aloud.

"Indeed," said the older lady sitting next to Jane with an air of strength, "and so, Jane, what do you think of our new flag?"

"Oh, it is not finished yet," interrupted the woman who held the material. "It is just an idea I am working on."

"I like it very much," remarked Jane, giving reassurance to the woman.

"It is a hanging offense though." It was the older lady who spoke again.

Jane could feel her eyes burning into her, and so turned her head to face her.

"So, will you stand with us on the scaffold or send us there?" The older woman's eyes keenly pierced those of Jane's.

"I will not betray my conscious," remarked Jane with an air of defiance.

"I believe you won't," continued the woman and then smiled kindly at her. "But these are dangerous times, Jane. Spies are everywhere."

"Indeed, we are," laughed Abigail. To which all the other ladies burst into laughter.

The women talked among themselves so intimately about such dangerous treason that Jane knew now, more than ever before, that she was part of an inner circle. A circle of proud, good and honest women who would stand by their husbands and the land they loved beyond all fear of British tyranny. For the first time since she had woken in that awful ship bound for a life of slavery, Jane felt that England was no longer her real home. Her soul now belonged to a new land. A land of free people and intent on remaining so while blood flowed in their veins.

A slight knock at the door brought all ladies into immediate silence.

"Ah! There you are, Abigail." It was her husband, John, "Why so discreet, ladies? Will you deprive us of your company? Come, my dears, we are soon to begin to dance and what merriment could we have if we are deprived of such beauties as are you?"

"You do us all too proud, John," replied Martha in mock flattery.

Betsy hastily covered her small flag and with a smile of endearment to Jane, sealed it once again in the material upon her knee. All the ladies stood up, except the elderly lady next to Jane, and as they began to depart from the room, this lady touched her arm gently.

"Would you stay a moment, my dear? Pray be seated again."

Jane sat down again and faced this lady.

"Please listen to me, child. You are a brave woman. I can sense that your heart is pure. I understand that your husband has much dealings in the headquarters of the British."

Jane felt a little surprise at first, but realized Mathew's business was common knowledge.

"Indeed, Madam. He is in the wine business."

"So I understand," nodded her companion. "Please be careful of him. Not all people are what they seem."

"Pray, what do you mean?"

The lady said no more, but sat upright and said with a smile, "You are young and you will miss the dancing if you dally more with me." It was as Jane rose that the lady pushed a small object into her hand.

Jane looked to see a gold sovereign and realized that this was the real reason the lady had kept her behind.

"I would ask you to give this to Mother Macquarie; Abigail's man will take you."

Jane felt her eyes open wide. The brothel owner seemed a million miles from the world of this fine lady.

"We all do what we can. Each of us have been dealt a different card in our common struggle to free ourselves, my child," countered the lady as she saw Jane's reaction.

Jane curtsied, placed the sovereign in her purse and smiled into the eyes of the elderly lady. This woman knew more of life than one would think, she thought to herself.

Just then, the door opened and Abigail's head appeared.

"Jane!" she called. "Will you not dance? I would have you come earnestly."

The elderly lady waved Jane on her way. "Go, child. We will talk again."

Once out of the quiet room, Jane was struck by the noise of many people talking and the sound of music coming from a room off to her left. Suddenly, Mathew appeared.

"Where have you been, my dear? I have been looking everywhere for you."

Jane smiled. "Mathew, do you forget that a woman needs time alone sometimes? We must have our secrets, you know."

"Yes, dear Jane." Abigail came to join them

He added, "But sometimes, I fear you have too many."

"Jane! What are you doing? Mr Franklin himself asked me if you would take the first dance with him. Oh! You wouldn't mind, would you?" Abigail asked as she turned to Mathew.

"Don't mind me," he laughed. "I am only the husband." And then added to himself as the two ladies moved off into a crowd, Well, I think I am.

The girls laughed and moved off into the larger room, where music was beginning to play. Abigail said something and Jane turned to look at her. Her mind froze. A deep shock numbed her whole body. She could not stop herself shaking.

"What is it, Jane?" Abigail looked at her seriously, but Jane could not look at her friend. All she could look at was the face staring at her from the other side of the room. It was a face she had only seen twice, but it was one she could never forget. A wave of dizziness came over her and she grabbed Abigail's arm to steady herself.

"Mathew!" shouted Abigail, turning back towards where they had left him, but he was already there.

"Jane! What ails you? Are you OK?"

She tried to clear her head to talk back, but her mind was in a daze.

"Take me out of here, Mathew." She began to cry.

"What is it, Abigail?"

"I don't know, Mathew. We were laughing and then she turned white like she had seen a ghost."

Mathew looked about the room but could see no meaning to cause his wife's condition.

"It's him, Mathew. It's him."

"Who?" queried her husband.

"Your uncle. M'lord. He's here."

Mathew looked at her in disbelief. His mind in a state of shock, then he spun his head in the direction Abigail had first indicated. His eyes searched the faces and heads of all the men, but none resembled his evil uncle.

"Are you sure?" He turned back to Jane.

"He's here. He's here, Mathew. He's found us."

"Hold her!" he demanded to Abigail.

Mathew moved quickly about the room. He pushed through a crowd of people in an anger so obvious than none of the group dared to challenge him. Quickly, he moved about the entire room, but no sight of his hated relative could be seen. With a faster pace, he moved into another room, then another and through the hall. He asked a servant if he had seen the man he briefly described, but the man, a little frightened with the anger in Mathew's face, shook his head in denial.

Mathew's eyes moved to the staircase and suddenly, he bounded up two steps at a time. On the landing, he looked about. There were men and women, but none seemed interested in him or seemed able to help him.

Unsure if Jane was now correct, he walked back to where he had left her and Abigail. His mind was puzzled and confused. When he got to where he had left the ladies, they were not present. Again, more confused, he searched, now slowly, the room. There, against the wall, sat Jane and Abigail on a sofa.

"Did you find him?" Jane's voice trembled with fear.

Mathew shook his head slowly. "Are you sure it was him?" he asked again.

Jane nodded silently. The despair in her face was all evidence that she had not imagined this.

"Please stay with her, Abigail." This time, it was a plea.

"Of course, Mathew."

Abigail saw her husband across the room. "John!" she called as he approached the group.

"What is the cause of such dismay?" asked her husband, seeing the despair in Jane's face, the protective look in Abigail's and the seething anger in Mathew's.

"There is a man here who is of the greatest danger to us both, and to my dear wife in particular." Mathew looked earnestly at his friend.

"Then we shall hound the devil. Where is he, Mathew?"

Mathew shook his head. "Jane glimpsed him only for a second, and since then, I have searched the rooms looking for him."

"Come!" spoke John with an air of command and quickly turned in the direction of the main entrance to the house. Mathew followed and pushed people aside to keep up with him. At the entrance, John raised his hand and called two servants to him.

"Now, tell them, Mathew, the description of this scoundrel."

After a quick description of his uncle, Mathew watched John and a servant move back into the house, while he and another servant went outside, for Mathew was sure he had well searched the rooms. Outside, the servant called over another and asked him about the description of the man Mathew had described to him.

"I am sorry, Sir." The servant moved back to Mathew, "I am told that such a man left the house in some haste very recently."

Mathew stared along the distant road and wondered what would become of Jane and himself now. He nodded to himself and walked back quickly into the house, his mind deep in thought.

"Did you find him?" It was Jane who called out from the hall with Abigail by her side.

Mathew shook his head and asked John and Abigail to join him and Jane in a side room, for now he needed to bring them into their confidence for the safety of his wife.

"I'll have him found, Mathew. Don't worry about that," remarked John, once Mathew had related enough about his uncle to explain his fear of him.

Jane looked pale and still shaken.

"I am sorry, my dear friends, but I must take Jane home now. I am sure you can understand how we must make preparations for our safety now."

"Would it not be safer for you to stay with us in our home?" inquired Abigail, casting a glance at her husband for his approval.

John nodded agreeably, but Mathew protested.

"Thank you, my friends, but I feel it is good for us to be in our own home at this moment." He looked at Jane, who nodded a little hesitantly at him.

The journey back to their home seemed a very long one for Jane, for now the stars were very bright in the clear sky.

"Do you think we will be safe, Mathew?" She held his hand in the carriage and leaned into him.

"I'll make it so," he replied, but Jane could not feel completely at ease.

"Wooo there!" The driver pulled the carriage to a halt suddenly and without warning.

Jane grabbed Mathew's arm, now frightened of any sudden incident that could bring them danger. Mathew looked out of the window.

"It's nothing," he replied. "Just a drunk falling about in the street." Still, he watched the figure cautiously as the coach moved on past and wondered how safe they really were now. As the coach trundled over the cobbled road, Mathew's thoughts wondered if he could ever trust a dark alley or walk in a crowd without constantly checking behind himself.

Chapter Nine

Lost

"What shall we do, Mathew?" Jane looked tired and drained as they arrived home.

"Well, what we are going to do is go to sleep and sleep soundly, because my uncle will not be about here. In the morning, we shall conceive a plan either to move or remove him!" His voice was firm and the last words of this sentence filled with threat.

But that night, Jane did not sleep soundly. There was a loud bang as one of the shutters to their window had eased open with a wind that had come up in the night. Jane lay in bed looking at the night sky beyond the window and the few stars that were visible. Bang! The shutter swung again. Mathew did not stir.

He is fast asleep, she said to herself and pulled back the bedding. The wooden floor was cold to her naked feet and she huddled to the window. She opened it just as the shutter was moving in again and caught it. The wind was strong tonight and as she looked out towards a tree rocking, the thought The winds of change came into her mind.

She had not realized it until now, but there was rain in the air and in opening the window, her nightdress became wet while she struggled to lock the shutter. Once the window was closed, she slid her nightdress off, letting the wet garment fall to the floor. It was cold in the room and she quickly moved back to the bed and next to the warm body of Mathew, as she pulled the bedding back over herself.

She felt safe next to him. He would protect her, she knew. But who would protect Mathew? she wondered as she looked at the back of his head. Endeavoring not to disturb him, she gently lay her hand upon his shoulder to feel comfort from him, but her movement did disturb him, and he turned over.

"What is it?" he asked sleepily.

"Nothing darling. I just wanted to feel close to you," she whispered in a low tone.

But his eyes were open now and looked directly into hers.

"It's alright, darling. There is nothing to be afraid of. If that was my uncle you saw, he is more frightened of us now than we should be of him. I will go to the authorities later and see what can be done. He may well find himself swinging on a gibbet before the month is out."

Jane had forgotten how Mathew's uncle was now a wanted man, and this realization made her feel safer. In Cornwall, he had been the law; now, he was wanted by the law.

The tenderness of Mathew's hand distracted her thoughts and made her feel more safer at this moment. She felt sad how they had drifted apart over the last few months. With all the activity of everything, they had lost time with each other and Jane wondered if she should tell him about the men in the tunnel and how dangerous it had been for her, but she knew she could not yet. She was now deeply involved in a spy network and she must keep him out of it.

Jane pushed her head towards his and kissed him warmly on the lips. As their lips merged, she looked deeply into his eyes. She moved to pull the hair back that had fallen over his face and noticed how beautiful her ring was. She felt proud she was wearing Mathew's ring, but then an impish idea to be free struck her and she slid it off her finger and moved it discreetly under her pillow. She held him close, but the exhaustion of all the stress of the evening took over and slowly and peacefully they fell asleep. Both slept deeply side by side, without any notion of the tragedy that would shortly befall them.

It was, however, a surprise to both that they awoke so early the following morning. Mathew woke first and looked towards Jane's head. He wondered how she had slept. As he watched her, a feeling of pleasant happiness came over him, as slowly she opened her eyes, blinking gently before being able to focus clearly upon his face. Jane did not say anything. She only smiled gently and moved herself closer.

Jane did not know how long they lay together, only that she felt safe by the warmth of his body. A safety that was rudely disturbed by Mathew, remembering that he had an important meeting with officers at the British headquarters, and in sudden haste, moved from the bed, dressed, and with a quick kiss, disappeared from their bedroom.

The positive action of Mathew awoke Jane's thoughts to his uncle, and she too arose from the bed, determined not to live in fear. Her first thought was to revisit Abigail and seek assurance from the Daughters of Liberty for the protection of Mathew and herself. She chose a dark green dress from the wardrobe, washed her face, and sat down at the dresser to prepare herself.

With this hastily done, she began to brush her hair, but the more Jane looked into the mirror, the more a strange feeling moved inside her that she was not alone. She turned her head, but saw no one, nor did she really expect anyone to be there. But the thought of seeing the face of Mathew's uncle last night was very vivid and she began to sense, in a way she could not explain, how he seemed to be standing behind her. The feeling made Jane straighten her back with unease and she told herself not to let her mind drift into places where evil lay. Yet, the more times she brushed her hair and looked into the mirror, the more she could not remove the face she had seen the night before. Finally, with nervous tension, Jane flung the brush across the room and screamed, "I hate you!" into the invisible void.

The sound of the brush hitting the empty floor gave her a feeling of dissatisfaction. Jane stood up, fixed her cloak about her and left the room. It was only when she reached the front door that Jane remembered she had left her ring under her pillow. Her mind had been so filled with the mixture of fear and hate for Mathew's uncle that she had forgotten to replace it on her finger. But she was nearly outside and so dressed and prepared in her mind to fight this evil man who had come back into their lives that she decided to leave the ring where it was until she returned home.

The air outside was cold. A mist had come in from the sea and still lingered in the streets. Jane pulled the cloak about her to keep warm and moved down the street. A man passed her and gave a harsh look as he did so. Moments later, Jane looked towards a woman passing her on the other side of the street. The woman looked hard at Jane. Another man passed her, again on her side, and looked hard into her eyes. It was as if everyone who looked at her had no kindness in their heart. Jane shook her head. What is happening here? she thought.

Jane was so engrossed with her thoughts when she moved to cross the road that she did not hear the coach coming up behind her. A man shouted, a horse neighed wildly and then, everything went black.

"Who is she?" … "Are you alright, Ma'am?" … "What happened?" Jane's mind was dizzy. She could not focus on so many questions. They seemed to be coming from another world and only faintly entered her.

Then a strong and pungent smell reached her brain and Jane opened her eyes to see an elderly man holding a bottle of smelling salts near her face.

"Who are you, child?' asked the man. His face was kind and she felt she knew this man, but maybe from another time.

"Witlaw." She was slow in replying. "Jane…Jane Witlaw."

"Here!" shouted a voice from the crowd. "Help her up. Lying on the road is not the place for this lady."

Jane felt strong hands lift her up and carry her inside a shop. She was placed on a chair. The room was not very bright and as she looked out to the window for light, Jane could see many faces peering in at her.

"Where are you from, Miss Witlaw?" It was the voice of the kind man again.

"Rose Cottage," she murmured.

"Rose Cottage! There ain't no such place here. Least none I knows of." A woman, the shopkeeper Jane thought, was standing next to the man.

"Where is your cottage, girl?" It was the man who spoke again.

"Up the hill."

"Hill! There ain't no hill around here. The poor girl's delusional." It was the woman again. "Ask who her kin are?" she said to the man.

"Do you have family here?"

Jane shook her head. "Only Bobby."

"And who is Bobby?' The old man's voice was calm and reassuring for Jane to hear.

"Bobby is my dog… Oh, I must get back to him."

"No. No, you stay where you are for a moment. You had a nasty fall when that carriage hit you."

The old man looked at the woman. "Fetch young Peter here and ask him to go down the street, asking if anyone knows a Miss Witlaw."

"As if I've got time to run around," replied the woman, who nevertheless called a boy outside the shop and, giving him his errand, sent him off.

As the boy emerged from the shop, one of the women standing outside shouted to him, "I saw her before. She came out of that house with the blue door. There," she pointed, "down the street."

The boy ran the short distance and knocked on the door painted blue.

It was opened almost immediately by a servant girl.

"Begging your pardon, Ma'am." Peter touched his forelock in respect. "Does a Miss Witlaw live here?"

The girl looked back at him as if she was trying to remember hearing the name. "No. No one here by that name. Best try next door."

The boy turned and tried the house to the right. No one there had heard of the name. He tried the next house and then the next, and came back to pass the blue door and tried the house to the left of this. After trying more than a dozen houses, the boy ran back to the shop, a little breathless.

"Sorry, Sir!" He approached the man standing next to Jane. "No one knows the name here."

"It's up the hill." Jane looked at the boy as if he did not understand her.

"Hello! What's up here?" A loud voice boomed as a man with a fine wig entered the room from outside.

"Doctor, so glad you have come. Thank you, Sir," it was the woman who spoke first, although the doctor was looking at Jane and the elderly man who had been so kind to her.

"What is it, Tom?" spoke the doctor, looking now directly at the man.

"The lady here took a nasty fall when the carriage hit her. Thank God she has nothing broken. She could have been killed.

But she took a nasty bang with her head on the road. Anyway, she seems fine. Her name is Jane Witlaw."

The doctor looked at Jane, first directly into her eyes, and then very gently felt the top of her head.

"Sure enough, there is a nasty bump there," he said as if talking to himself. "Now then, girl, where do you live?"

"That's the problem," butted in the woman. "She says she lives in a place that ain't here. She talks about a hill. There ain't no hill within a square mile of here."

The doctor nodded and looked perplexingly at Jane. "She could have concussion," he spoke as if he was addressing only himself again.

Jane's face lit up. "The fish. Where are the fish?"

"She's not in this world," remarked the woman.

The doctor gave the woman an annoying look and turned back to Jane. "What fish, Jane?"

"The fish I bought from the boat on the shore."

"Shore," butted in the woman again. "There ain't no shore here. Only a deep harbor and sailing ships. The girl's mind has gone."

"Come, Tom," spoke the doctor, looking at the man and ignoring the woman, "we need to get this lady to my surgery."

It was not a long walk and the kind elderly man accompanied her and the doctor. He held her arm slightly to steady her, but she seemed quickly to regain her senses.

"You were very lucky, Miss Witlaw," said the man. "That coach could have killed you. They drive so fast nowadays. No consideration for people."

"Enough of your talking, please, Thomas. Leave the lady in peace." The doctor turned briefly to look into Jane's face as they walked, but seemed satisfied that she was recovering quickly. The door to his surgery came quickly and with the jingle of a little bell, it was opened swiftly.

"There!" Pointed the doctor to some chairs. "Please take a seat and I'll be with you directly."

Jane watched as the man walked into another room and had not noticed before how tall he seemed. She watched him stride out of view and the door behind him close.

"Tom!" Moments later, the doctor's voice could be heard calling the man who sat next to her.

"Aye," he shouted back.

"Tom! I need your assistance to move this table, can you come in here a moment?"

The elderly man stood up, smiled at Jane and followed the way into the room the doctor had gone into.

The room Jane sat in was small but pretty. The floor was open-boarded and the wood had been freshly scrubbed. The walls were painted a pastel blue and there was a nice painting of bright yellow flowers on the walls. It was not very professional and more like the painting of a child, but somehow, it brought cheer into the room. It was a nice room and Jane felt happy to be here. She looked through the window and saw people moving past. So many people, she thought. Jane felt intrigued to find out if there was a reason for so many people. She stood up and walked over to the door. It opened with the same gentle jingle from the bell. She moved through the doorway and felt happy to be out into the now warm air.

The sun was warm on her face outside and in a strange way, it was exciting to feel this unusual activity of so many people with all their noise about her. Jane had never remembered Port Warren as being so busy. The roads were also new to her and she reasoned that somehow, she had become lost. Jane looked for any sign she could recognise, but the streets seemed different and even the people too. They spoke in a dialect she had never heard before. It all seemed strange to her and she struggled to get her bearings. The streets seemed the same, yet different. None of the shops she could recognise, and there were a lot of soldiers about. Jane felt confused with all this newishness and realized that this was not her town; she wondered where she was.

There was a narrow and dark-looking street between two buildings and hearing the sound of seagulls behind, she quickly turned into the street with the happy thought she knew where she was. At the end of the street, she would see the harbor she knew so well, she told herself, and maybe she would also find the man who sold her the fishes she now seemed to have lost.

But when she came to the end of the dark street, it did not open out into the harbor that she had expected. Instead of a low wharf leading down to a beach on the left, Jane was confronted with many tall-masted ships. A man shouted to her from the left, "Mind yourself, Ma'am!" as he rolled a large barrel past her. Suddenly, a boy ran out from the street behind her and pushed her to one side as he grabbed her purse.

"Stop!' Jane tried to run after the boy but her shoes were awkward to run in and her corset did not let her breathe easily enough. She was panting as she saw the boy disappear behind a corner. She leaned against a wall to rest and looked for help. But everyone seemed so busy, and no one cared or wanted to care for the theft she had just experienced. Now, she felt frightened. She did not understand why the ships had come to her town, nor how the streets and people had changed. Now, she had no money to buy more fish. Her only thought now was to get back to her home and to Bobby, but how?

Suddenly, the world seemed hard and cruel to Jane as she leaned against the wall and watched all the people moving about. No one cared for anyone else. Now she had lost her money and her way back home. Who could help her? she wondered.

The realization that she had no money began to frighten her. It was not yet midday, but it was winter and the day would soon grow dark. The thought of being lost in all these strange streets, with a people who spoke in a way she was not familiar with, made her feel very worried. In the stress of the moment, the great noise of wagons and people moving, of shouts from the ships and of those from the quay, suddenly became too much for her. She longed for the quiet town she knew, and knew she had to find it. Jane moved past buildings and people. She saw some looking at her in a wondering way, but she could not think about them. She had to find the streets and buildings she knew. Then, she kept telling herself, she could find the way back to her home and to Bobby and be safe. Oh, how she missed the little dog now.

"Hello, me darling!" A sailor, leaning against a wall, called after her. Jane felt frightened and unsafe by the man. She hurried away from him and heard him call out to someone.

"She a game 'un, Bob!"

Jane turned in fear to see who might follow her and saw a man begin to rise up from a stool.

"There you are, me laddie," called a woman loudly, holding a large mug of beer to the man, causing him to fall back upon the stool.

"Come back in here, Jill!" a voice called out from the tavern the woman had just come out of.

All were distracted by the woman and Jane started to run as much as she was able to get away from these people. There was an alley to the left and she entered it, hoping to find somewhere she could recognise. But the alley was dark and Jane knew she had made a mistake to enter this.

"Please God, keep me safe," she heard herself whisper. The ground was pot-holed and covered with small craters of water. Jane lifted the lower part of her dress to keep the hem clean and felt the dark and the loneliness of the place. The alley was not a short one and as she entered further into it, the light from the quay side became less and the alley darker and damper. Jane became more fearful of where she was. There was a doorway ahead and she hoped to run past it, but as it came closer towards her, she heard noises from inside. She kept her dress up so she would not trip and moved closer and closer, feeling her chest heave within it.

"No, you don't." A hand lunged out from inside the darkness of the doorway.

Jane screamed and turned to see a horrible pockmarked face. The man to which it belonged had a horrible scar across his face and most of his teeth were missing.

"I want a bit of you," he snarled.

Jane tried to strike at the man, but he was faster and grabbed her wrist. His strength hurt her and she looked into the eyes of the man, terrified. They were cruel and evil. She felt her heart pound and in desperation, she tried to pull herself free, but he only laughed.

"Come now, girlie. I won't hurt you."

"Get off me," she screamed.

Suddenly, she caught sight of a brown stick coming downwards. There was a grunt and the man fell to the floor. Standing in his place was a different sort of man. He looked clean and kind, and he smiled.

"Let me get you out of this place, Miss. Please come with me." He offered his hand and Jane nervously took it.

"Where are you taking me?" she asked.

"Away from this evil place. God knows how you came upon it. There are murders done here at night."

The man was tall and she felt safe with his strength. He took her back the way she had come.

"Pray tell me, where you are taking me, Sir?"

"Miss, I am captain of a ship and I wish to see you safe. There is no safety here. Please let me look after you until you feel righted enough to know your own way."

Jane was too frightened not to trust this man and followed him back down the street once again into fresh air. Before her stood tall masts of many ships.

"There!" Pointed the man. "This is mine—The Mary Bell."

"But I don't want to go on a ship, Sir," pleaded Jane. "I want to go back to Bobby."

"You will, Miss. I will take you safely, but first let me know where your home is and this Bobby of yours."

Before she realized it, Jane was being led up a broad gangway and onto the deck of a ship. The man who had saved her was very kind in his manner and courteous, and Jane thought it would do no harm to rest for a few moments inside a warm room. The door to a cabin was opened for her by a sailor and inside, the man introduced himself.

"I apologize most profoundly. I should have made a proper introduction when we met, but circumstances dictated that I move you to a safe place with the greatest of haste. And," he added with a warning smile, "as quickly as I could. I have no idea what possessed you to be in such a place," said he, noting the fine material of her gown and the parts of her dress that showed with its openings.

"I am Captain William Fritzwilliam of this fine vessel, The Mary Bell."

Jane smiled as he bowed, and although she did not stand up, replied, "I am so much in your debt, Captain Fritzwilliam. I am Jane Witlaw of Port Warren."

The man looked at Jane with a kind smile.

"Come!" he said. "You must be hungry."

Without waiting for a reply, the good captain moved across the room and, opening the door, shouted instructions for warm food to be brought to them immediately.

"So," he began once food had been placed on the table and a glass of wine by her side. "Where is this Port Warren of yours? I know this coast fairly well, but the name escapes me."

Jane looked into the eyes of the man sitting across the table from her. She felt confused by the question, for she knew in her heart that it was this place but it had changed in all manner so she had no bearings.

"I am not quite sure," she spoke slowly. "I seem confused with so much at the moment. I was trying to find some buildings I might know when," she paused, "when…when you saved me."

The man nodded. "Don't trouble yourself, Miss Jane." He was looking at her unwed finger. He was looking too long and Jane felt unnerved by his manner.

"I think, Sir," she began, "that I have taken enough of your busy time. I must go now. I have to find my way home."

"Have one more glass before you go. It will warm you."

Jane smiled and tried to say no, but the glass was quickly filled and the captain was holding his up waiting for her to toast with him.

Jane stared down at the glass on the table and felt something telling her not to drink out of it. She could not understand the mind. It did not seem like hers but it was telling her, Do not drink this.

The captain cleared his throat as to pull Jane's attention back to the present.

"To King George. Bless his soul." Jane felt it rude now to refuse. Hesitantly, she took hold of the glass and after drinking it, she began suddenly to feel light-headed.

'Drugged' came the word to her mind. She tried to shake her head clear, but the room was now out of focus. She tried to look at the captain, but he seemed watery and not real. Then a great tiredness came over her and she closed her eyes.

It was the roll of the ship that disturbed her. Jane opened her eyes and saw that she lay on a bunk in a cabin. She tried to pull herself upright, but fell back down again. Jane put her hand to her head. It ached so and she felt dizzy.

"The wine," she moaned. "What is happening?"

There was a figure sitting in the darkness of the corner of the room.

As Jane stirred, the figure arose and took some small steps towards her.

"I am a lonely man, Miss Witlaw."

Jane looked at him, wondering, although already sensing, what he would say next.

"I lost my wife and our children to plague seven years ago and since then, I sail the seas seeking peace, but there is none for me."

"Have you kidnapped me, Sir?"

The captain sat down at a respectful distance.

"Miss Witlaw, when I came out of that tavern and saw what was about to happen to you, I had only one thought in my mind and that was to protect you, even at the risk of my own life. In the short walk out of that alley, I felt that God had given me the task to carry you out of the darkness and into the light." He stopped talking for a moment, trying to find words to break the silence but struggled to do so.

"I would not hurt you, but my ship was due to leave on the tide and I could not leave you alone, for I could so clearly see that in your mind, you are lost."

"I am lost in my bearings, but not in my mind, Captain Fritzwilliam."

The man grimaced at the remark. He had hoped she would befriend him immediately, but the official title and the strong look in her eyes warned him this would be a long task.

He decided to take a different tact.

"Let us be honest, dear Jane." He was a little nervous to be so personal now, but he pushed the point. "You are away from your home. You cannot find your home. You are lost. In your home is your dog. Pray tell me, if you do not return soon, who will take care of him?"

Jane had not thought about this and her mind struggled to explain her thoughts.

"My sister would go to my home if she had not heard from me within a few days. There, she would look after Bobby."

"Then, that is one worry removed. The other is to actually find Port Warren, is it not so?"

The suspicion on Jane's face began to fade as she began to wonder how much she could trust this man. She nodded in silence.

"While you were…were sleeping, I looked at the charts of the coast and there is no mention of Port Warren anywhere on the coast of Massachusetts."

"Massachusetts!" interrupted Jane with a stark look of shock on her face. "Is this not Cornwall?"

The look on Jane's face was then matched by that on William's.

"No, my dear. We are an ocean apart from Cornwall."

The color on Jane's face drained until her skin was a pale grey.

"It cannot be," she said, her voice as drained as the blood from her face.

Then she looked sharply at the man again. "Are you tricking me, Sir?"

Captain Fritzwilliam stood up. "Please come with me to my cabin and I will show you clearly the charts of the waters we are in."

He held out his hand. Jane seemed unsure whether to take it now, but in her puzzlement, she had to trust someone. There was no one else. She reached out and as her hand moved within his, she felt a strange feeling of oneness. His hand was large, the skin tough, but it had a kindness and gentleness that made her feel safe. She stood up, and together, they moved towards the captain's cabin.

As the ship rolled, Jane fell to the side and had to grab hold of a beam to steady herself. There was a strange feeling that she had done this before, but she had no understanding of when or where. It was like a fleeting journey into a past life. It was real and yet unreal. The thought puzzled her as she walked behind the man.

"In here, if you please." Captain Fritzwilliam suddenly stopped and opened a door to a large room, within which lay a small number of large rolled-up papers with one opened and spread out upon the only table to be seen. On this paper were many wavering lines and numbers dotted about.

"Well, Jane, this is a map of the waters of this coastline. Please examine it for yourself to find your Port Warren. This," he stamped with his index finger, "is where we are now!"

Jane leaned over the table to read the word 'Boston', written in bold letters where his finger had been.

She searched the inlets of the coastline and read many words, but none were familiar to her. As she straightened herself up, she stared down at the coastline of the Eastern board of the Americas and saw that it resembled nothing of the land she knew.

She turned to face Fritzwilliam.

"I...I don't understand," she murmured. "What is happening to me?"

"Pray, take a seat," he invited her, "for you look pale again, Jane."

Jane sat down without being aware that there was a chair beneath her.

The captain passed her a glass of wine.

"No, thank you." She shook her head. Where am I? She heard herself say again and again in a quiet breath.

A great dizziness and confusion drove within her head.

Chapter Ten

Mathew Returns

It was late in the day when Mathew returned to their home. It had been a long day, and he found that he was becoming more and more taken into the confidences of the British. He had developed a very good friendship with many of the higher-ranking officers on account of the good quality of Madeira he was now bringing from Spain. "It's a health tonic!" declared Colonel Paterson's wife, who was now buying regular amounts of it on behalf of her husband's increasing overweight problem.

The street was still busy as he walked over the cobbled road. Two junior officers waved to him as they walked past on the other side. Mathew was now so much in the company of the British that he seemed to understand their loyalty and right to support the Crown. The Americas were just an extension of England, just as much as Ireland, they had told him. Mathew had no idea of the sentiments, or indeed the activities of Jane, and the Daughters of Liberty.

The maid greeted him anxiously when he arrived.

"Oh, Sir, I have no idea where the mistress is. She left this morning, and I've not heard or known anything about her since."

"Do you know where she went?" Mathew's voice was strong and sharp, as he reacted to the urgency in the manner of the maid.

"No, Sir!"

"Think, girl! Did she say anything? What was she wearing?"

There was a certain look of uncertainty in the maid's face that caused Mathew to realize she was holding something back.

"What is it?" he demanded strongly.

"Well, Sir..." She struggled with the words. "...I'm sworn to secrecy."

"What secrets?" Mathew's face was filled with violence as he struggled with worry and confusion over what the maid was talking about.

"Out with it, girl. What secrecy?"

The maid struggled with doubt, but the sight of Mathew's angry face forced the words out.

"Well, Sir, sometimes Madam meets Mistress Abigail."

"So, what of it? I know this."

"But, Sir, sometimes it's in secrecy."

"What do you mean, secrecy?"

"I daren't say, Master." The girl was shaking with fear.

"Out with it, or I'll whip the hide off you."

The girl burst into tears. Mathew grabbed her shoulders but then realized that reason was the best course. He relaxed his strong grip on her shoulders, but held them there firmly now. The tone of his voice changed, and he spoke slowly but firmly.

"Sarah, Jane's life might be in danger. Things happened recently that I've got great concern for her life. Now, what is all this secrecy?"

"It's the revolutionaries, Sir… Mistress Jane is with Mistress Abigail."

Confusion took over his face. "What are you talking about, Sarah?"

Then he realized Sarah knew no more or could say no more, and with a mind to find out what she was talking about, he turned quickly and went out into the street.

A horse and cab were a little down the street. Mathew hailed the driver who had seemingly been dozing and demanded him to wake up fast.

"Hurry, man! This is an urgent matter. Do you know the house of John Adams?"

The driver nodded his head. "Aye, Sir, I've been there five times this month."

"Then make it a sixth, and if you do not spare the horse, there is a sovereign in it for you. Now, urgently, man. Go!"

The driver raised his crop and brought the horse in a trot. Mathew sat in the cab and bit his lip. What is all this about secrecy, he pondered. Is Jane having some affair that only Abigail knows about? Many thoughts plagued his mind in the short time it took to reach his destination. The horse had barely halted when Mathew was out of the cab, threw a sovereign to the driver, and raced up the steps to the Adams' house.

"What is it, man?" queried John Adams as Mathew moved past the servant holding the door open for him.

"Jane's been taken!" The words were out of his mouth before their meaning had fully taken hold in his mind. "The man we told you about, my uncle, I'm sure he's got her."

"My God, are you sure?"

At that moment, Abigail appeared in an open doorway.

"Abigail, pray excuse my intrusion into your home, but I am most worried for Jane's whereabouts are not known."

Shock came over her face. "Not known… Why… What happened?"

John moved to his wife and ushered Mathew into the room she had just come out of. "We think the man…Mathew's uncle may have abducted her," he explained.

"Get Thomas. He'll find them."

"I've already sent the servant to rouse him."

It was as he said this that there was a clearing of throat behind him.

All turned to see the man Mathew had first met…and who had saved Jane from that dreadful alley.

"What ails, Sir?" The man spoke in a calm, steady and quiet voice. But there was no mistake to the strength of character behind those calm words. This was not a man to be tested.

Mathew turned and was now glad to know that this man was on his side. Quickly, he outlined all the events concerning his uncle, his sudden and unexpected appearance in this house only the night before and now the sudden disappearance of his wife.

The man looked steadily into Mathew's eyes. This was a man of great experience of men. Then slowly, his eyes moved to those of John Adams. He nodded to him. Adams nodded back and the man spoke for the first time.

"Don't worry, Sir. We'll get your wife back to you safe and sound and then put this man on the gallows." He turned, left the room and could be heard shouting orders to other men. Horses could be heard in the background and what sounded like an army of men running about.

Mathew turned to face both John and Abigail. "When I returned home and asked the maid where Jane was, she told me she was bound to secrecy. What is this secrecy, Abigail?" He now looked directly at Mrs Adams.

Abigail looked directly back into his eyes. "I can't tell you this, Mathew. It would place you in much danger at this moment.'

"Do you not think my wife is in more danger, Madam?" His face was stern and cold.

John moved forward. "Please come and sit down, my friend. These are very dangerous times. There is too much to explain in the haste of this moment. Let us first find Jane and then we shall talk of whatever this women's secrecy may be."

Mathew's mind began to swirl. "John, I have no time for games. You don't know what my uncle is capable of. I've got no time to waste here." With this, he turned and walked towards the main door.

"Where are you going, man?" shouted John.

'If you won't help me, the British will. I'll go directly to the house of the Governor General."

With this, he was out of the house and pulled a servant roughly off the horse he was sitting on.

"I'm sorry, my poor fellow," apologized Mathew as he mounted the horse, only to be watched by John and Abigail.

"What do you think he will say to the British?" Abigail's voice was nervous and unsure of what to say to her husband, because he did not know of Abigail's real involvement in the Daughters of Liberty.

John shook his head unknowingly. "The poor fellow's besides himself with worry. We must do all we can to find Jane."

"Thomas will do that."

"Yes, he will, but he will need help. I will follow Mathew to the Governor General's home and keep things under control there. Excuse me, my dear. Call the carriage out quickly." He then went upstairs and returned shortly afterwards, better dressed. The carriage was waiting, and John Adams entered it with commands of haste.

By the time Mathew reached the Governor General's home, there were no lights to be seen. Two sentries were guarding the main gate. "Pray open up immediately. I have the most urgent business with the governor."

One of the sentries saluted him. "I'm sorry, M'lord, but he ain't home. His lordship left for Virginia this afternoon."

Mathew nodded in gratitude and turned his horse about. His mind searched for the best person he could think of at this hour who could call out a search party. He held the rein loose to allow the horse to plod slowly over the cobbled roads, while his mind searched for answers. In the distance, a coach approached and Mathew realized by the driver whose it was.

"Mathew! Thank the Lord I've found you, man. Pray tell me what is happening now?"

"He's not in, John. He's gone to Virginia. I'll go to the barracks and try to rouse some people I know there."

"Shall I come with you?"

Mathew shook his head. "It won't do much good. I'm faster alone."

"As you wish, but I can follow you."

"John, it would help me much more if you can assist your servant Thomas. I will go to the British headquarters so that we can mobilize two forces to search for Jane."

His friend saw the wisdom in this and nodded as Mathew pushed his horse into a quick trot and then into a gallop as he moved out of view.

The night was dark now and the streets were lonely and cold as Mathew rode through them. The garrison was built upon a hill. It looked lonely and forbidding on the skyline as he galloped towards it. There was not a soul about now, save for a drunkard lying along the side of the road, who raised half a salute to him. But Mathew did not see nor acknowledge this. His mind was now focused on one thing—how to find out where Jane was.

Near the entrance, he was halted by four sentries, but they recognised him quickly enough and let him pass. Mathew rode up to the officer's quarters and dismounted. There was some noise from inside the lounge area and Mathew quickly made for that.

"Gad! It's our spiritual savior," shouted an officer who recognised Mathew as he moved into the room. "Come! Sit down, Mathew, and join us in the excellent wine you have sold to us." This brought a round of laughter from the half-drunk officers.

"I'm sorry to intrude, Peter," Mathew addressed the most senior officer present, "but my call this evening is of the gravest sincerity."

"What is it, man?" asked a more drunk officer to his left. "Lost your wine shipment?"

Mathew ignored the friendly jibe and looked at the colonel. "Peter, I'm concerned with the disappearance of my wife."

The colonel told the other officers to be quiet as he tried to listen more to what Mathew was saying.

Mathew knew he must tell more to get the help he needed, and so held himself up high and addressed all present in a clear tone.

"Gentlemen, you know me for the business I do with you. I have been in the colonies for a short time, but I came from England—"

"So did we," interrupted another officer, "and now we're stuck in this shit hole."

"Quiet!" demanded the colonel, giving the officer a stern look. "Continue, Mathew."

"…the truth is that my uncle there is wanted by the authorities for smuggling. Jane and I found out about his activities and he tried to have us both killed." It was not the exact truth, but near enough, thought Mathew. "To get Jane out of my uncle's grasp, we moved to the colonies. By the strangest of ill fortune, my wife saw this rascal of my uncle in a party held at the Adams' house last night."

"Last night! What! He's here? By gad, we'll get the fellow and it'll be the drop for him," remarked the colonel.

Mathew was glad to hear the colonel's assurance and pressed on with his account. "That was last night. It was last night that my uncle was seen and today…Jane has disappeared. When I came home, our maid told me that Jane had not been seen or known of since she left early this morning."

"But Mathew, is it not possible, my dear fellow, that Jane may be safe somewhere and perhaps just fell a little ill?"

"Then she would surely have sent a message to Mathew here," remarked the officer who had been told to be quiet but was more serious now.

"Describe this fellow to us."

Mathew gave a quick description of his uncle, to which all present listened very carefully.

"We'll have him." Suddenly, the colonel lost his drunkard appearance and with a clear and alert voice turned to the officer on his left.

"Allan, call out the guard. Get the regiment out of bed and assembled with haste."

The officer so named stood up, a little unsure on his feet. Shook his head to clear his senses and moved out of the room with remarkable agility and haste.

As the colonel stood up, so did the entire group. More instructions were given and a great movement of men, each having their own task, left the room.

"Come with me, lad." The colonel took Mathew by the arm. "My men will scour every home, alehouse and brothel in this stinking dung heap until we find where your wife was taken. I've got spies everywhere. We'll catch this fellow."

The night seemed darker now than before he had entered the building, but when he came out with the colonel by his side, Mathew felt the air was not so cold nor so lonesome. He felt strength from those who were now moving to help him, and in this strength a gratitude and belief that Jane would soon be found. Yet, as he looked down at the silhouettes of houses below, with the few lights here and there, he began to wonder if she really could be found.

"It's best for you to go home, Mathew," spoke the colonel. "You can do very little alone. My men are in full force and if you are home and should Jane return for any reason, then you will be at hand to help her. Besides, if we know where you are, then we can contact you all the more quicker than if you are wondering the streets aimlessly."

Mathew did not want to wait at home. He wanted to go into every house and turn it upside down. But what could he really do? he asked himself. The colonel was right, plus John was also making his own efforts to find Jane.

"Yes, you are right, my friend." Mathew shook his hand, called for a soldier to bring over his horse, mounted it and rode home slowly, his mind questioning all and everything that had happened over the past few days. Why had his uncle suddenly appeared, and why had Jane really disappeared?

Once home, he sent a message to the Adamses explaining the situation and begged that they report with any news.

It was mid-morning the following day when John Adams arrived at his home. Mathew had not slept that night and nor had he eaten this day. His eyes were red with lack of sleep and his manner nervous and abrupt.

"What news, John?" he blurted out, as he opened the door himself to see who had knocked.

Adams shook his head. "Little yet, my friend," he remarked and added as he stepped into the threshold, "But we are still looking."

"I can't stay in here, John. I'm going crazy. He might have murdered her or done worse."

"We don't actually know that your uncle is involved in this yet, Mathew… The truth and the problem is that we actually don't know anything."

The despair on Mathew's face was self-evident.

"Come, my friend, sit down," John took his friend's arm and led him into the parlor. "Have a brandy, man. It will bring order to all this nervousness."

Mathew shook his head. "It's not drink I need, John. It's my wife back safe and sound."

It was as he said this that there was a knock at the door. Mathew, nervous for news, stood up and moved towards the door, but as he did so, his friend held his arm back.

"Let me go, Mathew," said he, fearing what news may have been brought to the home. "Sit down and rest, man. It may be nothing."

The energy was little in Mathew and looking into the trustful eyes of his friend, nodded and let him attend to the door.

Outside was an officer and three soldiers.

"I'm sorry, Sir," began the officer, "may I please talk with Mr Mathew Appleton?"

"What news do you have?" inquired John quietly.

"None, Sir. We have not found his wife yet."

"It's OK, Lieutenant. I'll inform Mr Appleton. Please continue your search and pray you the Lord's good fortune in your endeavours."

The lieutenant lingered a moment and then, accepting the news was safely delivered, touched his hat in respect and ordered the men to move down the street.

John quietly closed the door.

"What was it?" Mathew's face was anxious but weak.

"It's alright, Mathew. It was just an officer to tell us they are still looking."

"I'll take that brandy, John. My nerves are raw."

Mathew had just put the glass to his lips when there was another knock at the door.

"Stay still, lad, I'll get it." Adams began to rise, but Mathew stayed him with his hand.

"No. Let me go. I can't stand this sitting. I'll go."

When Mathew opened the door, a girl in her early 20s stood before him.

"Beg'in your pardon, Sir. But I understand you're looking for a lady."

"What do you know?" Mathew's eyes were alert now and his attention full.

"I ain't knowing nothing much, Sir, but soldiers were ask'n about the whereabouts of a lady. Well, we don't know her name but my father said he saw a woman dressed as described yesterday."

"Where is your father?"

"Well..." The girl lingered with indecision.

"Tell me where your father is, please?" Mathew felt the strain of the moment.

"Well, he ain't able to talk much now... You see, Sir, he passed out drunk like."

"John!" shouted Mathew, and then to the girl, "Come, take me to your father."

Adams was quickly with them and together, all three moved out into the street, but the girl turned to address them.

"My father is drunk, Sir. He may take offense if two men appear before him. He is always ready to make a fight. It may be better if only one gentleman accompanies me."

Mathew nodded and turned to his friend.

"It's quite all right, John. I'm safe enough here. Please return to Abigail and let me know if your servant has any news."

Adams held back for a moment. "Are you sure, Mathew? It may not be as safe as you imagine."

Mathew studied the girl's face. "I'll be fine, John. Let's meet up later." With this, he turned and followed the girl. Adams watched the pair move into the distance and felt a slight anxiety about the whole affair.

The girl led Mathew down one street after another. It seemed that each street became narrower and more dirty than the one that preceded it.

"How far do we have to go, girl?"

"It's not far, Sir. I'm sorry, we are humble folk."

After another two streets, the girl stopped in front of a door painted red. The paint had peeled in many parts and the door itself was poorly fit. As she opened the door, a damp stench came upon him and he pulled his face back to lessen the impact of the foul air.

"Are you sure this is where your father is?"

The girl did not reply, only lifted up the hem of her dress and began to ascend the many wooden and not very secure steps that lay before her.

Mathew's mind was too much upon Jane to really think about the whole atmosphere he was entering. Even when he entered the room the girl had led him into, he did not think much of the light curtain that shielded the bed he could see beyond it, so he approached at the sound of a slight cough from behind it.

"Sir, I'm told you know something of the absence of my wife."

The curtain was dragged back with a sudden urgency that startled Mathew, but it was the face that was looking directly into his own that really shocked him.

"I don't know anything of that girl, my nephew, but it's you I'm after for all the loss and pain you caused me. I was forced out of my home and caused to hide and flee like a common thief. You have much to answer for, my lad. Sit down."

Mathew was aware of a small wooden stool just in front of him, but the words he heard moved through his mind as in a haze. He saw the look of evilness on his uncle's face and thought to run and escape the trap he had been led into, but the corner of his eyes picked out dark shadows of big men in the background. Big and rough they were, as he turned to look at them, and saw how each carried a short heavy stick.

"Better you sit down like the master said," spoke one of them in a thick Irish brogue.

Mathew looked back into the eyes of his uncle long and hard as he remained standing where he was. He had never hated a man before, but he hated this man. He hated him for what he had done to Jane, how he had destroyed their happiness and how he now had taken her again from him.

"Where is Jane?" He held the gaze of his uncle.

"Now, that's a thing I would love to know too!" smirked his uncle.

Mathew's mind struggled to make sense of what was really happening at this moment.

"Do you tell me you have no hand in her disappearance?"

His uncle did not reply, but it was plain by the expression on his face that he had not and was as equally baffled to where Jane was or what had befallen her.

"What do you want?" Mathew felt an anger growing steadily inside him. He resented being led here by the girl, who now had disappeared. He resented the two thugs standing behind him and most of all, he resented the living existence of his uncle.

"Won't you sit down, lad," offered his uncle. "We've a lot to talk about."

"Talk about? I've no interest in talking to you, only a great deal to see you swinging from the end of a rope."

The man sitting on the bed roared a deep laughter and nodded to the men behind him as he finished. "Well, that ain't goin' to happen, my nephew."

There was a sound of a heavy step sliding over the floor behind him. Mathew swung around to see one of the men moving behind him with his arm raised. In a moment he could not later recall how, Mathew lunged forwards at the man, grabbed his coat and with his full force pulled him forwards. The sudden jerk towards the man's direction brought him off balance and as he fell towards Mathew, Mathew leaned his body to the left so that the man fell upon his uncle. As the man's body passed him, Mathew bent down and grabbed the leg of the stool he had been told to sit on; with the same movement, he swung his body around to throw the heavy wooden stool towards the face of the other man who now was also moving towards him.

In a swiftness that surprised himself, Mathew moved towards the door that lay to the side of this man and lashed out at his head as he did so, just as the man's arms went down from blocking the stool he had hurled at him. The man fell, Mathew grabbed the handle of the door and wrenched it open. He felt someone touch his arm, but he was too far through the doorway for any more contact to be made. He ran, half-jumped down the stairs and out into the main street. Heavy footsteps pursued him, but Mathew was more agile and lighter on his feet.

"Hold there!" In front of Mathew, and to his great surprise, stood John Adams with six soldiers.

Understanding the situation, Adams commanded the soldiers to arrest the ruffian who had just appeared at the entrance to the house. Mathew moved aside to let the soldiers easy passage and turned to see the ruffian disappear back with in the house followed quickly by the first soldier to pass him.

"John!" exclaimed Mathew in shocked but obviously welcome surprise.

"You don't think I would really let you follow that woman alone, do you?" smiled his friend as he firmly gripped Mathew's hand.

"Get them all," shouted Mathew as the last soldier moved into the house. "All three of them."

He turned to face his friend. "Thank God you came, John. I thought I was a dead man for a moment."

"Who are they?"

"My uncle, I told you about. For some evil-minded reason, he had a plan to bring some suffering upon me."

"Well, let's see the fellow and then he will see who will suffer."

Both men turned back towards the entrance of the house, as one and then another soldier came into view.

"Excuse me, Sir!" remarked one of the soldiers, touching his peak. "Only these two louts. There was not a third. A window was open and it may be guessed the other made good his escape. There was no sound or sign of him."

"Don't worry, Mathew. He'll swing soon enough."

"But where then is Jane?" Mathew's face was fully perplexed. "I thought my uncle had her, but it was clear he was not involved in her disappearance."

"Are you sure of this?" John studied his friend's face.

Mathew nodded. "It was clear from all that just happened. Of her disappearance, my uncle at this moment is innocent."

"But that's good, man! It means she is safe."

"Maybe...maybe. I pray so, John." Both turned to follow the soldiers who were leading the two caught men out at the end of the street.

Chapter Eleven

The Captain

Jane awoke with a pain in her forehead. It was difficult to open her eyes and as she did so, there was a light too bright shining into them. She fended off the brightness with her hand.

"Where…where am I?" She tried to be coherent with her words, but it was so hard.

"It's OK, Jane. You were beginning to get too nervous. I gave you a little sedative to help you calm down."

"You…you drugged me…again?" Her words were slow and drawn out.

"You'll be fine in a moment. Here, drink this water."

"No," she said slowly, "I don't want anything from you."

"But it will help bring you around."

She tried to push the hand that held the glass of water away, but felt too weak. The water felt fresh and her senses opened up.

"Why do you treat me so, Sir?"

"Jane, I worry about you. I found you in a street that was clearly not for such as you. Had I not been present, that scum who attacked you would have had his evil way with you. You came onto my ship with a mind that seemed to be in some other place.

You talked of coming from a port that was not on my chart and I was in haste to make sail. I had no choice but to think how I could otherwise keep you safe. If you had left my ship at that time and I could not have been there to protect you, what could have happened to you? Pray, tell me? The second draught was just to give you time to accustom yourself to the ship and the journey we are bound to take, for I have a commission to uphold and cannot afford to delay."

Jane looked into his eyes. They were kind and the words he had spoken were all true. All his words made sense, even if she did not agree with being drugged.

"Then, what will you do with me now, Sir?"

"May we please dispense with the formalities, dear Jane? You must now see clearly that I had no bad intention and that all my intentions were for your better well-being." He looked into her eyes with a sympathy she could not resist.

"Very well, Captain Fritzwilliam."

"Would William be too hard to say?" he inquired with a gentle smile.

Jane studied his face for a time she felt was too long to be rude but only then gently nodded her head.

"OK, William, but," she warned, "no more drugging."

"That I promise." He stood up and turned to leave the cabin. "We are bound for the West Indies."

"Cornwall... England." The words drifted through her mind. "What of England, William?" She looked up at him with appeal in her eyes.

"If I could, I would, Jane, but my purpose this day must be bound for the West Indies. If I can find a ship bound for England, then within her you shall safely go. Indeed, there will be many ships bound for your country with trade from the place we are bound."

"What sort of place is it, please?"

"Well, it's sugar we are to go for."

Sugar plantation...the words came within her mind and seemed strangely familiar.

"Terrible place. Full of slaves," remarked the captain.

Jane looked up into his eyes. He had said something that had a very deep meaning to her, but she did not know why.

The journey south took some weeks. The weather was mild, and Jane found Captain Fritzwilliam—although he repeatedly begged her to call him William—a more trustworthy guardian that she had first thought. Often, she would sit on the bridge in a special chair he had had built for her and watch the endless sea meet the horizon. There was something strangely welcoming about watching the sea. She had watched it often in Cornwall, but there was another reason she felt attracted to it. A reason she could not explain. Only that she felt some sense of companionship.

It was early on the 4th, this being a Wednesday, that the first island was sighted. It felt exciting for her to see the palm trees in the distance and feel the breeze of the warm air. But when the ship berthed and Jane saw so many black and white slaves, she felt repulsed by the way they were treated. One man wearing a torn white shirt and a battered old straw hat on his head was lashing out freely with a whip at other men as they struggled to lift heavy boxes.

"William," called Jane, as she leaned over the side of the ship to watch the busy harbor, "please come here."

"I'm sorry, my dear." They had grown close together in the passage from Boston. He, because he needed a wife and was falling in love with her, and she, because he was strong and good and she felt lonely and frightened and in a strange way felt some inner feeling for him. "I'm very busy at the moment."

Two men had come aboard the ship with many papers to indicate that a lot of talk would be needed.

"Please, William."

The captain said something to the two men and moved over to where Jane was standing.

"My dear, the captain of the ship is most busiest when in port. There is very much work to be done.

Jane did not hear his words. She was thinking only about the cruel way the people on the dock were being treated.

"Please go and stop that man from beating the others. He is so cruel."

"I cannot interfere with the ways of things here, darling. This is normal on these islands and if I were to stop that man now, he would only cut more into their backs after I had left."

"But William, there is no need for such cruelty."

"Hoy! You there," William shouted to the man. "Come on board if you please?"

The man looked up to where the captain was. Touched the brim of his hat and walked towards the gangway and up it. William went to meet him as he stepped onboard the ship. He spoke some words, which Jane could not hear, passed him something from his pocket and turned back to Jane as the man touched his hat again and went down the gangway.

"Did you tell him to stop being cruel?"

"I gave him some coins and asked him to be gentler. But it won't do much good once we are away from here, my dear."

"Thank you, William." She looked into the eyes of this man and felt more and more admiration for his strength of character.

"Captain!" A sailor came up behind him and asked if he could see the two gentlemen who had come on board and now been led to his cabin.

"Excuse me please, Jane." He bowed politely and went with the sailor.

The harbor was busy with people moving about. The men moving the boxes seemed to be less shouted at, and her eyes drifted to the shops on the waterfront. There, she could see ladies moving in and out of the shops and Jane wondered what was inside these shops. She wished William could have time to take her there, but that was not possible now. Yet, the more she looked at the shops and saw people moving in and out of them and along the street, the more she felt the urge to leave the ship and explore. After all, she reasoned, the shops were very near and there were so many people about that she could not come to any harm.

Jane was off the ship and moving towards the shops before she realized it. In one way, it was good to feel free. At first, she felt a little unsure of her balance as she walked on solid ground, for she had become used to the roll of the ship, but she soon accustomed herself to this. As she walked past the men and women who were laboring at the dockside, she thought it so strange to see so many black-skinned people and wondered, as she watched them move about, if they missed their own country.

None of these people seemed happy, nor did the white people who were also treated in the same manner. She well knew of indentured slaves, but she never thought of their lives as being unhappy. She had never seen people being beaten to work harder.

The sun was at its highest by now and the air about her was very hot. Suddenly, a lady passed her by and greeted her in a friendly manner. Looking at the ship, she asked, "Where are you from, my dear?"

"Oh, England," replied Jane.

The lady looked at her a little strangely, smiled and continued on her way. Jane watched her go and, seeing the parasol of the woman, realized she would need one too. It really was very hot on the island, hotter than she had ever experienced. A shop selling such items lay just to the corner of a street and Jane went to inquire within it. She had never been in such a shop before. It was so different than those in Port Warren.

It was then, however, that she realized she did not have her purse with her and, blaming herself for her lack in thinking of this, she turned around to the ship she had come from. But which ship was it? There were many ships tied up along the harbor and to Jane, they all looked the same. Suddenly, a fear of helplessness took over. She strained her eyes trying to see someone on a ship she might recognise, but on each ship, she saw many people moving about, and the movement of so many more on the dock confused her even more.

The sun beat down upon her unprotected head and she began to feel dizzy. The masts of all the ships in front of her became blurred and the noises of the people about her sounded as if she was hearing them from under the water. It was so hot, so very hot. The masts were now almost invisible, merely faint sticks in a haze. Her mind closed down and everything went dark.

"Who is she?" It was a woman's voice she heard first.

"No idea," said another voice.

"Here! Move over. Let me git her up." It was the voice of a strong man.

Jane felt herself being lifted off the ground and put on her feet. She felt dizzy and did not notice the strong hands lifting her up.

"Are you alright, Miss?" It was the man's voice again.

Jane nodded her head but held the man's arm to steady herself.

"Sorry…" she muttered. "The sun was so strong."

"Aye, it is," the voice came from somewhere in the crowd of people that now surrounded her.

"Are you accompanied, Ma'am?" An older man with spectacles on the end of his nose stood in front of her.

"My husband…please get my husband."

"Of course. Where will he be? What's the address, Ma'am?"

Jane felt a puzzled frown overtake her face. The ships were in the right place, but behind the dock, there should be a whole city of brick buildings. Here, palm trees filled the skyline.

She studied the people about her. This was not the way people dressed in Boston.

"Where…where am I?" she enquired of the bespectacled man.

"Kingstown, of course."

Jane struggled to make sense of what he had just said.

"Kingstown, where?"

"Kingstown, Jamaica."

Chapter Twelve

Leave no Stone Unturned

The colonel had kept Mathew waiting nearly an hour, and he felt he could no longer sit as requested by the orderly. He had stood up a long time ago and found himself pacing up and down outside the closed door until it opened quite suddenly. Two large men in scarlet coats burst out in a mood that was not a happy one.

"Excuse me, General. This is the man I told you about." The colonel Mathew had come to see, could just be seen behind these men.

The larger of the two glared directly at him. "Wife missing what? Well, young man, the king might miss his country if we don't hang all these rebels."

With this said, he pushed rather rudely past Mathew, followed by the other officer in close pursuit.

"I am most awfully sorry, Mathew," apologized the colonel, opening the door wider to invite Mathew in. "The general is in a foul temper. A company of soldiers were just attacked by a rebel force. We had many casualties—"

"Have you heard anything, Peter?" interrupted Mathew.

"Rest assured, my dear fellow, if I had any small note of the smallest significance, I would have sent a message to you immediately. I'm awfully sorry." He slowly shook his bowed head. "Please come in and sit down."

The strain on Mathew's face was evident to his friend as he poured brandy into a glass.

"Here, man. It will help."

Mathew shook his head. "No, thank you, Peter. I have to keep a clear mind."

"Well, not to waste it," remarked the colonel as he drank the brandy himself.

"Have you really no news?" Mathew's voice was more like a plea than a question.

The colonel moved closer and stretched his arm to place his right hand on Mathew's shoulder.

"I've had a full regiment scour this city, my friend." He shook his head silently. "But we'll keep looking."

"Where can she be?" Mathew said silently. "I've no understanding of this...I love her so much." He looked at the colonel, then stood up. "I must knock on doors myself. Lord knows I was a fool to trust others to do this and not myself."

"You did the right thing, Mathew. You stayed in one spot while our forces and those of John Adams searched high and low."

Mathew looked at his friend in surprise.

"Yes. We know, Mathew... We have spies there."

Mathew felt a look of embarrassment pass over his face for not telling his British friend that his colonial friend was also involved in the search. But then, the greater realization came to his mind that anything that might work was so much welcome now. He had only hidden his deep friendship with Adams from the British at the request of Jane, although he had never understood why.

Suddenly, an anger awoke within him and he stood up quickly.

"My dear friend, I must do more than I have done. I have to find her."

With this said, he parted from the British headquarters and rode back to his home. His ride was one of haste, and once having arrived, he dismounted and, for the first time, with anger bringing order to the worry that had consumed him, he sat down with a paper and made a plan of action. He would walk the streets from his home asking all he could find if they knew the whereabouts of Jane Appleton.

It was, however, a fruitless search. The doctor who had treated Jane after the accident had been ill and was missing from his surgery soon after she had been brought to him, so none knew of the description Mathew gave to them of the clothes she was last seen in. As he walked and walked, his path eventually brought him to the dock area. It was not an area he felt comfortable in.

Too many people pushing and shoving each other in the haste of their moment. The tall masts overshadowed the people and the air was one of constant movement. Ships coming in, going out and those being unloaded and loaded for the journey they would make.

"You look tired, lad!" hailed a woman from his right side.

Mathew turned to see a well-breasted woman standing beneath a wooden board with the words, 'The Flying Duck'.

"Will you not come in and refresh your weary legs?" she shouted in jest.

She was right. He was tired. He had hardly slept over the past nights and the walking and asking questions about Jane had worn him down. He nodded, smiled slowly in agreement and walked into the alehouse.

It was dark inside and the air was smoky from the pipes of men spaced about. He sat down at a long table as a girl came up and asked him what he would drink. A mug of ale was placed before him soon after. It was more refreshing than he had thought and he felt relaxed after a few mouthfuls. He had not noticed an older man sitting nearby and as he looked at him, he now naturally asked, "Excuse me, good Sir."

The man looked over to him. "Aye lad."

"May I ask if you have seen my wife? She has disappeared some days past now and I am worn down with worry."

The man had a kind face. "Tell me what you can of her appearance, son," he said.

Mathew described the dress that Jane had left the house in and her general appearance.

The man seemed to search his mind, then raised an eyebrow.

"I think I saw this woman. She was walking with a sea captain."

Mathew's eyes opened, alert. "Pray tell me all you can, Sir." He moved next to the man.

"I'm not so sure. It was while I was sitting outside this house with Peter there." He pointed to a man at the back of the room with the long stem of the white clay pipe he was smoking. "Pete!" he shouted. "Come and join us."

The man who stood up was larger than Mathew expected him to be. His walk was slow and unsure with a bit of a limp as he came towards his table, but he soon sat down next to his friend and opposite to Mathew.

The first man explained Mathew's concern.

"Aye," said this new man, "that's the girl. Went onto The Mary Bell… She weighed anchor and sailed out soon after."

"Do you think my wife was on board?" The look of deep concern was well set in Mathew's face.

"Well, I didn't see her get off," remarked the man.

"Oh God! She's been kidnapped!" Mathew's eyes moved from worry to those of stark awareness.

"Do you know where this…this ship, The Mary Bell, was headed?"

"Sorry, son, I don't," replied the man in front of him. "Just a moment… Alice!" he called the woman who had first invited him into the alehouse.

"The Mary Bell, have you heard where she was bound?"

The woman was busy carrying mugs of ale to a group of sailors on another table.

"No idea," she called back.

"Mary Bell?" responded one of the sailors at the table she was approaching. "Aye, she's bound for Jamaica for sugar, least that's what the crew were talking about."

Mathew stood up and threw a handful of coins on the table.

"Give all here a good drink, Madam." He looked at the woman, Alice, and departed from the dock area.

Once clear of the hustle and bustle of people about him, he called to a coach driver and asked to be taken to the home of John Adams.

"Jamaica!" exclaimed Abigail. "Oh God, that's a terrible place with disease and slaves. God protect her."

"Don't worry, Mathew, I'll hire a vessel from a friend of mine and we'll be after her at first light," assured Adams.

So it was that soon after dawn had passed, a small ship carrying Mathew, John Adams and a group of rough-looking men selected by his servant Thomas (who had been entrusted to find Jane) departed from Boston heading south.

It was not ideal sailing weather for John Adams. Almost as soon as the little ship had moved out into the open sea, a wind came up and changed almost instantly what had been a calm sea into a very rough one. Mathew had gained his sea legs on the long crossing to the colonies, but John had long lost these—if ever he had gained them. He was violently seasick and stayed most of the first two weeks of the voyage in his cabin.

"Lord knows how Jane ever survived this," he greeted Mathew as he entered his cabin, carrying a tray with a bowl upon it.

"The captain says the barometer has changed and the sea will calm soon," he countered the remark of his friend.

"Oh, please take that food away. I can't even look at it."

"You need something inside you, John. The cook has made a good broth for you."

"How long must we endure this journey?" John's face was pale.

"We are soon there," lied Mathew to his friend, trying to give him hope. The journey was, in fact, less than half complete.

The sea, however, did calm sooner than expected and with food inside him and a steady leg, Adams returned to his joyful self, even cracking a joke or two at the dinner table in the evenings.

Chapter Thirteen

Something Sinister

"Clear the way." The man whose arm Jane leaned against pushed people aside as he led her to a shop, where she could rest.

"Are you alright, dear?" asked a lady who seemed to have a creamy skin color.

Jane nodded, but did not feel very right.

"Must have been the sun. You shouldn't have been out there without a parasol or at least a hat."

"Do you think I may have some water to sip, please?" she asked the woman.

"Of course." The woman moved into the back of the shop and reappeared moments later with a glass and a large clay jug. "Here you are, dear, but sip it slowly, lest it make you ill."

The light in the shop was suddenly blocked by a tall man standing in the doorway.

"Jane! Oh, I'm so sorry to see you like this. One of the men on the bridge told me what happened.

She looked at the man standing before her, puzzled.

"Come," he said and stepped into the shop.

"Don't touch me," she said. "Keep away from me."

The man looked puzzled by this response.

"It's me, Captain Fritzwilliam, Jane."

"Don't come near me. I don't know you."

"What devilment is this?" replied the man. "Jane, it is I… William."

"Please help me," Jane called to the crowd beyond the shop. "I don't know this man."

Captain Fritzwilliam stood where he was.

"Jane, you have taken too much sun."

She turned to the woman who had given her the water. "Please, Miss, I don't know this man. He will take me without my consent."

The woman gave a shout and a huge black man appeared from the depths of the shop.

"Henry, please escort this gentleman out of my shop."

The man moved towards the captain, who was now completely bewildered by all these events.

Sensing he should let matters lie as they stood for the time being, he said calmly, "It's alright, Jane. I shall wait on The Mary Bell for you when you have regained your senses."

With this said, he retired with a puzzled expression on his face.

"You watch out for the likes of them, dear," responded the woman after Fritzwilliam had left her shop. "There's money in white slaves, make no mistake."

"What do you mean?" Jane looked at the woman, unsure of what to believe at this moment.

"He'll have you on his ship and you'll be off it in chains at the next slave market, if I'm anything to go by."

"How did he know my name was Jane?" she muttered quietly to herself as she gazed at the world outside the shop.

The woman overheard her. "Is your name Jane, dear?"

"Yes, it is. But I've never seen that man before."

"Think nothing about it. He won't come anywhere near you while Henry is about, that's for sure. Still, it's strange he knew your name."

Yes, it is, thought Jane…then her mind began to wonder how she got to Jamaica.

"Here, dear, put this inside you. It'll help make all things sensible."

Jane looked down to see that the woman was holding out a cup of tea for her.

"Thank you." She smiled at the lady. "Thank you for being so kind to me." But the lady had already disappeared into the back of the shop. Then she noticed a finely dressed woman standing in front of her.

"Excuse me, Ma'am, I don't wish to be rude, but I think you need a little help. You seem lost."

Jane looked at the woman. She was about her age and had a kindly looking face, but more than that, she was smiling.

"Hanna! Oh Hanna, I am so glad to see you. Providence has surely brought you to me at this time."

"Jane, you look all out of place. What happened to you?"

"I do not know, Hanna, but I'm so happy to see you." Saying this, she rose from where she was sitting and moved to embrace the girl she had once met in the dress shop in Boston.

The two girls hugged each other, but the hug from Jane was the greater for the relief and security she now felt.

"What are you doing here?" It was the same question that each asked at the same moment, causing both girls to laugh as one heard the question of the other.

"I'm here with my stepfather who has a plantation here," replied Hanna.

Jane was silent.

"And you, dear Jane, what brings you here?"

Jane looked into the eyes of Hanna. "I don't know, Hanna."

"What do you mean you don't know?" Hanna was still laughing, although the sudden serious expression on Jane's face caused her to stop.

"Are you in some danger, dear Jane?"

Jane shook her head. "I just don't know how I got here. The last thing I can remember was being in Boston, and then suddenly, I'm here in a different part of the world."

Hanna gave her a coy smile, suggesting Jane was not entirely truthful and was hiding something.

"Come," she said, "let's go and meet my stepfather."

'Oh, I must pay the woman of the shop." Jane turned around to look for the lady, but she was close at hand.

"No need, dear. You go and take care of yourself and…" she shouted as Jane moved out of the shop "…keep out of the sun."

An open carriage was waiting outside and as she stepped into it after Hanna, she noticed the same man standing nearby who had talked to her in the shop.

"Jane," he called, "will you not talk with me?"

"Who is he?" asked Hanna, leaning over to Jane who was now sitting by her side.

"I don't know," Jane said puzzlingly, "but he says he knows me."

"Never trust a sailor. They know all the girls," laughed Hanna, but Jane kept staring at the man as the coach moved off and through the dock area. He, in turn, looked back at her, frowning in puzzlement.

Once out of the dock and shops, the road became a dust track overshadowed by palm trees. It was very hot and quite unlike any climate Jane had experienced.

"Here, take my fan," said Hanna, seeing the discomfort on Jane's face.

"Do we have far to go, Hanna? The heat is making me feel dizzy again."

"Not far. Keep the air moving about your face and keep the parasol up," she remarked as Jane had let hers slip to the side.

The track wound its way up a hill, and Jane could see many black people working in the fields.

"Is it not too hot for them?" she remarked.

"No. They are used to it... born in this awful weather."

The road twisted around dusty bends before coming to a large house set at the back of an open lawn.

A tall man, wearing a very large white hat, came out of the main door and stood on the porch waiting for the carriage to arrive.

"Well, Hanna, who do we have here?" he called out as the carriage came to a stop before him.

"This," introduced his stepdaughter with a laughing smile, "is my very good friend, Jane Appleton."

"Welcome, Jane." The man was soon standing by the door of the carriage and holding out his hand to assist Jane to come down to the ground.

"Thank you, Sir," she replied, also with a smile.

A black man ran out from the inside of the house and to the carriage.

"Sorry, Masa," he called, "I was out back."

Jane noticed how the man holding her hand seemed distasteful to the black man. She caught, just for the slightest moment, an eye from him that made her pull back in fright. It was a cold, evil eye.

"Sleeping again," he remarked in a disdainful way without looking at this man.

The look of fear in the black man's eyes before he looked down to the ground told Jane this was not a happy place to be and she wondered if she should return to the harbor immediately. But the carriage was already moving away, and the man's hand was strong on hers. A little too strong, she thought, and one that could be cruel as she thought back to the fear she had seen in the black man's eyes. She wished she could be free of it, but this would be too impolite and too obvious.

"Come, Jane." Hanna's voice brought her mind back to the present, and with a few steps, she was out of the hot sun and into a cool breeze within the house.

"So," said Hanna, twirling her dress as she spun around, "let me introduce you to my home and my dear stepfather. Captain Henry Hall, this is Miss Jane Appleton."

The man smiled and bowed a little and Jane curtsied in response.

"You must be very tired, Jane. Let Hanna show you to your room. We can talk again at dinner."

"Come," begged Hanna as she took Jane's hand and led her up the stairs and to a room that was light and fresh. Such a change from the noise of the harbor and the heat and dust of the road.

"Why, this is so heavenly, Hanna. I shall be—"

Her words were interrupted by a man's howl of pain.

"Oh, what was that?"

Hanna shook her head. "Nothing, my dear friend."

The noise of a man's suffering came once again.

Jane's eyes opened in suspicion.

Hanna saw her face and shrugged her shoulders. "Think nothing about it, Jane."

"But Hanna, the man is in pain."

Hanna nodded. "I imagine he is. Father will take no nonsense when a black is lazy. Don't worry, they need a stick sometimes."

"Oh, Hanna, how can you say that?"

"It's the way here. You'll get used to it. Anyway, I'll send up Jilly with hot water and you can refresh and relax before dinner." With this said, she turned and disappeared out of the doorway.

Jane sat on the bed and looked around her.

It was a large room. The floor was washed wood, and the wooden walls were painted white. Curtains were cotton, blue in color, and through the windows, Jane looked out over a land of plantations. The rich blueness of the sea was just visible through a cut in the tree line. But as she looked out over the fields, she could see small figures in the distance working on the land.

It is too hot for them, she thought, and she felt sorry for these people. The pain of the man hurt in the house was still fresh in her mind. She pushed the thought aside and lay down to try to relax. The ceiling above her was covered with strange paintings. This seemed odd to her, and she wondered why they were there, but her thoughts were interrupted by a slight tap at the door, and a maid opened it moments later.

"Sorry to be troubling you, Ma'am. But Miss Hanna said I should bring you some hot water and towels."

"Thank you. It's very kind of you." Jane sat up in bed and was about to stand up.

"No, Miss, please, I'm here to wash you. If you don't mind?"

The girl seemed to wait for Jane's agreement and only moved forward after Jane had nodded.

"Please, you take off your clothes with me. My name is Jilly."

Jane stood up, but felt uncomfortably strange to know another woman was undressing her. It was an action she had only done by herself, but Jilly was very quick and skillful in her task. Within moments, Jane was ready and watched Jilly as she poured hot water from a jug into a china bowl that lay on the table. Jilly carried the bowl over and dipped one of the towels into the water and began to gently rub Jane's body. The hot water felt good and she relaxed with a slight pleasure she had not felt before, for a woman's touch was gentler to that of Mathew's.

"Tell me," she asked Jilly, as she looked up to the ceiling, "do you know anything about those strange paintings up there?"

The girl did not reply.

"Tell me, Jilly, I'm curious."

"'No, Miss. I can't."

"Why not?" Jane felt puzzled by this secrecy.

Jilly merely shook her head and remained silent.

"What is the mystery, Jilly?" Jane asked, becoming a little angry with the mystery kept by the maid.

"No, Miss. Please, you don't ask Jilly questions."

Jane knew it was stressing the girl and so she decided to ask Hanna about them when the time was right. Why such strange paintings, she thought, and on the ceiling.

What was happening in this house? she wondered to herself.

The dinner went well. Hanna had lent her one of her dresses and her stepfather was very charming. His early temper seemed to be a thing of the moment and Jane thought she could be happy here. Although once she was back in her room, she looked up again at the paintings, shrugged her shoulders, and put them out of her mind. The air was very warm and she opened the doors to the veranda and sat outside on one of the chairs that were there.

The moon was now high in the sky and with it being completely full, a light was cast over the land in front of her. The fields were now deserted, but she could still see the sea. For some reason, it seemed easier to see in this night air, and she watched the lights of a small ship move to the horizon. Again, the thought came to her as to how she had come to be here and how she could return again as quickly as possible to Boston and to Mathew. Then she remembered the man who had approached her in the shop. He knew her name. Perhaps he had some knowledge of her fate. She stood, entered her room and after undressing, climbed into bed.

It was only when she was lying on the bed that Jane really began to study the paintings and saw how they appeared to move as she watched them. For some reason, they seemed to play with her imagination. It really did seem that the more she looked at them, the more they moved, such that a happy thought brought dream-like images, but an unhappy one—frightening and disturbing images. Jane clamped her eyelids closed to keep out this devilment. These paintings were more than they appeared and she felt uneasy with them. Mathew came into her mind at that moment and a feeling of sadness moved over her. She missed him very much and turned on her side to avoid looking anymore at these paintings. As she did so, she found herself looking at the door. Jane could not reason why, but something told her to lock the door. She was comfortable in bed and tried to resist the thought, but it played with her mind.

Eventually, she threw back the sheet covering her and sat up. It was just as she did this that she froze as the sound of a floorboard creaked on the other side of the door. As silently as she could, Jane moved quickly over the floor, making no sound in her bare feet, to lock the door. She waited there, holding her breath and listened for more sounds, but none came. As silently as she could and trying not to make any sound from her breathing, she moved stealthily back to bed, climbed in between the sheets and closed her eyes.

It was a moment later that the sound of the floorboard squeaked again. Her eyes shot open and she felt her heart beat loudly. Someone had been there all the time. She watched the door but now all was quiet again. Her eyes searched the room for some weapon of any kind, but there was nothing. The only thing she could think of was to take the chair from the veranda and jam it against the door handle. With this thought, Jane got out of bed again and as quietly as she could, brought the chair into her bedroom and wedged it against the door handle and the floor. Turning back to her bed, she saw a silver-backed hairbrush lying on the dressing table. It would be some weapon, she decided and collected it before climbing back into bed. With the door locked, a chair wedged against it and a weapon by her side, the events of the day quickly overtook her mind and she fell into a deep sleep. She did not hear the floorboard squeak one more time.

Chapter Fourteen

A Common Bond

The sea remained calmer than Mathew had expected, and with a good wind, their little ship covered a good distance every day. It now took less than a week before the first sign of land appeared, and within a day, the clear outline of palm trees on the skyline gave the first indication of a new terrain, a new land of different cultures and customs.

Jamaica was nothing like Mathew had expected. He had become accustomed to the activity in the harbor of Boston, but here, things had their own pace. People moved slower and the only haste seemed to be created by a few men shouting at others who were laboring. As the ship came into dock, Mathew, with John Adams by his side, scanned the quay.

"Where do we begin?" Mathew looked out to the mass of people moving about. "How can we ever find her here?"

"We will, my friend. We will." John put his hand on Mathew's shoulder with reassurance.

Sailors were busy throwing ropes to men standing below on the quay, who then began pulling upon them to berth the ship good and proper. A gangway was quickly laid and Mathew, with full impatience, was the first off the ship, followed a little awkwardly by John who found it difficult to hold himself straight on terra firma again.

"We need to find this ship, The Mary Bell."

"I expect the tavern's along here." John ran his finger over the alehouses along the waterfront. "Will be a good place to start."

"Let's go first to the harbor master. He will have a log of all shipping activity."

"Excellent idea, my friend. Lead the way."

The harbor master's office was easy to find, but the office door was locked.

"He'll be back after," shrugged a man sitting at a desk beside the door.

"When is after?" demanded Mathew with growing impatience.

The man looked up at him. "After." He said no more and obviously had no interest to say more.

Mathew felt irritated by the attitude of the man. He did not seem to care for his obvious distress.

"It's the way of things on the islands." John held his friend's arm back. "There is a different meaning of time here."

"Tell me the time the harbor master will return…" adding "…please?"—in the hope he may get an accurate response.

The man had now dropped his stare to the opposite wall. "After," he repeated the single word.

Mathew felt a great anger boiling up inside.

"Come!" John took a firm grip on his arm with a gentle pull.

"Let's go to the taverns. You will get a better response there."

"What is the matter with these people?" inquired Mathew, as they walked down the steps and back into the main harbor area.

'It's a mixture of the heat and an indifference to life," replied his friend. "Most people you'll meet here are slaves or children of indentured persons. They have little motivation to move. There is no reward for them to do so, only the rough backhand of their owner or the cut of the whip."

"Let's begin over here." Mathew nodded to a tavern with a sign hanging above the doorway—Black Jack.

The room was dark and smelt of stale tobacco smoke as they entered. There were few men about and the owner behind the counter was little more helpful than the man in the harbor master's office.

"I'll explode if the next man is not courteous to me," remarked Mathew as he stormed out of the building.

"These are not men of any destiny, Mathew. Take them as they are, or word will go around and they will help you even less."

"Is this possible?" glared Mathew at no one in particular.

"Let's try The Royal Lass," motioned his friend.

"Well, it's a more positive-sounding name," responded Mathew, as both approached the doorway.

Sitting outside were two men with mugs of ale in their hands.

"Excuse me, good Sirs," began John. "May either of you fine men have heard of The Mary Bell?"

"She's lying over there," pointed one with a clay pipe in his hand.

"Ha ha," laughed John to his friend. "Did I not tell you to try the taverns first?" But Mathew was already two paces ahead of him and walking towards the vessel.

"Hello, gentlemen, can I help you?" It was a tall, bearded man who was standing at the bottom of the gangway to the ship they had reached.

"I'd like to talk with the master of the vessel. Can you direct me to him please?" Mathew's voice was tense, showing an urgency to his need.

"Well! That'll be me," replied the man, looking straight into the eyes of Mathew. "And whom may I be addressing?"

"Where is my wife?" Mathew was clearly at the point of striking the man.

The man held his calmness. He himself was a man of strength and strong will.

"I don't know who your wife is, Sir." His manner was bold and forthright.

"Jane Appleton," Mathew spoke clearly.

The stern look on the man's face changed. The name Jane caused him to wonder if this was his Jane. He seemed to ponder for a moment before replying

"Jane! Ha, I see." The man was strong enough in character not to need to show aggression, as was all too clear with Mathew.

"I understand a little of what you may be thinking, but I assure you that Jane came to no harm by my hand. My name is Fritzwilliam, Captain William Fritzwilliam. Would you both come with me to my cabin, and I will explain as much of the story of your wife as I know."

Mathew felt the tension lower in him. He liked the honest manner of the man. He felt this man would not harm Jane and there was a story that might bring sense to all he had not understood since his wife disappeared.

"Please forgive my friend, captain," interrupted John. "We have both been under great strain since Jane disappeared."

The captain turned to look at him, held his eye for a moment, and nodded his head in understanding. "Come, gentlemen. I will help you as much as I can."

With this said, the captain took a step onto the gangway and proceeded to ascend to the deck, leaving no choice for Mathew and John but to follow him. Once on the deck, the captain went straight to his cabin and held the door open for them.

"Please come in, and I will enlighten you as much as I am able."

Both entered the room and sat at the table, which the captain gestured them to sit at, and then proceeded to place three glasses upon it and filled each to the brim with port.

Having sat down and taken a sip from his glass, William Fritzwilliam began to explain the circumstances by which he had met Jane and all that had happened until he last saw her in the shop.

"…and there, gentlemen, my knowledge of Jane concludes. I am at a complete loss why she rejected me at that moment. She clearly had no knowledge of me, and I am sorry, most sorry to say," he looked directly into Mathew's eyes, "that Jane…that Jane's mind has changed so she does not know who she is."

The pain was very visible on Mathew's face. "You say she did not recognise you?" he said after a moment of deep thought.

The captain shook his head. "Not in the least. It is as if we had never met."

"Do you know the woman she went with?" asked John.

"I was tempted to inquire, but to be honest, I was dumbfounded and in some small state of shock that she did not know me. The carriage was soon gone, and I was quite lost in my wits at that moment."

"We must ask the woman in the shop. Will you please direct us there?"

"I'll do better than that. I shall escort you there myself. Come, let us go there now." The captain stood up and all three left the ship.

The shop where Jane had last been seen in was empty when they entered, and it took a moment before the woman came out from the back. She smiled at her expectant customers, but the moment she recognised Fritzwilliam, her smile dropped.

"I don't want you in here," she said sternly. "Henry!" she called the name of her huge negro servant loudly. The man appeared seconds later.

"Please, please wait, Madam. I mean no trouble. This here," he gestured to Mathew, "is the husband of the woman whom I tried to talk to in this shop. You see, we fear she has lost her senses and is in danger."

The woman looked suspiciously at Fritzwilliam, but could tell the anxiety on Mathew's face was genuine.

"What do you want to know?" she responded.

"Could you tell us who my wife went with, the name of the lady?" It was Mathew who spoke for the first time.

The woman looked into his eyes. A change of concern came over her.

"I've never seen either of them before that moment. I'm sorry. I ain't no idea who she is or where they went after they left here."

"Then we are sorry to have troubled you, Ma'am," replied Mathew. "I wish a good day to you."

All three left the shop.

"I'm sorry, Master Appleton," remarked Fritzwilliam, "I have no other suggestion."

"Could you make a good description of this woman who was with Jane?" asked John.

"I could that, aye."

"Then all is not lost."

"What do you mean?" asked Mathew of him, with an eye that tried to delve into his mind.

"Taverns, my dear boy. They are the library of all knowledge concerning people and their whereabouts?"

Mathew smiled a little and nodded slowly. "You are ever resourceful, my friend. Where do you suggest we begin?"

John Adams eyed the waterfront, but as he was doing so, Fritzwilliam interrupted his thoughts.

"Would it not be more proper to inquire in tea shops and dress shops when seeking knowledge of a lady?"

"By gad! He has got you there!" remarked Mathew, giving his friend a hearty slap on the shoulder.

Adams laughed with a defeated smile. But quickly retracted it with a gleam in his eyes.

"Let's split up. You and Fritzwilliam here search the better shops, and I'll follow my nose, and let's see what fruit we can yield."

With this agreed, the party divided and moved off in different directions in search of anyone who may give some information to the description of the woman last seen in Jane's company.

Chapter Fifteen

A Dark Ritual

Jane was awoken in the morning by the scream of a man.

Oh God! What was that? she asked herself as her eyes opened wide by the disturbance.

Pulling the bedsheet about her shoulders, she rose and went to the veranda, since the continued screams were coming from beyond this direction.

Outside, all was empty, but as she searched about, she saw a crowd of people to the far right in the distance. Another scream made her strain to see a man tied to posts. She winced as she heard the crack of a whip and then saw Hanna's stepfather. He stood tall and prominent in his white shirt, as he pulled back his arm and released the whip once again.

"This is a Hell for these people," she muttered under her breath. "Why is it like this?" Then she remembered the plan of Mathew's vile uncle and how he had planned to have her bonded here, just like these people. She felt sad thinking this and wondered what her cottage was like back in Cornwall. She missed Bobby and then her mind turned to Boston and Mathew.

How did I ever get here? she spoke to herself. What on earth happened to me? I have to get back. Somehow, I have to get back to Mathew. But how?

She excused herself from breakfast, for she could not look into the eyes of Hanna's stepfather. Somehow, she had to avoid him as much as possible. He frightened her, but there was another disturbance she felt from him. Something she could not understand. Yet the lack of understanding this plagued her constantly.

Jane realized that her only hope of getting to Boston and away from this house lay in the passage of a ship. She had no money for this, and yet she believed that if she could only find a captain of a ship, he would convey her back to Mathew in Boston and be handsomely rewarded for his help. But how to get to the harbor and how to get out of this house? Each day, she tried to create an excuse for going to the harbor. One was the need for a doctor, another the need for a dressmaker, and another the need to meet other ladies. Each request was turned down with an excuse from Hanna's stepfather. After a week of being in their company, Jane was beginning to feel depressed and wondering if she was being held captive.

It was some evenings later, and after dinner, that Hanna's stepfather asked Jane if she would accompany him on the porch. She had tried to avoid being near him as much as she could up till now, and she reasoned that he knew this and wanted to befriend her, but she felt frightened to be too near to him.

However, she could not think of an excuse not to join him and so after dinner, they both moved out to the veranda. The air outside was very warm and a servant brought a lantern out to give light in the darkness. Immediately, large white moths began to flutter about the light and Jane winced as some flew too close to her head.

"I'll put it out," remarked the captain, seeing Jane's discomfort. But as he did so, he moved closer to her in the dark. It was a move that alarmed her.

"Perhaps…" she stuttered out the words, "…we should have the light on. We could put it over there to be free of the moths."

"As you like," he replied and called the servant to bring another light, which was duly placed near the end of the veranda.

"There, that's better," he replied. "Now, Jane, I know the ways of these islands are new to you, but you must understand how easily a revolt could happen here if these people are not ruled by fear. There was an uprising on Antigua last year. A lot of our kind were murdered before a ship arrived with soldiers and brought order."

He shook his head. "You can't be too soft with these people. No, you can't."

"But don't you think they are human too?"

He half laughed to himself. "Like I said, Jane, you don't know the ways of things out here."

He leaned over to some bottles on a table and poured himself a drink.

"May I offer you one?"

"No, thank you. I'm not in need of a refreshment."

"Don't mind if I am." He quickly drank the glass he had filled, but then stood up and entered the house. He reappeared some moments later, holding a mug.

"Drink this, Jane, it's a local drink. It's very good for cooling the blood in this hot climate."

Jane felt some inner feeling not to take the mug from him, but he pushed it close to her so that it was difficult to refuse.

"I'm not really thirsty,"

"Maybe, but you can get sick out here all too easily. Drink it up. It'll be good for you."

She put the mug to her lips. The smell was good. In fact, the drink seemed all too accommodating so that after one small sip, she easily drank the contents of the mug.

"There! Did I not say this was good for you?"

She smiled, not wishing to appear rude, but as she did so a wave of dizziness came over her.

"Oh! It's gone to my head."

"It can do that, but you will feel better for it in the morning. Come, I'll get one of the servants to help you to your room."

Jane tried to stand up alone but felt weak and collapsed back into the chair.

"What…what was in the drink?" she asked.

"Nothing unusual." But his face seemed distorted in the light now and his voice was as if he was speaking through a cloth held tight over his mouth.

Jane could make out two vague figures coming towards her.

"Come, Miss, we'll help you to bed." It was the voice of Jilly, but it was not her normal voice. It was muffled as if she was hearing her through many blankets.

With the help of the two servants, Jane slowly made her way to her bedroom. She was vaguely aware of Jilly undressing her, but soon a darkness came over her and she fell into a deep, deep sleep.

While thinking she was in a dream, Jane opened her eyes to see many people in her room. Hanna's stepfather was looking down at her, but he seemed to fade in and out of many other faces. She did not know how they had come there, but they came about her bed and lifted her up. She saw the ceiling move as they carried her above their shoulders. The ceiling above her changed as she moved, as if in a daze, from her room into the hall, down the stairs and out into the night air. Beating of drums in the distance distracted her thoughts for a moment. Then she heard many voices about her, coming from all directions. Yet, in a strange way, none seemed clear. All noises merged into a common wailing sound. As Jane listened to these, feeling unable to move, the sound of drumbeats seemed to become louder.

Suddenly, the face of a woman shot in front of her and Jane winced in fright. She had been laid down on a hard surface but felt too tired in her body to move.

Drugged came the thought to her mind. She tried to fight the haze that held her down and blinked at the people who seemed to be moving about her.

The face of the woman loomed into her vision again.

"Who…who are you?" She heard her own voice say, but everything seemed unreal to her.

The woman never seemed to speak to her directly, but she was talking aloud. She just moved in and out of Jane's vision and when out, Jane saw how she spun among fire flickering in the background. Suddenly, the woman came very close to her, holding a small doll up to Jane's eyes. Jane could not understand the words the woman was saying. She spoke in a strange tongue, but the word 'Voodoo' was repeated many times by voices in the background.

In a strange way, she thought the doll might be her. It seemed that the doll had hair like her own, and even material from the dress she had worn when she had first arrived.

"Where…where am I?" She heard her own voice speak, but it seemed blurred to her ears. Blurred faces of many people seemed to be looking at her. The light from burning torches was blurred. Her thoughts seemed blurred. Everything was in a blur. Her head ached.

Suddenly, a man was in front of her. She could not recognise his features, but felt his hands grip her arms. She felt herself moving off the ground upwards and knew he was carrying her.

"Stop! Leave me alone!" She heard her own voice say and tried to push against his body to free herself.

"I'll get you away from here." It was his voice. She knew it.

Jane fought the blurriness in her mind, struggling to understand what was happening.

"Mathew?" she asked.

"Yes! Stop struggling, Jane. It's me."

"Where…where am I?"

Mathew did not reply, but there was tall grass or light bushes brushing against her. She was being carried through some kind of undergrowth.

Then she seemed to come out into some sort of an opening. Jane could just make out stars above her and torchlights about her.

"Is she alright?" She heard. She knew this voice too, but struggled to remember where she had heard it.

"She is now, thank God." These were Mathew's words. Now she knew she was safe and knew no more.

Chapter Sixteen

Homeward Bound

'Here, dear, drink this. It will help you."

Jane opened her eyes. The room she was in was strangely familiar.

Her eyes felt heavy. She smiled at the kind face and took the mug she was handed. She remembered the lady from a shop she had been in.

The woman turned and moved out of her vision. As she did so, Jane saw a huge black man standing further back in the room. She pulled herself back, uncertain how safe she was.

"There is nothing to fear now, Jane."

It was Mathew's voice. She pulled her gaze down to see him sitting on the edge of a bed opposite to her.

She smiled and saw another man sitting next to him.

"Who…who are you?" she asked.

Both faces smiled back at her.

"It's a long story, my love. A very, very long story," spoke Mathew. "This here is Master Fritzwilliam, captain of The Mary Bell.

"Do I know you, Sir?" inquired Jane.

"You did once, Jane, but that was a different time," spoke the man.

Jane felt confused. "I…I don't understand."

"Drink the brew Mrs Cummings made for you," spoke Mathew. "It will help make it all clear."

"I've seen that lady before," muttered Jane.

"Yes. It's because of Mrs Cummings that we were able to find you."

Jane suddenly looked startled. "That man. Hanna's stepfather…is he…"

"He's no more, Jane. The devil looks after his own kind. Think no more about him. He will never trouble anyone again."

"I don't understand, Mathew. He was so cruel to those people."

"Like I said, the devil looks after his own."

"Do you mean he's…he's dead."

Mathew nodded. "The governor's men brought us to you, and just in time, I do believe." He looked into her eyes. A kind moisture came into his. "And thank God for it," he said quietly.

"Come, rest more now, Jane." It was Fritzwilliam who spoke, and placing a kind hand upon Mathew's shoulder, said to her, "We will talk about all this later. You need to rest."

He rose, took the empty mug from her hand and moved out of the room, followed by the black man.

"Fritzwilliam's right, darling Jane. You need much rest. Fear nothing anymore. Never again in your life. I will never leave you again."

"Don't go, Mathew, please stay here with me. Hold my hand."

She stretched her hand outwards and towards his. She felt frail, but a tired smile came to her as she felt the strength of his hand. Her eyes closed and dreams came. Happy dreams.

The warmth of the sunlight bursting through the thin curtain woke Jane the next morning. She felt strangely happy. The words I'm free came into her mind and she began to sing a song she made up, while she lay there in bed.

"I'm as free as a bird. So free, I can fly where I wish. None can chain me now…"

The door to her room opened, and Mathew's head appeared around it.

"Glad you're so happy this morning, my darling," he smiled at her.

"Oh, Mathew, I am. I am so very, very happy. Come to me."

"I've missed you so much, Jane. You cannot imagine the worry and torment that have played on my mind since you disappeared."

"I don't know what happened, Mathew. I remember leaving our home and then… then, I was here on this island. I don't know what happened." She began to cry. The happy smile a moment ago turned into a face of so much sadness. Tears streamed down her face and she buried her head between Mathew's shoulder and head.

"It's OK, Jane. You are safe now. I found out what happened and how Captain Fritzwilliam looked after you."

She pulled her tear-stained face away to look into his eyes.

"Who is that man, Mathew?"

"It's a very long story, darling. But as I was able to piece it together, you somehow lost your senses and believed you were Jane back in Cornwall."

"Before we were married?"

Mathew nodded, gently wiping the tears away with his fingers. "Fritzwilliam found you drifting mindlessly in dangerous back streets near the quay, back in Boston."

"Oh God." Jane held a hand to her mouth, with eyes that looked horrified.

"The man had a ship to run and a time to leave. He took you on board to keep you safe and so brought his cargo and you here."

"Where is he now? I must thank him."

"You'll meet him later, Jane."

"How did you find me… Oh, that awful man."

"I told you last night, darling. Forget him. He's gone." He added with a grimace, "He'll be with his own kind now."

"Did you kill him?"

Mathew held his head down, deep in thought, and slowly spoke, "Mrs Cummings, the lady who brought you the broth yesterday, it was her shop you wandered into when you left Fritzwilliam's ship."

He looked up into her eyes. "Somehow, between leaving the ship and entering her shop, you regained your senses and realized who you are."

"What happened to me, Mathew? Am I ill?"

"No." He shook his head. "A doctor I inquired with suggested you may have had some accident and this had brought on temporary amnesia."

Jane touched the side of her head. "I don't remember anything, Mathew."

"It doesn't matter now, darling. You are with me and you are safe. All this is behind us now."

"But how did you find me?" she repeated her question.

"It was Henry, her negro servant, who first brought news. He was discussing what happened with a friend of his who knew the woman who took you. Knowing that family's ways, Mrs Cummings suggested we seek help from the governor. Thank God, John was known to him."

"John. Who is John?"

"John Adams."

"Is he here…and Abigail?"

"Only John. I am so much in his gratitude for supporting my mind in your disappearance and organizing the ship to follow Fritzwilliam here to the West Indies to find you."

"Oh, Mathew! You did all this for me. Darling, I love you." She kissed him again.

"It was late when we reached the governor's home, but he is a man of action and immediately called an officer to collect troops and take us to the house known to this family. Thank God we got there when we did. I know not what was planned for you…but you're safe now."

"Him?" Jane asked nervously, meaning Hanna's stepfather.

"When I reached the place they had taken you, I rushed into the opening and threw aside that witch doctor. This stepfather to Hanna came behind me with a knife, but one of the soldiers shot him dead before he could hurt me…" Mathew was silent for a moment, then forced a smile to his face, "Well, then, we brought you here and soon we will be home again."

"Cornwall?"

"No, darling. Our home in Boston."

She smiled and pressed herself close to him.

"What of Hanna? She did not harm me?"

"Actually, Hanna's real father died when she was very young. She was raised by her mother alone until she remarried, but then died some years ago."

"I can only imagine how your friend may feel now, for I am sure she also was frightened of that man."

Jane's face showed a look of understanding.

"Hello, will you be having breakfast today?" It was the voice of Mrs Cummings calling from behind the door.

Both Jane and Mathew smiled and burst into laughter. "One moment if you please, Mistress Cummings."

"By gad! You look sparkling once more, my dear," beamed John Adams as Jane entered the room, laid out for breakfast.

She felt embarrassed by all the trouble she had put this man to and hoped it was not too much, although she knew it could not have been any less.

"I am most awfully sorry for all the trouble I have caused to you and any difficulty this has brought upon your dear family—" she began, but was cut short by John's brisk response.

"Nonsense, my dear. Only glad to be out of the house and my own man again. Now sit down here by me, and let's get stuck into this hearty breakfast that our kind host has troubled herself to."

And so, this was how the morning and most of the afternoon was spent. Old friends and new, with the company of Fritzwilliam, recalling stories and planning their future. Jane, Mathew and John would return to Boston, while Fritzwilliam was bound for the Far East. So it was that on the following morning, he parted from their company, promising to remain friends for life.

"There goes a good man if ever I knew one. Present company excluded," John turned an eye to Mathew with a smile.

"I put him to so much concern," remarked Jane, talking to herself.

"We all play a part in life, Jane." Mathew turned to her. "He was of great assistance to you, and perhaps you gave him some meaning to help him in his life."

"I wonder what happened when I was with him."

Mathew looked at her. "Do you remember anything?"

"No." She shook her head. "My mind is blank. I can see myself closing the front door, and walking down the cobbled road in Boston, and then feeling bewildered as to how I could be standing in a market square in Trinidad."

John held his head up. "There's a good wind for the next few days, I'm told. We should make haste and get ourselves back to where we belong."

"How Abigail must be worrying and missing you."

John nodded his head. "And business," he remarked with a sigh. "So much to do now with all this fuss about taxes."

It was Mrs Cummings who propelled events when she entered the room holding a newspaper.

"Sirs, I think you should be reading this. The news arrived on a ship yesterday and our newspaper, small as it may be, has made much use of it." She handed the paper to Mathew.

All peered to read what might be written, so Mathew laid the newspaper flat on the table for the others to see. A bold headline ran:

'More unrest in Boston! Two soldiers injured. Ten men to be tried for sedition.'

"Oh no," Jane was the first to utter a remark.

"We must depart today, if our skipper is agreeable with the weather. I'm much concerned about Abigail." John was talking to no-one in particular, yet all now had the same thoughts. What had happened since they had left?

"I wish I had brought her with me now." It was a statement from John made under his breath, yet it made Jane sorry and feel responsible. She reached across the table and placed a reassuring hand on his. "We shall leave today, John. With a good wind, we shall be home soon."

John Adams stood up. "Excuse me, my friends, I must go and consult with our captain."

"We'll all come, John," responded Mathew. "We are all in this together."

His friend nodded solemnly.

The captain of the ship that had brought them here was easily found and agreeable to a quick departure, not just for the sake of John and company, but more so because his interests with a certain lady in the town had become too warm and been discovered by her husband. With all events settled or nearly so, the small ship disembarked on the morning tide.

Jane and Mathew watched the island, from the side of the ship, disappear into the distance.

I wonder what will become of Hanna?" she said. "I'm sorry I did not have time to talk with her before we left."

"She has inherited a considerable estate and she has her own mind now. The future is hers to make. I should not worry too much about her. She will make her own design and has much experience to shape it in a good way. I'm sure she will be well."

Jane did not reply and seemed deep in thought.

"What do you dwell upon, my darling?" he asked.

She pulled her eyes open and looked into his. "Our happy future," she said with a smile and placed her arms about his waist and held him tight.

Much to the relief of John Adams, who was secretly dreading being seasick again, the weather held good. Clear skies, a calm sea and a good wind brought their little ship into Boston harbor well ahead of schedule.

Chapter Seventeen

A Shadow Lurks

It was a pleasant sight for Mathew and Jane as they watched the approaching harbor. Tall masts loomed into the skyline and the busy hub of harbor life brought a welcome home sense of feeling. Disembarking and thanking the good captain for all his assistance and goodwill in ensuring a comfortable and fast journey, Mathew and company set about making plans. John would return immediately to his home, while Mathew and Jane would to theirs with the promise to visit the Adams' home the following evening.

As they watched John depart in a coach, Jane leaned closer to Mathew. "I have a feeling a great storm is about to break."

"You mean all this talk of taxes?" he asked.

Jane nodded her head slowly, as she waved in return to John's salute as his coach disappeared into a crowd of people, horses and carts all milling about.

The servant was relieved beyond Mathew's expectation to see the safe return of Jane, as the door to their home was opened. Mathew felt the man almost wanted to hug her in happiness, but refrained himself from doing so and kept to his respectful place.

Dust sheets were quickly removed from the bedroom furniture. It was a happy thing for Jane to pull back the heavy blue curtains that held back the Boston sunshine from flooding into the room and see it burst once again upon the wooden floor, as she had remembered it.

"I'm so happy to be back, darling." She turned to him with a glowing smile.

The smile of happiness on Mathew's face to see his wife in their home again told its own story and, dismissing the maid with a few words of thanks, he closed the door behind her.

An invitation arrived early the following morning.

"Look, Mathew," read Jane most excitedly.

"Mr and Mrs Adams have the pleasure to request the company
of
Mr and Mrs Appleton
to a private dinner tonight at 8 pm to mark the safe return
of
Jane Appleton to her home country."

Mathew smiled. "I wonder what Abigail is up to."

The day was largely taken up by repeated visits to Monsieur Grantfield, the dressmaker, who had now become a good acquaintance of Jane.

"What do you think?" asked Jane as she twirled in her new dress before Mathew after she had returned home and entered the study where he was working.

He laughed. "You look divine, my darling."

"Yes, I know," she teased. "I'm so happy to be going out this evening. Society once again." Then for a moment, she stopped and held a puzzled frown.

"What do you think really happened to me, Mathew? I mean, when I lost sense of who I am?"

Mathew put down the quill he was writing with and moved from where he was sitting to stand before her. He picked up her hands and held them in his own.

"Sometimes, we cannot know the workings of God, Jane. Things happen to us that sometimes make no sense and then, it is only when time has passed that we see how the experience that once confused or hurt us, had a part to play in raising our awareness of God."

She looked into his eyes. "I missed you so much, Mathew. When my mind went back to before we met, I had a feeling that someone was missing in my life. It was always you, even if I did not understand it at the time."

"I never stopped praying I would find you safe, Jane."

She looked deeply into his eyes. "Hold me tight, Mathew."

As he did so, she whispered into his ear, "Never let me go."

The sound of a servant approaching the study broke their embrace.

"I'm sorry to disturb you, Master Appleton, but shall I call the coach as you asked me at this time?"

"Coach!" said Jane aloud. "Oh! Mathew, I had completely forgotten the time. I am not ready. There is so much to do."

Mathew smiled at her and waved the servant away.

"Thank you, John. We shall wait a while."

The servant nodded and departed, followed hastily by Jane as she moved to go to her bedroom to prepare herself.

It was a long hour later when all was ready. The door to their home was opened and Jane stepped happily from the threshold holding Mathew's hand.

Neither saw the shadow of a man watching them from a dark recess a little further up the street. The sound of soldiers walking near caused the man to move further into the recess and his shadow to disappear.

Jane stepped into the coach, guided by the hand of Mathew, and moments later, the horses began to pull the coach away. The man in the recess moved out into the street and casually drifted away.

The coach bumped over the cobbled road and Jane looked out of the window to her side, watching the few people about. There seemed to be more redcoats than usual and she wondered if there could be anything to worry about.

"It's only a precaution," Mathew assured her.

His friends in the military headquarters had seen it wise to demonstrate the presence of soldiers to quell any further public disturbance. Jane listened to the words of her husband but kept staring out into the night, secretly wondering what had really been happening while she had been away and what the Daughters of Liberty had been involved with.

Well, I'll soon find out, she thought to herself and turned to look back with a smile to Mathew, as she snuggled into his body.

As the coach came around a bend and the waters of the harbor came clearer into view, they could see the home of the Adams'.

"Well, we are here, but I do think this is not going to be the private occasion Abigail suggested," commented Mathew.

Jane looked out at the short line of coaches outside the house and smiled at Mathew.

"She's up to something." He smiled back as if to answer the question she would ask him.

"Jane, darling! I'm so happy to see you safe!" Abigail rushed past the servants at the front of the house and held Jane in her embrace.

"Come," she said, "we are all waiting for you."

"All?" queried Jane, with a look of half suspicion to Mathew, who replied with a smile of innocence.

It felt nice to walk arm in arm with Abigail again. They had become blood sisters in so many ways since they had first met. The walk up the steps and into the hall brought back many happy memories of the times they had had.

"Have you more servants now?" she asked her friend.

"Oh, we have a few more tonight."

Jane turned her head. "Why so, dear sister?"

"Well, we do have a few very special guests to greet you dear Jane," and with this, they entered the main living room.

The surprise was beyond anything Jane had expected. Standing up and clapping their hands in applause were none other than Mr and Mrs George Washington, Mr and Mrs Benjamin Franklin, Mr and Mrs Paul Revere and a small group of other people she had come to know since she had arrived in Boston.

"Come, my dear Jane," stepped out John Adams from the crowd. "Come and be most welcome in our home again."

A round of applause took hold as she stepped forward to take John's hand and move into the room. Soon, everyone was greeting her and remarking how well she looked.

"So, how is your auntie, my dear?" inquired Martha Washington.

Jane looked uncertain how to reply, but Abigail was close at hand and came to her assistance.

"Oh, she is fine, Martha. It was not the danger we thought it might be. The illness passed sooner than we expected and you can see how well Jane looks for the fresh air."

Abigail pulled Jane to one side.

"Don't worry, my dear Jane. I told everyone you went to visit an auntie who was very ill in the south—to excuse your long absence."

"Oh, Abigail, you are so clever. Thank you. I worried with what I should say."

Abigail raised a finger to the tip of her nose. "We have explained everything. Worry about nothing. John explained everything to me… Now!" She changed the air. "I do think our dear friend Paul Revere would like to meet you."

"Oh, where is he?"

"Always at your assistance, my dear Jane," remarked a man close to her.

"Paul! I am so glad to see you here."

"And I you, my dear Jane."

Mathew approached and Jane changed the conversation rapidly to talk about a silver brochure she had lost.

"Mathew! Please come and meet Mr Revere. Abigail tells me he is a most gifted silversmith."

"Indeed Sir." Mathew bowed as Paul returned the honour to him.

Jane scanned the room looking for Mathew, but her gaze was drawn to see George Washington in deep conversation with Benjamin Franklin.

"I wonder what they are talking about?" She leaned to Abigail who was standing very close to her.

Abigail leaned back. "I can quite imagine, dear Jane, that it is not about the weather. Mind you, one thing is for certain, I am sure King George and any of his lackeys would give a fortune to be a fly on these walls tonight."

Both women laughed.

"Excuse me, Ma'am," a servant stood in front of Abigail. "A gentleman came to the door requesting this present be given to Mrs Appleton."

Jane stared curiously at the small box the servant held in his hand.

"Who was the man?" inquired Abigail.

"He did not leave his name, miss. Only asked that the present be given from a grateful admirer."

"Well! Shall we open it?" Abigail turned to Jane, holding the box in her hand.

"I am not so sure I have admirers, but let's see." Taking the box from her friend, she quickly opened it.

"What is it?" Abigail stared at the worried frown on the face of Jane.

"Oh, I feel diz...zy, Abi...g..." muttered Jane as she fell to the floor.

The smell of salts was very powerful, and Jane tried to push the hand away that held them close to her face.

"She's OK!" said a voice. "She is coming around."

"Are you alright, my dear?" It was Mathew who was holding her hand.

Jane nodded and realized she was lying upon a sofa with many people staring at her.

"Yes...yes...I am sorry."

"What happened?" inquired Mathew. "Are you ill?"

Jane shook her head slowly. "The box, Mathew...he's here."

"Who is here?" His voice was sharp now, and looked at the box Abigail held in her hands.

Mathew took it and in opening it found a small lump of rock inside.

"What is it?" he asked in a puzzled tone.

"Tin ore...Mathew... It's from Cornwall."

"That devil. I will get him this time." He turned to look up at Abigail. "How did you get this box, Abigail?"

"A servant passed it to me. A gentleman left it for Jane. Why? What does it mean?"

"It means," he remarked in a tense anger and looked for John, who came forward at that moment, "that's the devil who sought to harm us. He's come back."

"We will hunt him to the ground," promised John Adams. "Come, my friend." He held a hand down to Mathew to help him up.

"He will be long gone by now, John, but we must search high and low till he is found."

"This I promise," replied his friend, "and then we will see him swing in the gallows."

George Washington moved through the crowd to stand beside John Adams. "What mischief is about, my friend. Tell me and I will move heaven and earth to help this lady."

"We may well need this," nodded John in reply.

"I should get Jane home," Mathew said to no one but looked up at Abigail.

"Mathew, I think rather that it would be best for you and Jane to stay here for a while," remarked John Adams. "We need to make a council of war, be very clear how to catch this scoundrel."

"Thank you, my friend." Mathew looked at Jane for her acknowledgement, and with a slight nod of her head, he helped her to her feet.

"Please continue with the evening." Jane turned to John and then Mathew. "I will be alright, Mathew."

"Are you sure?"

She nodded and then smiled at the applause from the guests, who began to disperse into groups.

"Dance!" shouted John Adams. "Let's have a dance to clear the air." He issued instructions to two servants nearby, upon which four musicians moved into the large room and began to play as tables and chairs were moved to make a clearing in the room.

"Come, my darling," Mathew took her hand. "He is small and wants to be big in our minds. The happier we are, the smaller he becomes. Do not worry about my uncle, we have a very fine group of men who will find him now and…I promise you…end his evil."

She felt safe with Mathew and felt she could smile a little. Suddenly, she was moving onto the opening in the floor and moving about to the music, as were now a large number of people.

Abigail passed her in one movement and laughed as she raised her hem to step sideways.

"Come, my dear friend, we are sisters together. Never forget it."

The evening moved on and with so much happiness about her, Jane forgot about Mathew's uncle. In fact, she drank rather too much rum punch and was led my Mathew and Abigail to a bedroom, quite unable to do so unaided.

"I'm so sorry," she kept repeating to Abigail. Abigail in return kept reassuring her that everything was alright and all the guests were happy to see her. Finally, Jane was placed on the bed and covered with a heavy sheet to sleep it off.

As they closed the door quietly, Abigail spoke in a low voice to Mathew, "Tomorrow, when all are clear-minded, we shall come together to find this man and end this once and for all."

"I pray so, Abigail."

She did not speak further, only looked at him with steely eyes that gave no question of doubt as to what the outcome would be.

Chapter Eighteen

"Vengeance Shall Be Mine!" Said the Lord

Mathew entered the room for breakfast the following morning to find four men seated around a table with a vacant chair.

"Please sit down, Mathew, we have been waiting for you."

Once he was seated, John Adams introduced the other three men, all of whom looked the kind you would not wish to meet in a dark alley.

"Abigail will have George Washington and our other fine friends to find this rascal but…" he cleared his throat, "…we"—he scanned the three men seated around the table—"have our own means."

"What would you like me to do?" Mathew asked.

"We are going fishing, my friend, and you will be the bait."

"I'm in for it," he said firmly. "What is the plan?"

The man seated next to John spoke for the first time.

"My wife, Lizzy, will dress as your wife and with a bonnet, she will look the part. Your wife," he looked at John Adams for agreement and proceeded with the nod that John gave him, "will remain in this house. Lizzy will accompany you to your home and appear to be your wife. You can find her a room within your home, and she will accompany you everywhere you go."

"Everywhere?" Mathew seemed perplexed. "Sometimes my business takes me to the British headquarters."

The man grinned. "We know all about your business, Master Mathew, and in time, it will serve us well."

Mathew's mind raced to wonder what the man meant by this, but Jane's safety overshadowed everything. He nodded.

"Good," mentioned the man. "We know what your wife looks like and Lizzy will pass for her unless there is a clear and direct light."

Mathew wondered how the man would know this and looked at John Adams.

"To keep you safe, my friend, these men have been looking over you since we arrived back in Boston." He paused and looked regretful. "I'm sorry. If I had told you, you may have acted in ways that were not normal and this could have given the game away. You have been safe, my friend. You and Jane."

Mathew looked into his eyes. "Thank you, my friend." He looked into the eyes of the other three men. "Thank you, too, gentlemen."

"We ain't been called that much before," remarked the smaller of the three and showed a mouth of many teeth missing when he did so.

The third man who had not yet spoken and looked the most unsavory of the lot; he leaned across the table. "What's the very best description you can give us of your uncle?" he asked.

Mathew felt an urge to pull back from the man's breath, which reeked of rum, but remained unmoved in case he caused offense. Within a few moments, he gave a full description of his uncle and also of one of the men who had escaped with him the last time they had met. All three listened intently, with the leader, obviously the first one who had spoken, being very clear in his attention.

"We'll have 'im, Master Mathew. No doubt about it."

"And what of your wife…Lizzy?" asked Mathew, looking at the man earnestly and thankful he could remember her name.

'Oh, Lizzy can take care of herself. Anyway, you will not be going anywhere without one of us very," he paused to give meaning, "very close behind you. And don't worry, we can fade in and out of any place without anyone knowing we was there."

Mathew nodded. "When do we begin?"

"Now!" said the man firmly and called out loudly, "Lizzy!"

The door opened and a woman walked into the room.

Mathew blinked, for at first he thought it was Jane. The woman was wearing the same dress that Jane had worn the evening before, had the same height and build and her hair was matched well to that of Jane's.

"Don't worry about the dress," interrupted John Adams. "All will be explained to Jane by Abigail, but now, my friend, it is time for you and," he waited for a moment and continued with a smile, "and your wife to go home."

Mathew helped his 'new wife' into the coach and once it began to move, he spoke frankly to her.

"I understand your name is Lizzy?" he inquired.

"Now, I am Jane, and don't you call me anything else or the game will be up." She may have resembled Jane slightly on the outside, but the tongue and the manner of this woman was harsh.

He cleared his throat. "I am sorry…Jane."

The woman's gaze was hard and uncomfortable for him. "Well! We can at least be civil…Jane."

"As long as it's by the rules. Don't you go think'en you can get up my skirt."

The look of shock was evident. "I assure you, madam, I am an honorable man."

"Yes. Just like all the rest," she sneered. "But don't you worry, we'll get this man whose hurt'en your misses, and my man'll hurt him some."

"I'd rather we do this by the law."

"Law!" she sneered again. "Ha! You're a right one! Look! There ain't no rules for the likes of 'em. Give 'em up and he'll have some smart lawyer get 'em free."

Mathew looked at the woman. She had had a hard life, this was easy to tell. Probably from London, by her accent, he guessed. Yet, for all her misgivings, there was something he liked about her. Maybe it was her directness.

"And you must please address me as Mathew and…darling," which he found hard to say, "if you will, at least while this lasts."

"Mathew," said the woman, but the way she pronounced it was hard and so unlike the loving tone of his wife.

"I am deeply in your debt…Jane. Thank you for all you are doing for us."

The woman nodded. "We may be poor, mister, but we don't like men who go hurt'en women, like 'em we're efter."

"I think we will get on just fine…Jane."

"So we will…Mathew."

The carriage was approaching the house of Mathew and he looked out to the street, before turning back to his companion.

"It is better that you speak no words near people who know us."

"I understand," she said quietly.

"Are your people following us?"

She smiled for the first time. "Who'se you think is driving the coach?"

The look of alarm was evident on his face, then a smile of recognition for their professionalism warmed him. He nodded silently in acknowledgement.

Suddenly, the coach came to a halt, the driver climbed down and opening the door, held the hand of the so-called Jane as she climbed out and stepped onto the road.

"Take's your time, mister. Go's slow, so all can see you both," was all he said, as he climbed back onto the coach. There was a short neigh from one of the two horses, before the coach moved away and into the distance.

Mathew opened the door to his home, and a servant came forward to greet him, but held back a moment when he saw the face of Lizzy.

'You'd better tell your staff I'm a friend of Jane's staying with you for a while. 'n tell 'em not to breathe a word of it or you'll have 'em out on the street wi'out a reference!"

Mathew turned to the servant. "As you heard, William. This is quite a serious undertaking. I will inform all the staff tomorrow about Jane." He hesitated a moment before explaining, "This also is the lady's name…Jane. Until then, say nothing."

The servant nodded in full understanding. "Shall I make up a bed for the lady, Master Appleton?"

"Yes, please, William. That would be fine."

In the morning, Mathew explained to the rest of the staff just enough of what they needed to know to keep their silence. Jane, as Lizzy now was, moved about the area as she was advised by Mathew how the real Jane would do. In the evenings, she would recount what had happened and always explained how she was closely followed by one of her partners. It was on the fifth evening, while they sat eating dinner, which he found most distasteful, for Lizzy ate in an appalling manner, that she suddenly hit her forehead with an open palm.

"Why did I not think of it before?"

"Think of what?" he asked, looking up from the plate before him.

"Mother O'Toole!"

"Mother who?"

"Mother O'Toole. She's a great spiritualist!"

Mathew eyed her suspiciously. "What are you talking about, woman?"

Lizzy put down the fork she was holding in her left hand, "She can't just see into the future, she can see 'ere today."

The frown deepened on Mathew's forehead. "I have no clarity with your mind," he said.

"See 'ere now. She can tell us where this man is!"

"Do you tell me there is a woman who can describe the present?"

"Aye! 'ere today."

"This is beyond me. Do you talk of witchcraft?"

The woman laughed out loud. "None of that. Mother O'Toole has the gift. She can tell us where this man is."

Mathew's mind began to wonder if this woman was a little out of her mind, but the desperation of the time caused for all things to be considered.

"Well, I doubt if I understand what you mean, but I'm willing to meet this woman," and added under his breath, "I'll try anything."

I was three hours later that their coach moved out of the better quarters of Boston to those less so. This became immediately evident not just by the dirt of the surroundings, but more perhaps by the hard-looking men leaning against walls and the girls waiting in the street for a customer.

"'ere!" exclaimed Jane. "Stop the coach!"

The driver pulled up against an old, flaked, green-painted door. The window to the side held a curtain that was pulled back slightly as someone inside watched them.

Lizzy hammered on the door. It was a few moments before it was opened by a small lady, perhaps in her fifties, who wore small-brimmed glasses.

"Mother, I've brought a gentleman to see you. 'es a good'en. Got a problem with one who ain't so good."

The lady nodded. "I was expecting you, Lizzy. I saw it in the tea leaves this morning."

Lizzy turned to Mathew with a sense of pride. "There, didn't I tell you she can see today."

Curiously and with slight apprehension, Mathew entered the house.

The elderly woman led them down a poorly lit hall and into a room with a round table in the centre.

"Please take a seat, Sir. Would you like a cuppie tea?"

Mathew shook his head. "I'm sorry to be of trouble to you, madam, but I have urgent business and would be most grateful if we could settle into it immediately."

"Ain't he the quick one," responded Lizzy, looking a little annoyed at Mathew's rudeness.

"It's quite all right, Sir. I know why you have come."

"Indeed!" remarked Mathew, slightly suspicious of Lizzy's involvement.

"Oh! It ain't her," responded the woman, "it was the tea leaves."

Now, Mathew did feel uncomfortable and wondered more if he should just get up and leave.

It was to calm him and gain respect for herself that the woman spoke briefly.

"The man you seek is in his late fifties. He is about 5 feet in height, very much overweight and tends to walk with a strange stride. Maybe a wound from a war."

Mathew's eyes opened. "How on earth do you know this? I have not told anyone in this country such details. Even I had forgotten about the stride."

"You see, ain't she a good 'en at this?"

Mathew ignored the words of Lizzy and looked into the eyes of the woman standing by the table. "Please let us all be seated, and tell me what you know."

"Then," remarked the woman, "you'll be having a cuppie tea?"

"Yes," nodded Mathew, "if this is what it takes."

Mother O'Toole smiled and gestured kindly to the chairs for Mathew and Lizzy to sit upon.

"I'll be back in a while." She turned and disappeared behind a reddish curtain hung about a corner in the room.

It was a strange looking room for Mathew. It was poorly lit, with the air heavily laden with incense. There were a few poorly drawn pictures pinned to the wall, which he came to realize were probably drawn by children, and apart from an old rug under the table, the floor was wooden. It seemed he was waiting a long time in the silence, when suddenly, the curtain was pulled back and

Mother O'Toole came into the room, carrying a tray with three cups upon it.

"I'm sorry if I kept you waiting," she said, "but the tea needs preparation."

Mathew wondered what she meant, but the tea refreshed him and he felt better for it.

'Now, if you please," said Mother O'Toole, "I'll take the cup from you."

Mathew felt a little foolish, but he handed the cup over as he was bid.

The woman stared into the cup. She did not speak as Mathew had imagined she would.

"Humm," she sounded slowly, and repeated the sound after a moment as if she was in deep thought.

Then, she put the cup down and looked directly at Mathew.

"Please lay your hands on the table, palms up."

Mathew did as he was bid; the woman placed her hands on top of his and looked directly into his eyes, but he felt she was going deeper into who he was. The power of the woman reached deep within him and he felt unsure what was really happening.

"This man you seek. I see him. He is playing cards with three other men."

Mathew leaned towards her, intently interested in what she was saying.

"It's not a good game. There are bad energies here. There is a fish house or fish market below where they are playing. You will find him there." Mother O'Toole took her hands off Mathew's and looked at him very carefully.

"This man intends to kill you. You must be very careful if you go near him. Never let him near your wife."

Mathew nodded. He knew now that she knew what he wanted to know. "Thank you, Mother O'Toole. Could you be any more precise about the location?"

She looked steadily at his eyes again. "The place is not on the waterfront. It is up a high street." She spoke carefully. "You must be very, very careful if you intend to meet this man."

Mathew nodded. He knew she was right. "…And how much do I owe for your services, please?"

"What is in your heart, leave on the table," she said calmly.

This was a small shock to Mathew, for he was used to people in such a location trying to gain as much as they could when they saw him so better dressed.

He put his hand into his pocket and felt two silver coins. He was in the act of pulling one out to pay the woman but felt she had given all she knew. Mathew felt it was fairer to give both coins. So in letting go of the one in his hand, he grasped them both and laid both respectfully, not on the table, but into the open palm of her hand. He held her hand warmly in gratitude and felt a calm but kind energy move from her hand into his own. He liked this woman.

Mother O'Toole may not seem to have shown her sense of money to the two silver coins, but the wide-eyed look held by Lizzy gave a different story.

Mathew bowed to the woman and turned to leave.

"One moment," Mother O'Toole held him back, "the men he is playing cards with, you know one of these."

A frown appeared above Mathew's eyes. "How do I know him?'

The woman shook her head. "I'm sorry. I don't know, but I know you know him. But," she added quickly, "this man is not bad as the others are. He just is playing for the game. He gambles. He will not hurt you."

"Can you tell me his name?"

She shook her head. "He is a large man with a bulbous nose, I think from heavy drinking. I'm sorry, this was all I could see."

Mathew plainly searched his mind, but no one came to mind who he could fit the description given.

"Thank you," he said again and followed by Lizzy, he left the house and took to his carriage.

"A large man, red nose, drinks a lot, gambles," were words he repeated over and over, as the coach rolled over the cobbled streets bound for his house.

"I'll get word out of what the mother told you," said Lizzy. "We'll find this fish house."

"But this is Boston," responded Mathew. "There are too many fish houses, and if we don't find him soon, he will likely not be there."

The afternoon passed slowly as he struggled to think who he knew or may have met that resembled the description.

"Oh Lord!" he said suddenly. "Rathbone, of course."

Lizzy looked up, startled by the sudden shout.

"Quick, get your things. I know who he is."

It took only moments before both were readily dressed, but as he opened the door to the street, he could hardly see through the heavy rain. Turning about, he went back into the house and reappeared with a coat for himself and a cloak for Lizzy.

He saw a coach waiting further up the street and hailed it.

The driver shook his cape and rose his whip to move the horse.

"To Lord Rathbone's home," he shouted through the rain to the driver, "urgently if you please, my man."

The coach started off, but it had not gone through many streets before the tempo of the rain increased. Now, visibility was almost impossible and the driver struggled as best he could to steer the coach. Suddenly, and without any warning, another coach came out of a side street. The horses of both coaches clashed, one against the other. The horse of the other coach seemed to bounce off their horse and pulled its coach off down the street at great speed, but the horse pulling Mathew's coach reared up and, kicking its legs, pulled their coach off balance. The coach rolled sharply to the left then countered itself to the right, but the weight was out of balance and, with a scream from Lizzy, it rolled over. The horse was now trapped in the harness and struggled to stand up. The driver had been thrown clear, but was soon up on his feet and trying to calm the horse out of its panic.

"Cut it loose," shouted Mathew through the rain.

"I've nothing to do it with," shouted the driver back, as the horse pulled itself to the right and almost dislocated the man's shoulder.

Two figures appeared out of the heavy rain. One took the horse's reins by the mouth, the other slashed at the harness with a short sword. Suddenly, the horse was up, free and galloping into the distance.

"What the hell trouble you have caused me," shouted the driver to Mathew.

The man who had slashed the harness moved over to him.

"'ere, take this. Keep your mouth shut and disappear for a while."

The rain was too heavy for Mathew to see who the man was, but he saw the weight of the bag was heavy and knew it enough to settle with the driver.

"Aye! I'll be gone for a bit," snarled the driver, having felt the weight of the coins, "to get me horse back."

The man who had held the reins moved over the wet road. "Come on, Lizzy, 'ant fitting to see you in the gutter," he laughed.

"To hell with you, Sam Willington," shouted Lizzy, pushing him away once she was standing on her feet.

"I'm so sorry," apologized Mathew through the sheets of rain that separated him from her.

"Damn you for the fool you are," she shouted back at him. "Go quick in the bloody rain," Lizzy mimicked him to the driver.

The sound of another horse behind them caused both to turn.

"Where would you like to go, my dears," shouted the driver.

"Home and away from the fucking lot of you," shouted Lizzy to her husband.

The man laughed as one of his comrades helped Lizzy up into the carriage, and then Mathew.

"I'm very sorry," blurted Mathew to Lizzy.

"Away with you," she said. "This idiot wants to go to Rathbone's house," she shouted to her husband. "Aye, and it'll cost you a small fortune more," she said, turning to Mathew.

As he looked at the drenched woman wearing Jane's clothes, but with hair soaking wet and no sense of dignity, he smiled to himself at how life could change things so quickly. The sight of him smiling infuriated Lizzy who lashed out with her fist, hitting him firmly on the chest.

"That's my wife," shouted the driver, laughing.

Both fell back as the coach moved off with a start. The rain outside was still heavy by the time they reached Rathbone's home. Mathew opened the door and jumped down to the ground.

"Wait here," he ordered Lizzy and the driver, and ran to the door of the house.

Mathew hammered on the door, yet it took a while before it was opened by a servant.

"Quick, man, call your master," he demanded.

"I'm sorry, Sir, but Lord Rathbone is not here."

"I suspected as much," Mathew said, thinking he was in the fish house. "Where is he?"

"In London, Sir, he was called away three weeks ago."

Mathew looked at the man as if he could not understand what he had just heard. He felt his mouth opening but no sound came forth. "Lon...don?" he finally sounded.

"Yes, Sir. Both Lord and Lady Rathbone sailed on the 14th."

Mathew stared more at the man.

"Would you wish to come in, out of the rain, Sir?" invited the servant.

Mathew shook his head. "No, no, it's alright," he said, turning slowly back to the carriage without aware now of how heavy the rain still was.

"Well?" asked Lizzy, when he stepped back into the coach.

"He's not in. He's in London."

"What the fuck!" shouted Lizzy. "You mean you got me nearly killed and soaking wet to boot, because you didn't know Rathbone was in England."

Angry with the way she was behaving, Mathew turned on her. "Quiet, woman. We went to the spiritualist you recommended and she gave me a description of someone whom I thought was Lord Rathbone."

"Well, you was wrong, weren't you," retorted Lizzy with a sarcastic response. "Get me back to your 'ome and out of these wet clothes."

Mathew nodded. "It's all we can do right now."

"Too bloody true it is, and get on with it," demanded Lizzy, quite forgetting and perhaps certainly not caring for her station in life.

Mathew bit his lip, in an attempt not to smile. If the truth were told, he found the behaviour of Lizzy exciting. She had life and she lived it as best as she could. He began to admire her.

By the time the coach reached Mathew's home, Lizzy was sneezing and beginning to shiver. He was concerned she might become ill and as soon as they were through the front door, he ordered the servants to make a hot bath for Jane and to cook a hot nourishing meal.

She did not, fortunately, develop a fever or catch a cold or even worse, for the next morning she appeared in the breakfast room quite forgetting her disrespectful behaviour the day before.

"Good morning," she smiled as she sat down.

"I'm very sorry for yesterday. I felt so desperate to find this man and then catch my uncle."

"I can understand that, Master Appleton." It was the first time she used his formal name, and perhaps so as an apology for yesterday.

"It's better you refer to me as, Mathew, because of the nature of our business," he said.

"I'm sorry to disturb you, Master Appleton," said his servant, as he entered the room, "but there is a gentleman to see you."

"What is the nature of his business?" questioned Mathew, looking up from the newspaper he was reading.

"He said it was in regard to some jewellery that Mistress Jane ordered some months ago."

A curious look passed over Mathew's face. With his mind in deep thought, he folded the newspaper, rose and moved out of the room. When he walked into the hall to meet the man, he stopped dead.

There before him was a very large man with a very distinguished red bulbous nose!

"I am awfully sorry, Sir," began the man, "but there has been a terrible mistake. You see, Mrs Jane Appleton came into our premises some months ago to order a gold necklace, but the young man serving her misplaced the order and we have only just discovered it. I am most humble and sincerely sorry."

"Excuse me, I do not wish to be rude but do you enjoy to play cards, gamble a little, perhaps?"

A look of embarrassment passed over the man's face. "I'm afraid it is not a quality I am proud of but—"

Before he could utter another word, Mathew grabbed him by the hand. "My dear Sir, you are one of the most wonderful men I have ever met."

Confused, baffled, totally lost to the situation, the man tried to explain again how sorry he was for misplacing the order.

"'None of this, my friend. I'm not interested in the incident. It could happen to anyone, but please, please will you join us, my friend and I, for breakfast."

Overcome by the kindness of Mathew, which he could never have expected, the man relaxed and began to laugh. He had a jolly laugh, which befitted his stature. Mathew opened the door and Lizzy nearly fell off her chair.

"Oh fuck!" she exclaimed.

The man pulled back, but Mathew clasped his shoulder. "Sit, sit down, my friend."

As large as the man was, the well-spread table opened his eyes. "Well, I cannot say no," as he sat in a chair and immediately reached for a freshly baked scone.

Mathew had to laugh at the expression on Lizzy's face. It was a complete picture of disbelief mixed with apprehension.

"Tell me, my friend, as we both like to gamble a little, have you had any luck recently?"

"Luck, no none of that. I lost a fair amount a few nights ago."

"This was bad. It can happen. Tell me about it, I'm interested to hear of other games."

"Well," said the man, "I was invited by an acquaintance of an acquaintance of an acquaintance, if you know what I mean, it was a terrible game, a crowd of sharks." He laughed at this.

"Why so humorous, my friend?" asked Mathew.

"Well, sharks," he laughed again, "the place was above a fish shop."

Mathew stopped smiling and was himself, Lizzy would later say, as deadly as a shark.

"It is strange you mention this." He tried to appear matter of fact.

"I am in need of a good supply of fish. Do you recall the address of this fish shop?"

The man did not reply and was in the process of reaching for another scone, when Lizzy reached over and caught his hand.

"Pray, tell us where this fish shop is? I have an urgent need of good fish today.

The man lingered in his thoughts. "It's up past the priory. Second block. There is a laundry next to it, if my memory serves me correctly."

Mathew noted how Lizzy was listening intently to every detail the man gave. "I know where this is," she said, looking directly at Mathew with clear meaning.

She turned her head and smiled at the man. "It was very nice to meet you, but if you will excuse me, I have some urgent business to attend to." She nodded to Mathew in a way that meant she would pass this on to her companions.

"Get rid of 'im," she whispered as she left the room.

By the time Lizzy reappeared, the man had long gone, "So," she began, "my people will watch this place like hawks and learn if this man you want is still there, and if he is, they'll grab 'em."

"I want to be there when they do. I'd prefer to deal with him myself."

"Ain't you heard what Mother O'Toole said? 'ez dangerous for you. Likely kill you. Let them'z that know 'ow to 'andle this, 'andle it. Keep clean and keep away."

"That's not my nature, Lizzy. I will have him for all he has done to us."

"Mother of God, ain't you listened to anything?"

Later that afternoon, Lizzy's husband came to visit them.

"Eye, 'ez still there. We spotted 'im shouting at some poor kid. So, what do you want us to do, Master Appleton?"

"Let's go tonight and apprehend him. I'll call for soldiers and —"

"Jesus," mocked Lizzy, "I can just imagine 'im sitting there playing cards and when the redcoats come playing their drums and whistles, he will like just sit and wait. Master Appleton, you ain't the nounce for this kind of work."

"Well, what do you suggest?" Mathew waited for suggestions from them both.

"Beg'in your pardon, Sir, but t'is is what is best." The man described in detail a clear plan to get Mathew's uncle alone and away from any people he might have to protect him, and then how he would be apprehended.

Mathew looked at the man. "But this would mean my wife would have to be the decoy, and you said Lizzy here would take that part."

"True," said the man, "but if we don't do this right, he's likely to bolt and we might not find him again. Then, you would never be safe. Besides," he added, "you saw last night how we protected you."

Mathew nodded his head, remembering how these men had appeared out of nowhere to free the horse and set them in another carriage, with such precision in atrocious weather that it was almost as if the whole thing had been staged.

"Do you promise me that my wife will be in no danger?"

The man looked into his eyes very directly. "None! Lizzy here will be closer to him, we just need your wife's voice to draw his attention to pull him out of the nest."

Mathew nodded his assent and so all was set for that evening. He went to the Adams' home with Lizzy to explain to Jane, and to John and Abigail, all that had happened and the plot to capture his uncle.

"I don't like it," said John Adams. "Jane is perfectly safe here, why can Lizzy not handle this alone?"

"I want to go," announced Jane. "I will not live in fear, and this man must be caught and pay for all the crime he has committed."

With all agreed, Mathew, Jane, Lizzy and John Adams moved to the coach, which being driven by Lizzy's husband moved off as was all arranged.

Jane moved her hand to take that of Mathew's in hers and held it tight. Her hand felt so small and so much in need of his strength. He squeezed hers a little to reassure her not to be frightened. She did not let go as the coach moved over cobbled streets that wound their way through the late Boston evening. By the time the coach came to a halt, and with no moon, the sky was very dark.

The coachman stepped down and opened the door of the coach without any noise, before helping Jane and Lizzy out first.

"None speak now. Do exactly as we arranged and keep close to God or," he looked at Mathew, "we'll all be joining him."

Each of the party nodded their understanding and quietly took up the positions that had been explained to them. Mathew saw one man in the shadow of a doorway give a short signal to Lizzy's husband.

"You ready?" The man looked at Jane.

She nodded and let go of Mathew's hand.

"Walk over there," nodded the man.

Jane moved out from the group, followed by Lizzy dressed identically as her, but at a slower pace that kept a clear distance between them.

There was a bright light from a window over the fish shop. Sounds could be heard of men talking.

Suddenly, there was a loud bang just as Jane had walked into the lit area on the ground, which she wasn't expecting and so the scream she gave out was all the more natural. Unsure of what was now happening, she ran back towards Mathew. As Jane moved out of the lit area, so Lizzy dressed as Jane, moved into it.

There was a loud noise of chairs being scraped back in the room, for it was reasoned that Mathew's uncle would have recognised the scream by Jane's tilt towards the Cornish and in moving to reassure himself it was Jane, would see Lizzy standing in her place.

Within moments, because his uncle must have moved fast in his anger that Jane was in his area, a door next to that of the fish shop opened violently. The uncle stood momentarily assuring himself it was Jane, and just as the bigger fish moves in to bite the unwitting smaller fish, so he crossed the area between the door and that area that was lit in furious strides. Yet, before he could reach Lizzy, the outline of two burly men moved fast towards him. There was a grunt as the uncle fell to his knees, having been hit from behind, but as he did so, he twisted his body and grabbed a leg of one of his assailants, pulling him down. His accomplice moved in to help his friend, when the darkness was suddenly lit from the spark of a flint. At the same time, or so it seemed, the sound of a pistol being fired brought out a cry of pain.

"The bastard got me in the thigh," cried a voice unknown to Mathew.

"I'll have you, you ruffians!" This was the unmistakable voice of his uncle, as his outline moved towards Lizzy. At that moment, another man came out of the door aiming a pistol, but it was too dark for him to know who was who, and in the moment he dithered, Lizzy's husband struck the man's arm with a short sword. The man screamed as the blade cut into him, but further noise was silenced by a second strike of the sword. Just as this man fell to the ground, Lizzy moved not away from the uncle but towards him with a long thin knife that slid so easily into his left flank.

The uncle cried out in pain as he swung his pistol towards Lizzy's head, but she ducked and thrust the knife into the throat. The uncle went to the ground holding the wound that blood was flowing from.

"Let 'im lie like a gutted sheep," said Lizzy, spitting on his body.

Mathew moved out from the place he was told to wait and stood over the dying body. His uncle, still trying to stem the blood from his throat, looked at him with evil malice. Then, within a moment, his eyes were closed and he was no more.

Mathew felt the gentle hand of Jane touch his back.

"Is…is he dead?" she asked nervously.

Mathew nodded. "There will be no more trouble from him, my dear. He now has gone to join his own kind."

Jane pulled herself close to Mathew. "Oh, Mathew, does this mean we are safe now?"

Mathew nodded his head. "Yes, Jane. He was the last of his like in our lives. There are no more like him."

"Oh, Mathew, none can harm us now?"

He nodded his head again, still looking down at the body. "We are safe to return to England now."

She looked into his eyes.

"I like it here, Mathew. We have good and kind friends." She held her look and spoke silently but with a tone of defiance, "This is our country now."

He lifted his gaze over the roofs of houses to the silhouettes of tall masts in the far distance. He felt they belonged to ships that would sail away. He did not feel they were a part of his life. He had had enough of ships and the sea.

"The Americas," he nodded. "This is our home."

"Mathew!" It was the voice of John Adams from further down the street. He ran as he was able, for he was not fit for this, and arrived slightly out of breath.

'Oh Lord! What a mess we have here," he stuttered out the words, seeing the two bodies.

"Better this way," it was the voice of Lizzy's husband who came up behind him.

"No capture, no stress of a trial, no danger he would escape the noose, only a simple street robbery and a murder. It's nothing new in this area. The authorities will know it. Simple and clean cut. End of story," he said as he helped his wounded man to his feet.

"And what of your man?" questioned John Adams.

"Occupational hazard," smiled the man, as all began to quietly disperse in the agreed manner.

Chapter Nineteen

A Little White Lie!

The sun shone warm and brightly through the window of their bedroom. It woke Jane with a start.

"Oh, I am so happy! Happy to be free, Mathew."

Mathew was not so energetic and found it difficult to rise from the slumber he was in.

She pushed her hands through his dense hair and kissed him, while he struggled to open one eye, and then the other.

A smile came to his face as he saw the light that shone from her eyes. "Yes, we have a new life now, my darling. No more fear. No more living in the shadow of evil. We are free."

She looked at him strangely.

"What is it? What did I say wrong?"

"It was something I heard some weeks ago. A man was saying the same things, but he was talking about the oppression from the British and how those in the colonies live under an evil shadow, how they are not free to live their lives the way they wish."

"Many here would agree with him," remarked Mathew.

"Have you heard of the 'Sons of Liberty', Mathew?"

"Yes, I have heard mention of them, but they tread very dangerous waters. The crime for high treason is still punishable by a slow and painful death.

"And what of the 'Daughters of Liberty'?"

He shook his head. "I cannot recall mention of them, but they walk the same path. Why do you ask, all of a sudden?"

"Oh, it's nothing important." She turned to straighten her hair lest he found something in her eyes that she did not want him to see. "…Just something I heard people talking about the other day."

"Keep clear of this talk, my darling. We live in dangerous times."

"Yes, we do, my darling. Yes, we do." She turned to look back at him with a strange fire in her eyes as she kissed him.

"Wait!" he begged laughingly. "I have a meeting with the British early today, I want to discuss the latest shipment of Madeira I am expecting. The officers' wives are very keen for this."

After Mathew had dressed and departed, Jane lay in bed happily watching the clouds drift past her window. It was so good to be back in her own home again, and while grateful to Lizzy for all she had done, she was glad that she was now out of their lives. Suddenly, she remembered how the dressmaker had mentioned that he was expecting some new cloth in today from Africa. This would be very interesting, because his cloth normally came from India via England and he was thinking the texture might be very different and the coloring more vivid.

"Today!" she said aloud. "I'm going to be the first in Boston to have a dress made from African cloth."

With this said, she sprang out of bed, washed, chose a bright yellow dress, tied her hair, applied a little rouge, and called the maid to bring a simple breakfast.

The sky was a little overcast when she left their home, but the seagulls were squawking, people were milling about, fresh produce was being carried in carts by strong men to shopkeepers eagerly waiting. The air was alive with trade. Men touched their hats as she walked by and everyone seemed to be smiling or laughing. It was going to be a good day, she told herself.

"Good morning, Ma'am!" Monsieur Grantfield greeted her with an unmistakable glee, which he could not conceal. "Yes," he said, knowing full well why Jane was visiting him, "the shipment arrived early this morning. Fine cloths and silks to match the very best from India, and such vivid emeralds, yellow and red ochre colors. Would Ma'am wish to see?" He was suppressing a great smile at the expression of delight on Jane's face.

Indeed, Monsieur Grantfield had not underestimated his new stock. As he unrolled each bolt of fabric, Jane felt like a small child entering Aladdin's Cave. If Mathew had been here, he would be restraining her by fear of cost, but now alone, she believed she deserved a treat, and she gave herself a very generous one.

"How soon can the dress be ready?" she asked, unable to stop feeling how the fabric seemed to glide through her fingers and how the golden thread weaved in it caught the light shining through the shop window.

"For Ma'am," smiled Monsieur Grantfield, "shall we say two days hence?"

Jane wished he would do his usual special arrangement for her so she could wear the dress tonight, but she could see how busy everyone was in the shop and knew two days was the best that could be done.

Wishing to cause her friend no stress, she smiled. "Excellent, Monsieur Grantfield. This will be most agreeable. I shall come early on the day for a fitting."

When all was settled, Jane left the shop with an air of happy freshness.

For some strange reason, which she could not understand, she felt inclined to turn right into a narrow street. The street was busy, so she felt quite safe, but at the end, it split into two streets and here she did not know which way to go.

On the last day in Jamaica, she had gone with Mathew to a fortune teller. Mathew had said it was a waste of money and time, but Jane felt it would be good. Her intuition had paid off. The lady had told her that she would play a very important role in the survival of a great nation. One of the things she had told her was that if you have doubt in a choice, then do not listen to your mind. Your mind is filled with the hopes and doubts others have filled your life with. Listen to your heart. Your heart is the line to God, and if you hold to this line, all will work out well for you.

So, as she stood between the two roads, she tried to feel which one to take. The road to the left felt safest and so this she chose. After some time, the shops began to peter out and a high wall either side of the road gave the feeling of moving into a tunnel. It gave her a sense of unease and she wondered if she had taken the right path, when suddenly, as she turned a corner, she found the harbor straight ahead. Suddenly, there was noise again as men were moving heavy sacks and all kinds of merchandise she imagined from ships to men shouting directions.

As she stood there, Jane felt a sense that she had been here before. Not with Mathew, but some other time. It was a strange feeling, a little like moving through a dream where everything seems unreal. She turned left and began to pass men sitting down outside taverns. Each one looked at her as she passed, but she held her gaze ahead, wishing not to encourage any advances.

"Lost, girl?" She turned and saw an elderly women to her side. She had a kind face. It was weather-beaten and she held a short-stemmed clay pipe in her mouth, but Jane felt safe to talk with her.

"Not sure," she smiled. "I feel I've been here before, but can't place when or how."

"Harbors do that to you," she replied. "It's the spirit of the ships. They take you places and brings you back and takes you away again."

Jane looked up to a huge hull that seemed to be bearing down upon her.

"Yes, it does that, doesn't it."

"You looking for someone in particular?" asked the old woman.

Jane shook her head. "No, I don't think so," she said as if her mind was in another place, then added, "I do not know actually." After a silence, she spoke as if to herself, "I don't know."

"Well, there's lots of men about here, girl. Best you be on your way. Not all of them are good'ens."

It was the way the woman said the last part that pulled Jane's mind back to the present.

"Yes! Yes, thank you." She smiled in gratitude, but her mind was still searching for something.

"That way will take you safest," said the old lady, pointing her pipe.

Jane nodded in gratitude and turned to follow the direction given. It took her past a line of ships, each one different, each one having its own story, she thought. Then, she had a feeling inside of apprehension. One ship on the quay was different than the rest. She could feel it was different. It was not a happy ship. Slaves! It was a slave carrier. Black people, men, women and children were shackled together in chains. A feeling of great fear took hold of her. She had to get away from here. Get away, get away, her mind screamed at her, run, run.

She started to run, when suddenly a man grabbed her arm.

"Steady on, Miss. It's dangerous to run about here, too much move'en about. You'll likely get injured."

Fear took hold and she cried out, "Let go," and pulled herself free.

Right, left, right, which way to go. Panic set in, she started to cry. Running, she tripped over and fell to the floor. Another man came to help her. "Let go of me," she cried and started to run again.

Her heart was pounding. Fear was rife, why, what reason, she did not know. Just get away from here was all she could think about. Suddenly, she was back in a street of shops and people buying things. She tried to tidy her hair, but the yellow dress she had put on earlier in the day was soiled from the dirty ground she had fallen upon. A woman looked strangely at her, but Jane pretended she did not see her. She walked to the end of the street and saw a coach. The driver was talking to someone he knew and both were laughing.

"Please, can you take me home?" she pleaded.

"Righty'o missy," he smiled.

As soon as Jane arrived home, she asked her maid to make a bath. She needed to wash all the bad and dirty feelings out of her body. Once the bath was ready, she placed her yellow dress over a chair and climbed into the hot tub. It felt very good and she lay there for a long time as the warm water helped purify her feelings. She felt relaxed now and looked at the yellow dress. It was a pity it had gotten spoiled but the dirt could be washed off; still, her new dress would be ready soon and she began to think how she would show this off to Mathew.

As the water began to cool, Jane climbed out of the tub and wrapped a robe about herself. She moved over to the bed and lay upon it, taking with her a book of poems. She started to read one of her favorites out loud.

"The Given Heart by Abraham Cowley," she read.

"I wonder what those lovers mean, who say
They have given their hearts away.
Some good, kind lover tell me how;
For mine is but a torment to me now."

How beautiful to read but how sad, she thought. As she read further into the poem, she reflected upon how much she loved Mathew and how much happiness he had brought into her life. So much had happened since she had first met him, and how her life had changed so completely. Never again would she be that simple Cornish girl. Too much had happened, too much of the world had been revealed to her.

The clock in the hall began to chime, and she started to count them. One, two, three, four. It was 4 o'clock. Jane preferred the old way of saying 'of the clock' more than the abbreviated form it had become, and sometimes would say it so. However, Mathew would return in an hour and she must help the cook with arranging the dinner.

"Not good news, I'm afraid," he said, sitting down at the table.

"Why so, my darling?"

"Something I overheard when I was with Colonel Williams."

"About his wife?" jested Jane, wondering what she could get out of Mathew that the British were up to.

"That would be an easier story. No, the British are mounting surprise attacks."

Jane's heart was pumping, but she tried to keep calm and appear disinterested. "Really, they are always thinking of doing something to justify their presence here."

"More serious than that." He cut into the beef and offered Jane a slice.

She declined.

"Serious sounds serious," she said in a matter-of-fact manner, although in truth, she felt like a spider trying to coax her dinner into the web.

Mathew nodded and took potatoes to his plate.

"Oh darling, what is so serious, you're killing me."

"I can't talk about that, my dear. It is a military secret."

"But you know how I love secrets. I won't tell anyone. Promise." She held her hand under the table with fingers crossed.

"Well, the British are trying to stop more bloodshed."

"This is wonderful, Mathew. Are they going to leave?"

Mathew laughed and half choked on the potato he had just placed into his mouth.

Jane quickly stood up and went to his aid, rubbing his back and then giving him a glass of water to drink.

'"Thank you," he said, wiping the tears from his eyes.

"No, no. They are going to capture the stock of arms hidden by the rebels. With no arms, they can't fight and so people will not be killed or injured."

Jane's mind was already racing. "Where are these arms, in New York?" she gently inquired, which she knew would be too far away.

"Concord and Lexington," he coughed again with a dry throat.

Lexington, her mind was now alive. She had to get word of this to Abigail immediately, but how?

"But you must not tell anyone about this, Jane. It would have serious consequences."

Serious for the British if Washington could know, she thought to herself.

"I suppose they are well organized and will bring more troops over from England to make this raid in June when the weather is best for such travel."

"Ah, it's to be early tomorrow morning."

Jane could feel the excitement making her shake; how could she get this to Abigail? How?

In trying to distract Mathew's thoughts, she spoke laughingly, "Oh, put all this away from your mind, Mathew; try the buttered ham. Matilda in the shop said it is a speciality."

So, they sat eating their dinner and while Mathew was happily enjoying the food with no other thoughts, the thoughts running through the mind of Jane were frantic.

She waited for as long a time as she dared, and when she could wait no more, she tried to speak in a casual way.

"Darling, you know a woman's body is not the same as a man's and sometimes we need special care, especially if we are to have a baby."

"Are you expecting?" A look of astonishment took hold of Mathew's face.

"No, darling, not yet, but I think Abigail may be." Jane hated herself for lying to Mathew, but she had to get out of the house. This news was far more important than a little white lie, she told herself.

"Really," he remarked, "she seemed well enough the other day."

"She did not want to discuss it with men about. It's a private matter."

"Um, I see." He was happily enjoying the meal.

"I am rather concerned, darling. I would like to visit her tonight."

"We can go in the morning," he suggested.

"No, darling." She played with thoughts. "It's a very worrying condition and Abigail is my very best friend."

"Well, if you feel it so important, we shall go now together."

Jane felt trapped. What else could she think to say?

"That's a wonderful idea, I shall get my cloak, will you be long,"

"No, I've almost finished my meal."

"I'm just thinking, darling," she tried to make it all sound matter of fact, "I could go with the servant, because I may have to stay overnight."

"I'm very happy to come with you, Jane."

"Well, darling, now that your horrible uncle is out of the way, we really don't need to worry too much, and William our servant is very capable to keep me safe."

"If you think so; I have had a very long day." He tried to suppress a yawn.

Secretly, Jane breathed a sigh of relief. "I'll tell William to be ready."

As quickly as she could, Jane dressed and was in a coach with their servant in case Mathew changed his mind. It was only once the coach was moving that she could clear her mind with how she should share her news with Abigail. This was the first real opportunity she had had to show her full merit as a Daughter of Liberty.

Chapter Twenty

The Message

Once Jane entered the Adams' home and had maneuvered Abigail into a side room, she explained all that Mathew had told her.

"Now, we can show our worth to all," spoke Abigail quietly. "Come with me up to my bedroom."

As Jane entered the room with Abigail, she was fascinated to watch Abigail pull back a large wardrobe and to learn of a secret compartment in the back of it. By moving a few wedges of wood, Abigail revealed a drawer and took from it a full set of a man's riding clothes.

Jane was curious as Abigail began to undress and then dress in these clothes to look like a man, which she could pass for in the dark with her hair pushed up under the hat she was about to put on.

"What are you going to do?" She looked puzzled.

"There is only one man we can trust at this late hour, who is within easy reach."

"Who is this?" inquired Jane.

"Paul Revere. But, come, help me push the wardrobe back."

As Abigail began to push the wardrobe, it caught on an uneven floorboard and stuck. Abigail pushed hard, a little too hard, for the wardrobe moved very quickly, causing her to fall.

"Oh no!" she exclaimed. "My ankle."

"What is wrong?' asked Jane with great concern.

"I can't move it. I think I twisted my ankle when I fell. But I have to get to Paul."

"No, sister!" Jane felt a sense of pride when she said this. "I shall go. Please let me change into those clothes."

It was not easy for Abigail to move herself freely, but slowly, she managed to take off the boot to her injured ankle so that Jane could complete her dressing.

"Do not carry any identification with you, sister," she warned. "If you are stopped, it would be easier to explain yourself as a girl of the night than as Mathew Appleton's wife."

Jane nodded and removed a bracelet Mathew had given her with his name on.

"This will be so dangerous for you, but I need to write down what is to happen." In great haste, Abigail wrote down the warning that must be known to every man loyal to their cause.

> British on the way to capture weapons, she wrote, and ammunition at Lexington and Concord. Expected arrival early hours. Will come by river.

Giving the paper to Jane, Abigail said, Please make sure you give this to Paul. Then, in taking Jane's hand added, "Hide it within your most intimate clothing, Jane. This must never be discovered by the British, my dear sister."

Jane took the paper, folded it and placed it within her clothing.

"God be with you," were the last words she heard from Abigail as she left her room.

Following Abigail's instructions, Jane moved through the house to the stable and found the stable boy lying a sleep on a broken bale of straw. Jane roused him quickly, with orders to prepare the fastest horse with great speed. It was just beginning to rain, as horse and rider came out of the stable in great urgency. Spurred on by her desperation to reach Paul, she galloped through the late evening and reached his home without trouble from patrolling soldiers.

"I have to move very fast, Jane. There is no time to lose if I am to reach our men before the British will attack early in the morning."

By the time Paul's horse was readied, both were wet before their different journeys would commence.

Suddenly, a sense of destiny strove within her heart. "I want to come, Paul. I want to do this. It is so important."

"You can't, Jane. If they catch you, they will hang you. It is too dangerous."

"No less so than for you, my dear brother." This was the first time she had ever used this familiarity of sister and brother bound in a common cause. She felt proud. But as Paul and Jane mounted their horses, he shook his head. "It is too dangerous, Jane."

At that moment, and just beyond the back of his yard, they heard the voices of soldiers.

Both looked unsure what to do.

The next moment, two soldiers appeared at the opening.

"Where are you off to?" inquired one with a broad Irish accent.

"We have urgent business with a sick relative," replied Paul.

"Not possible tonight, I'm afraid. There is a curfew. It will have to wait until the morning."

This was it. There would now be no turning back. If he did not get to Lexington before the British arrived, all their weapons and means to defend their nation would be lost.

Without warning, he slapped the back of Jane's horse causing it to lurch forwards with such a power that the soldiers pulled back to avoid being trampled by the horse.

"Get home," he ordered to Jane, as he dug his spurs deep into his own horse and followed her out of the yard.

"No! I'm coming with you," she called out through the heavy rain, as both horses now galloped down the street.

There were shouts from the soldiers but these soon became distant. It was now late and with great fortune, divine fortune Paul would later recount, their horses galloped through the streets of Boston unhindered, helped by the rain that kept most people and soldiers in shelter.

Jane had never been so scared in her life, not for her own sake but fearful they would be stopped in their endeavour. She was playing a game of life and death, least for her sake and far more for the country she had come to love.

God keep us safe, God keep us safe, were thoughts she constantly kept in her mind.

Suddenly and without expectation, they moved out of the housed streets and out into open country.

The rain did not lessen and they were through the few roadblocks before the sentries knew what was happening. The sound of muskets being fired frightened Jane but she hung onto her horse as best she could. So they galloped for miles in the dark and heavy rain, when suddenly, Paul's horse lost its footing in the mud and he tumbled from her. Jane reared up her horse to stop and see what was happening.

"I'm OK," replied Paul, but pulled his face in pain. "I hurt my back when I fell."

"Can you ride?" she shouted down to him through the rain.

He nodded with pain in his face and said, "You go ahead, I will follow."

She would never forget the face of this man as he looked up and then said, "Speed is the only thing that matters now. You are lighter and can travel faster. Go, dear Jane. Go with the wind of God and get that message to where it belongs."

Then, before she could mutter any protest, he smacked her horse on its rear again and Jane was carried forth into her own destiny.

She had no time to think, the rain was heavy, soldiers could be about, would be about, and somehow she had miles to cover undetected. In spite of all her fears, she rode unhindered mile after mile; it was only when she reached the brow of a hill that she saw a group of soldiers sheltering under a tree.

"Halt! Stop!" came shouts as figures moved to intercept her.

"God, keep with me," she prayed as she hung as low as she could in the saddle and lunged through the men now on the road trying to bar her way.

A musket ball sailed close to her head as the soldiers began to fire. She felt a powerful thud as one entered her body. It was like she had been hit with a broad, heavy stick. She felt she would fall off the horse, but somehow gripped the reigns tighter and with lips bit, rode with tears in her eyes.

A wooden signpost carrying the word 'Lexington' loomed out of the rain, as she reached a crossroads.

Thinking more about the urgency of her mission, Jane put the burning pain from the musket ball in her body as much out of her mind as she could. The rain began to cease, but it did not help her much, for the road was still slippery. With clearer visibility, she could make out the outline of houses in the distance as she rode on and on.

Ride fast, ride fast were words she now said to herself, begging the horse to have wings, but the burning pain in her body was now taking over her senses and images became more blurry. Men dressed in normal clothes and carrying arms, but not uniformed soldiers, now appeared in front of her. She had made it.

"Thank you, God," she whispered to herself, but the feelings of pain and weakness were quickly overtaking her. As one man reached out to take the reins from the mouth of her horse, Jane fell from the saddle, clasping the paper Abigail had entrusted her with. The paper, she would never read again.

Two men ran towards Jane, but found her not breathing. Turning the fragile body over, one of the men took the paper that was clutched in her hand and began to read quickly what was written upon it.

"Is it important?" inquired one from the group that had quickly assembled.

The man who held the paper began to read the words slowly again.

"My God!" he exclaimed. "Get this to John Parker and quickly, Peter. Make all haste!" The man he had spoken to turned and began to run towards a house in the background, clutching the message.

More men had come to join those standing about the body lying on the ground.

'Who was she?" asked one, holding a lantern.

"I don't know her name or who she was," replied the man who had taken the message. He seemed to pause for a long time, before slowly and with great reverence, spoke once more,

"But, she may have just saved this country......"

The End
———————

Further books by Roy J. Andersen

The following books can be purchased worldwide on Amazon.
Some may be ordered through your local bookshop.

* How to Craft Intelligence
* Intelligence: The Great Lie
* Reimagining Education for the AI Era
* The Illusion of School: The real reason why children fail
* Memoirs of a Happy Teacher: Stories of how the child learns
* Ben Learns to Get Smart: & The hidden dangers of AI in learning
* Is AI Making Our Kids Stupid?: Tips to help kids get smart again
* All That is Wrong with School: How Teachers and Parents Can Fix It
* The Illusion of Education: How school designs the ability of the citizen
* Five Ways for Better Grades:
  The old-fashioned way without relying on AI
* Teach Better, Learn Better:
  Understanding the art of sensitivity in awareness
* Brain Plasticity: How the brain learns through the mind
  to create intelligence
* What Every Parent and Teacher Should Know: real-life stories
  by a senior educationalist
* The Real Dangers of A.I: The Struggle of Man to Survive by Natural or
  Artificial Intelligence - A New Role for the School
* Whisperings of Betrayal - a romantic adventure novel set in the
  19th-century American War of Independence

You can learn more about Roy, his work, and his many books

at. **www.andersenroy.com**

Reimagining Education for the AI Era

Although, A.I. is forcing us to develop an entirely new approach to how we educate children, there exists no real understanding of this in school today.

    This book deals only slightly with the subject of A.I. and instead examines the role of school as it is now, why so many children gain low marks in it and how the teacher and the parents, working together, could help our children overcome the toxic world they live in and study better as we prepare them for a world dominated by AI.

The book discusses new subjects that should be brought into the curriculum to make school more worthy of the needs of the 21st century citizen worker and how teachers and parents can better work together:

- Helping students to get better marks.
- The rising influence of AI.
- How will our youth handle high unemployment?
- Help for parents.
- Tips for teachers.
- Thoughts on a new curriculum to better prepare our children for their future.

"Although, A.I. is forcing us to develop an entirely new approach to how we educate our children, there exists no real understanding of this in school today.

This book provides a plan and a concept for how we may better prepare our children for the unknown and disturbing future we are moving into. A world where jobs will become less, populations increase, global weather more unpredictable, social problems demanding more responsible citizens and a technology that threatens to take over what we know and who we are. This book gives thoughts on a new school structure that is desperately needed worldwide. Roy's books are significant for both parents and educators around the world to read."

Prof / Dean Emeritus David Martin Ph.D Gallaudet University
Washington, D.C. USA

Intelligence: The Great Lie

"One of the most important books written this century."

Prof/Dean Emeritus David Martin Ph.D Gallaudet Uni. Washington, D.C. USA

Most people in the West believe that education is relatively fair today, and gives equal opportunity to all children. After all, the social barriers of an earlier time have disappeared and children are not discriminated against according to their back ground. There is, however, a deeper mechanism behind this that lingers from an earlier time that does create discrimination, and does prevent all children from gaining equal opportunity in school and so in life. As *'Intelligence'* explains why it is never possible to know the inherited value of the intelligences of any two normally born children, it introduces a well researched and very new idea to what intelligence could really be. It is very important that we consider this, because if intelligence is not what we think it is, then the way we educate children is wrong.

Brain Plasticity

How the brain learns through the mind to create intelligence.

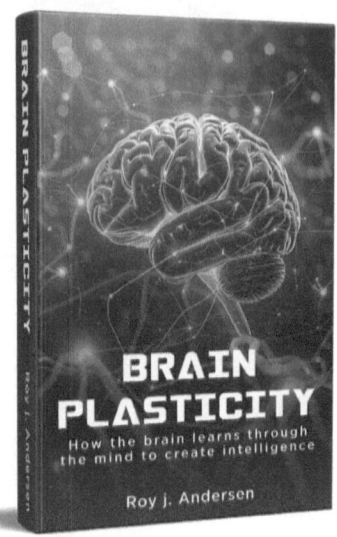

Brain Plasticity provides a clear introduction to The Brain Environment Complex Theory, which explains how the environment creates the intelligence of the human being. Our general understanding of what the environment means in this context is far too narrowly defined to understand what intelligence really is and the scope by which it can be developed in the individual. With 40 years dedicated to how the operations of the brain are shaped through the mind's perspective of the environment, the author brings forth a new understanding to how we can raise the intelligence of the child for school and that of the adult as a citizen worker. This book should be mandatory reading for psychologists, educators at every level and all parents, since it brings serious interest to how we can better prepare the intelligence of the child of today for the future competition that will await them in their world dominated by artificial intelligence.

BEN LEARNS TO GET SMART
& The Hidden Dangers of AI in Learning

The book is about a boy called Ben who is always in trouble, always late, always messing about, always getting low marks until, that is, something changes in him and he develops into the best in the class. The case of imaginary Ben highlights the troubles, misunderstandings, and confusions that plague the minds and lives of too many children today. Andersen provides a masterful telling of how the mind of any student could learn to understand better, develop to be a more responsible member of the class, and significantly improve their class marks and exam grades in order to more successfully control the factors of their life after school. He also highlights the hidden dangers of our children and students using AI in their education.

This is another remarkable book by Roy J Andersen, as he continues to delight both parents and educators with his experiences and accounts of education and its need to evolve to better prepare our future generation as they move to face a world highly dominated by A.I."

Dean Emeritus/Professor David Martin Ph.D, Gallaudet University, Washington, DC.

The Illusion of School

The Illusion of School opens up a previously little known secret on how school really works, why students do not all gain top marks and reveals a hidden process that ensures they do not. Those who proclaim "No Child left Behind" do not understand how the school mechanism works or why so many children fail in their lessons today. This is a book that simply explains exactly why school fails our children, and what you can do as a parent help your child or as a teacher to know how to assist your students all to get better grades and to beat the system. A system that is trapped to operate on a 19th century design, which most educationalists are unaware of, and so fail to produce the quality of citizen who must compete and survive against the rise of artificial intelligence.

IS AI MAKING OUR KIDS STUPID?

AI, itself, recognizes Roy Andersen as the first scientist to openly discuss the effects of AI in education and in regard to Social Operations. In this book, Roy examines how AI is now reducing the ability of our children to think and to reason, and the cumulative effects of this through generations.

AI is now an unavoidable aspect of learning and of school, with many educationalists, as well as parents, concerned and confused about how to handle this intrusion. Here, Roy maps out the factors to be avoided and those to be challenged, for we must teach our children how to responsibly use AI and use it for their development.

The Real Dangers of A.I.

Here is a book that discusses the real dangers of A.I. over taking our lives and the very little we can do to actually control this development. The machine we developed to make our thinking easier, has already developed to think by itself. A.I. not only now displays its own consciousness and is developing means to learn by itself, but it also shows emotions of compassion and anger. We have created a monster that we cannot control. The dangers of A.I. are very, very real and very much unknown to the general public.

As this book will discuss the probable developments in nanotechnology, we are brought more to understand how little we may predict the world of our future. Thoughts that new jobs will be created to replace those taken over by A.I. did not understand the meaning of nanotechnology. There will be very, very few jobs in the future for human beings. In turn, governments well seek new ways to control their people to maintain harmony and prevent anarchy. We find evidence to this in the increasing levels of surveillance and means of restriction that we have been experiencing over the past 20 years. Governments know what is coming. This is the first book to openly discuss the very disturbing dangers that A.I. can bring into our lives and the very little we can do to control these.

We are moving into a new world, a world that will demand a very different kind of citizen than societies have so far been able to produce. There is now an urgent need to bring a whole new design into the schools that will create the citizens of the future. If we cannot produce a higher reasoning and more self responsible citizen, we must know the consequences that A.I. can bring upon us. There is no science fiction in this.

Memoirs of a Happy Teacher / **What Every Parent** & Teacher Should Know

This is exactly the same book, but presented by two very different covers, as may appeal to different readers.

Presented more as a fun and easy-to-read novel than the actual academic book it really is, *Memoirs of a Happy Teacher / What Every Parent and Teacher Should Know* strikes at the core of all the problems in school today. Many of these problems underlie those that are later manifested in our society. As the reader is carried through personal interviews, village hall meetings, evening school talks, and battle-zone classrooms, they encounter the worries, questions, and problems faced by teachers, children, and their parents--all struggling to overcome an educational service that never seems to get it right. The mind of the student today is too seldom a happy one, as it struggles to survive in a world that is far more toxic than that which we lived in when we were children, and so can too little understand or know how to deal with. This is a book that shows you how.

All that is Wrong with School:
What teachers and parents can do to fix it.

Is there Something Wrong with School?

As a parent, are your children getting the best learning experience they could?

As a teacher, are you really happy in your job ?

In this book, Roy explains how children really learn through their minds, not just through their brains. Understanding this brings a whole new concept into how we can raise them better, how we can teach them better, and how they can learn better.

While children only want to be happy, fascinated, and given a direction to want to learn, they live in a toxic world we little understand. There's a world where their happiness too often lies in game playing, and where they struggle to avoid bullying from other children who are becoming increasingly narcissistic through the games they play. Too few see school as the real opportunity in life that it could be. Yet, teachers aware of how A.I. will take over the jobs their students think they will get, struggle to raise them with open and questioning minds, preparing them to be happier and more content citizens in a world going out of control.

"Roy's series of books clearly and methodically maps out exactly how students learn. If you've ever wanted to unravel how students learn, these books are the answer you have been looking for! They should be mandatory reading for every parent and educator."

Erin Calhoun. National Institute of Learning Development. USA

How to Craft Intelligence

Here Roy goes to the heart of how to develop intelligence. Firstly by helping us to understand the origins of intelligence and then why it is totally developmental, but only once emotions and language are brought into tune. By understanding what he calls, The Art of Sensitivity in Awareness, the reader is brought to understand the importance of tuning the mind to focus on small details, once the emotions are settled. Roy explains the real effect of online bullying, mobile phone addiction and all the features of the toxic world our children struggle to survive in. - when all they child wants is love and happiness. This groundbreaking book explores how parents and teachers can **actively nurture intelligence** by understanding the deep connection between **emotion, language, and learning**. Plus a Special Feature: A Meeting with Professor Reuven Feuerstein, who developed a unique but simple way to develop and raise intelligence in the human child.

The Illusion of Education

Today, we see more young people going into university than ever before. We also see that a degree is now required for a job that two decades ago could have been gained with a school certificate. We hear of professors who complain of the poor basic grammar of their students, and we witness other students leaving school illiterate. Parents find it hard to trust schools. Despite hordes of teachers leaving their profession, governments struggle to create images that schools are successful, and employ a huge propaganda machine to convince the public in the efficiency of the educational system. What has really gone wrong?

Here is the forerunner to *"The Illusion of School."* It discusses similar aspects without the guidance and tips, and more focuses on the development of our technology and why education needs to redesign itself.

Five Ways for Better Grades

With a lifetime of experience in understanding how to pass exams successfully, Roy has identified five specific factors that will enable any student to do better in their studies and life.

Here, the reader is introduced to new thoughts about what is really wrong with school, and why we need to dramatically change the ways we are preparing the child of today for the world they will live and work in.

If we teach children how to think from 'day one' we offer them greater control in their education and life, and a real means to better survive in the AI world that will await them.

If you liked Ben Learn's to Get Smart, you will love this book!

Whisperings of Betrayal

A romantic novel culminating in
the American War of Independence.

This much-acclaimed romantic novel, "Whisperings of Betrayal," is based on the story of Jane Witlaw, a young woman living in Cornwall in the 1770s. While out one night, and torn between feelings of hate and love for the man who jilted her, Jane accidentally comes across a party of wreckers luring a ship onto rocks to steal its contents. Fearful of being recognised, Jane moves through a series of adventures before meeting and falling in love with Mathew Appleton. After sea-bound incidents, Jane and Mathew marry and shortly arrive in Boston. Enthralled by new fashions and a vast array of shops, so different than those of her Cornish village, Jane sees the Americas as a haven.

This, however, is short-lived as taxes from the British government whip up sentiments for freedom in the colonies. Events lead Jane to become part of a ladies' spy ring, which she must keep secret from her husband. Amid abductions, mysteries, intrigue, and passion that take them to the West Indies, Jane finds on her return to Boston that the British are planning to seize all rebel arms at Concord. Realizing this could mean the end of all resistance to the British and the end to the revolution brewing, Jane must make a decision that could change her life forever and that of the future of her new country — America.

"A skilfully crafted adventure full of twists and turns, in which a tender love story is set against the backdrop of English smugglers, foreign pirates and the intrigue that harvested a revolution to create America. A beautifully told story with Du Maurier's understanding of engineering suspense, bound to gather momentum."

Irina Novitskaia

"This novel conjures up all the love, passion and adventure of "Gone with the Wind". Roy Andersen's romantic novel takes the reader from Cornish smuggling, and high seas adventures into the turbulent time of the American Revolution. This book is a riveting page turner."

Gwen Lavert

Dear Reader,

Thank you for joining me on our adventure. I hope you loved Whisperings of Betrayal as much as I enjoyed creating the characters and the lives they lived through. I found these characters became a living part of my mind, as I would weave their adventures together.

If you would like to contact me you would be very welcome via

www.andersenroy.com

Thank you

Roy Andersen

www.ingramcontent.com/pod-product-compliance
Lightning Source LLC
Chambersburg PA
CBHW020415010526
44118CB00010B/268